White Supremacist Violence

White Supremacist Violence is a powerful resource for education and mental health professionals who are developing the tools and skills needed to slow the progress of the fast-growing hate movement in the United States.

Chapters immerse the reader in a hybrid of research, historical reviews, current events, social media and online content, case studies, and personal experiences. The first half of the text explores the ways in which individuals become increasingly indoctrinated through the exploitation of cognitive openings, perceptions of real or imagined marginalization, exposure to political rhetoric and manipulation, as well as an examination of social media and commerce sites that create a climate ripe for recruitment. The second half of the book walks the reader through three cases studies and offers treatment considerations to assist mental-health professionals and those developing education and prevention-based programming.

White Supremacist Violence gives readers useful perspectives and insights into the white supremacy movement while offering clinicians, threat-assessment professionals, and K-12 and university educators and administrators practical guidance on treatment and prevention efforts.

Brian Van Brunt is the creative director at D-Prep, where he consults on threat assessment, crisis preparedness, crisis response, emergency operations, behavioral intervention, mental health, and DEI.

Lisa Pescara-Kovach, PhD, is the director for the Center for Education in Mass Violence and Suicide and a professor of educational psychology specializing in prevention through postvention related to mass violence, domestic terrorism, and suicide.

Bethany Van Brunt owns Looking Glass Consulting and Design and is the CEO of InterACTT, a subscription service supporting counseling, disability services, student conduct, law enforcement, CARE/threat teams, and diversity, equity, and inclusion.

White Supremacist Violence

Understanding the Resurgence and Stopping the Spread

Brian Van Brunt, Lisa Pescara-Kovach, and Bethany Van Brunt

Routledge
Taylor & Francis Group
NEW YORK AND LONDON

Cover image: Getty Image

First published 2023
by Routledge
605 Third Avenue, New York, NY 10158

and by Routledge
4 Park Square, Milton Park, Abingdon, Oxon OX14 4RN

Routledge is an imprint of the Taylor & Francis Group, an informa business

Library of Congress Cataloging-in-Publication Data
Names: Van Brunt, Brian, author. | Pescara-Kovach, Lisa, author. | Van Brunt, Bethany S., author.
Title: White supremacist violence : understanding the resurgence and stopping the spread / Brian Van Brunt, Ed.D., Lisa Pescara-Kovach, Ph.D., Bethany S. Van Brunt.
Description: New York, NY : Routledge, 2023. | Includes bibliographical references and index. |
Identifiers: LCCN 2022022195 (print) | LCCN 2022022196 (ebook) |
Subjects: LCSH: Radicalism--United States. | White nationalism--United States. | White supremacy movements--United States. | Violence--United States. | Hate crimes--United States.
Classification: LCC HN90.R3 V36 2023 (print) | LCC HN90.R3 (ebook) | DDC 320.530973--dc23/eng/20220721
LC record available at https://lccn.loc.gov/2022022195
LC ebook record available at https://lccn.loc.gov/2022022196

ISBN: 978-1-032-05886-3 (hbk)
ISBN: 978-1-032-05885-6 (pbk)
ISBN: 978-1-003-19965-6 (ebk)

DOI: 10.4324/9781003199656

Typeset in Goudy
by Taylor & Francis Books

Dedicated to Stuart Frisch (the man who taught them how to do it), for teaching this guy about Jewish Culture and in honor of the work you have done training and defending the Jewish community here and in Israel.

Brian Van Brunt

Dedicated to Quirino DiPillo,

My grandfather, who fought against hate as an Italian civilian in World War II. By hiding British and American soldiers from Hitler's SS, he willingly jeopardized his family to save lives.

And to my parents in heaven, Elvio and Elveria Pescara, who experienced hate as immigrants in the US, but decided to fight hard against it to ensure everyone felt love and acceptance. Thank you for giving me a childhood home full of diversity.

And, of course, I am forever grateful to my husband, David, who has to listen to me talk nonstop about unpleasant topics, yet somehow remains peaceful.

Taylor, Justin, Gabriel, and Tatiana – Thank you for living with a mom who, at times, seems to check out mentally while working. You have never complained about sharing the piece of me that helps others, sometimes at the expense of my time with you. I promise you, even then, you are first in my mind and heart and will be forever.

Lisa Pescara-Kovach

Dedicated to James and Sharon Smith. Thank you, Mom and Dad, for instilling a love of learning and the need to stand with those who are oppressed.

Bethany Van Brunt

Contents

Figures

Tables

Boxes

Preface

Before we begin, we would like to express our gratitude for your service. Whether you are an educator, mental health professional, parent, law enforcement officer, student, or member of a threat or CARE team, we are honored to share our knowledge of white supremacy with you. Although we possess insight and knowledge on this subject matter, you bring skills to the table that we need and appreciate; skills needed by our partners who join us in the fight against hate.

White Supremacist Violence: Understanding the Resurgence and Stopping the Spread provides anyone involved in raising, educating, or counseling young people the tools it takes to slow down the progress of a fast-growing hate movement in our nation. The book takes the reader on a journey that spans from the history of politics and religion that drove hate, to today's reality of white supremacists' use of mainstream social media and networking sites as they attempt to grow in strength and number. The reader will be immersed in a hybrid of research, historical reviews, current events, case studies, and personal experiences as they walk from the dark parts of history toward the light of threat assessment and ways to help those on the pathway to violence. *White Supremacist Violence: Understanding the Resurgence and Stopping the Spread* offers facts and solutions toward helping marginalized groups who are often targeted by white supremacists. The book is not fatalistic in nature, despite what we face in our nation today. Rather, upon reading the book, the reader will possess deep knowledge and tangible skills on how to fight white supremacy along with us.

Contributors

Dr. Amy Murphy, serves as an assistant professor of student development and higher education leadership at Angelo State University. She is also the program coordinator for the M.Ed. in student development and leadership in higher education, as well as the graduate certificate in academic advising, both fully online programs. Amy has been in the role of full-time, tenure-track faculty member at Angelo State since 2016. In this role, she regularly designs and teaches courses on educational law, student affairs administration, program administration and assessment, and academic advising. The degree program is nationally recognized and ranked among the best in the US for quality and affordability by multiple online higher education guides.

Dr. Murphy writes and presents to campus practitioners and educators on behavioral intervention, sexual misconduct, student conduct, threat and violence risk assessment, and other student affairs issues and topics. She co-authored *A Staff Guide to Addressing Disruptive and Dangerous Behavior On Campus* and a second book, *Uprooting Sexual Violence in Higher Education*. Her research includes the joint development of the ERIS: Extremist Risk Intervention Scale as well as other tools and resources for behavioral intervention teams in schools and universities. She has authored more than ten different book chapters and several peer-reviewed journal articles on related topics. Amy is a Past President of NABITA, the National Association for Behavioral Intervention and Threat Assessment, and past managing editor of the *Journal of Campus Behavioral Intervention* (J-BIT). During her time on the NABITA advisory board, she supported the development of standards for behavioral intervention teams and for case management practices through her research and writing.

Amy has more than 20 years of experience in higher education and student affairs. She is formerly the dean of students and managing director of the Center for Campus Life at Texas Tech University. Her experiences include, chair of the school's behavioral intervention team, oversight of prevention and response activities for gender-based violence and discrimination as the deputy Title IX coordinator for students, as well as administrative involvement in student conduct, disability services, counseling, and enrollment management. Amy provided leadership to a wide array of co-curricular and extracurricular student involvement activities, including a system of more than 450 registered student organizations, including 50 inter/national fraternities and sororities.

Amy's experiences in postsecondary education include diverse involvement in a number of complex and transformative projects, including a task force for Greek culture and task force for sexual harassment and sexual assault, new academic program proposal and development, strategic enrollment planning, and many special projects dedicated to the creation of innovative, research-based services and programs. Amy received her Ph.D. in higher education administration from Texas Tech University in 2010. She currently lives and works in San Angelo, TX.

A native of Buffalo, NY, **Edward Janak** received his B.A. (English) from SUNY-Fredonia and both M.Ed. (secondary education) and Ph. D. (foundations of education) from the University of South Carolina. He taught high school in South Carolina for almost a decade before becoming a scholar in the historical foundations of education and educational life writing. His current line of research during his "day job" explores the intersection of General Education Board funding on historically marginalized populations in the US West. His "night job" finds him examining the role of popular culture texts as both informal and formal educational media. He is the "Education, Teaching, History and Popular Culture" area chair for the Popular Culture Association and co-series editor (with Ludovic Sourdot) of the *Education and Popular Culture* series for Lexington Books. He co-edited three collections on popular culture and education: 2013's *The Pedagogy of Pop: Using Pop Culture to Improve Instruction*, 2018's *Educating through Popular Culture: You're Not Cool Just Because You Teach with Comics*, and 2022's *Kevin Costner, America's Teacher*, all with Lexington Press. He has published articles tapping popular culture in *Dialogue: The Interdisciplinary Journal of Popular Culture and Pedagogy*, *TechTrends*, the *Journal of Thought*, and the *Journal of American Culture*.

Candice Seiple is a current doctoral student and teaching assistant in the educational psychology program at the University of Toledo, where she teaches applied psychology for teachers. She also assists Dr. Lisa Pescara-Kovach in the Center for Education in Mass Violence and Suicide. Candice obtained her B.A. in psychology and

Women's Studies from Kent State University and earned her master's degree in Psychology from Tiffin University. She has experience in the field of mental health prevention and postvention with children and adolescents.

What's Inside? A Glimpse into the Content and Organization

Part 1: The Wolf at the Door

Chapters 1 through 3 provide the reality of white supremacy and related domestic terrorism through a review of the history of maltreatment and violence directed at Black, Jewish, LGBTQI+, and Asian members of society. The Tuskegee experiment, genocide of innocent Jews in World War II, and cruel experiments conducted on Black slave women will shock, yet inform the reader of the atrocities that we are working to avoid from happening again. The reality of where this started as well as startling statistics provide the foundation for our rationale in getting ahead of this growing threat.

Part 2: Down the Rabbit Hole

Chapters 4 through 6 allow the reader direct knowledge of the predominant terms, symbols, and gestures used by various white supremacy groups. The reader will also gain an understanding of the role the internet, including popular sites like Amazon and Facebook, in fostering a climate of information collecting, sharing, and recruitment. This section ends with an examination of cognitive openings and what makes some individuals more vulnerable than others in seeking to connect with hate groups.

Part 3: Case Studies

Within Chapters 7 and 8, the reader is immersed in the use of case studies toward becoming better skilled at understanding the risk and protective factors involved in this issue. Case studies are introduced toward allowing the reader to get insight on behaviors of concern as well as gain insight into an individual's likelihood of walking the pathway toward violence. Not all who come to our attention pose serious threats to our safety. As a result, it is of great importance to examine cases toward familiarizing yourselves with what should and should not raise concern.

Part 4: Assessing the Risk

Chapters 9 through 12 provide critical knowledge in identifying risk and protective factors. The reader will gain access of the newly introduced indoctrination rubric created by Dr. Brian Van Brunt. Brian is the pioneer of several tools related to threat assessment, including InterACTT's newly introduced Navigator (see www.InterACTT.org for more information on the Navigator). *White Supremacist Violence: Understanding the Resurgence and Stopping the Spread* serves as the launchpad for the indoctrination rubric that will be of great use to those moving forward in fields related to domestic terrorism. Within this section of the book, you will be able to conduct a hypothetical violence risk assessment.

Part 5: Treatment

Perhaps the most common question that arises upon a completed risk assessment is, "Now what?" This section affords the reader the opportunity to get a glimpse at risk level-specific case management plans.

Part 6: Educational Prevention Programming

As the final section, Part 6 provides national and international level resources and agencies dedicated to the fight against white supremacy, terrorism, and related violence. We are stronger in numbers and stand by the organizations within.

1 White Supremacy

A Growing Threat

Box 1.1 Key Take-aways

1. White supremacy is not a new problem and remains a growing trend worldwide, threatening the safety, security, and lives of those seen as different from the white supremacist standards.
2. Hate groups make use of the internet, political unrest, and fear to drive negative messaging against people of color, Jews, women, Asians, Muslims, and LGBTQ+I individuals.
3. Many factors contribute to the growth of this problem, including a system rooted in systemic inequity, a law enforcement focus on terrorism abroad following the 9/11 attacks, and a rise in access of materials on social media.
4. Key terminology is identified to set the foundation for the following chapters. These terms include the alternative-right (commonly known as alt-right), domestic terrorism and extremist groups, the extreme/far/radical right, hate crimes, neo-Nazis, racist skinheads, terrorism, white nationalism, white supremacy, and traditional white supremacy.

White supremacist marches, growing hate speech, and the push for a return to so-called traditional values flood our televisions, radios, and cell phones. All point out the obvious: an increasing political divide analogous to a simmer that is getting hotter with each day. Although 2020 and 2021 left little uncovered in discussions of race, politics, mask usage, vaccine mandates, mass shootings, and political conflict, a particularly concerning trend has re-emerged in global history: the rise of the white supremacist agenda. It is time we understand that the greatest threat to the safety and security of our nation resides in our own neighborhoods.

Many believe this to be in our past. We ended slavery, moved past Jim Crow laws and segregation, fought a world war that ended the Holocaust, and even elected an African American president. Surely, white supremacy has faded and is not the threat it once was. Unfortunately, this has

DOI: 10.4324/9781003199656-1

not been borne out, and we are seeing this threat rise and grow. In a 2019 meeting of the United Nations Security Council, Secretary General António Guterres warned of the growing threat posed by violent extremism and their increased use of social media and the dark web for coordination, dissemination, and recruitment (United Nations Meetings Coverage and Press Releases, 2019).

Antisemitism certainly did not end with the Second World War. January 27, 2020, marked the 75th anniversary of the liberation of the Auschwitz–Birkenau death camp. In the span of five years, some 1.1 million people died within the confines of Auschwitz–Birkenau (Gera, 2020), about one-sixth of the estimated 6 million Jews killed during the Holocaust. Political leaders, along with a few remaining survivors and their families, commemorated the occasion. In the commemoration, though, was also a warning. In his speech, United States Ambassador to the Organization of American States Carlos Trujillo spoke to this growing threat:

> "The United States is also deeply concerned by continued high levels of—and in some places increasing incidents of—antisemitism in many countries as well as rising trends in anti-Muslim and anti-minority sentiment. Overall, there were reports of physical assaults; verbal harassment; vandalism, including desecration of Jewish property and places of worship; and hate speech on the internet and in social media. The frequency and intensity of online antisemitic hate speech and harassment remains of great concern to the U.S. government."
>
> (Trujillo, 2020, para 10)

Make no mistake, white supremacy is a growing force. Whether this occurs in the form of neo-Nazi groups, gangs of racist skinheads, or in the online chatrooms of the alt-right, today's hate groups are willing and able to commit acts of violence. Critical evaluation of these groups is essential to understand and mitigate this risk. This is particularly important as the groups themselves employ misleading terms such as "patriot" or "protector of the Constitution" as they engage in acts of violence against America and the constitution.

What the Numbers Say

Hate Groups

The Southern Poverty Law Center (SPLC) (Hankes and Janik, 2021) reported that in 2020 there were 838 hate groups operating within the United States. This is a decline from 2019, where there were 940 groups, as well the 1,020 in 2018 (SPLC). Although this decline might seem like good news, we would suggest another interpretation. Each organization and their corresponding membership engage in savvy ways of misleading the public. Flanagan et al. (2019) described the use of social media platforms, both on the mainstream Internet and the dark web, to share their views, recruit members, and incite violence. Although Facebook has stated that it takes the matter seriously, leaders of hate groups are tech savvy. They use traditional social media platforms such as Facebook, Twitter, TikTok, and YouTube along with such chat sites as 8chan, 4chan, Telegram, and iFunny to spread their messages (Flanagan et al., 2019).

The lower estimates obscure the fact that hate groups have begun to consolidate their ranks, employ technical counter measures, and exist in greater number than those tracked by statistical counts. They are savvy enough to move from mainstream media to the dark web, conniving enough to shut down white supremacist merchandise sites that then reappear under other names, clever enough to wear Nazi symbols unrecognized by most, and bold enough to act on their feelings of hate. Homeland Secretary Chad Wolf made an alarming and realistic statement in his 2020 *Homeland Threat Assessment*: "I am particularly concerned about white supremacist violent extremists who have been exceptionally lethal in their abhorrent, targeted attacks in recent years." (Department of Homeland Security, 2020, p. 3). The fact that the Department of Homeland Security (DHS) is explicitly discussing and targeting domestic violent extremists testifies to where we find ourselves today. Gone are the days when foreign terrorist organizations were our only concern.

Hate Crimes

In October 2021 the Federal Bureau of Investigation (FBI) released updated 2020 hate crime data (Federal Bureau of Investigation, 2021b) that paints an increasingly grim picture. Specifically, there were 8,052 hate crimes stemming from a single category of bias, with 11,126 victims. This is a significant increase from 2019, where there were 7,103 single-bias hate crimes with 8,552 victims. The four main perpetrator biases that led to the crimes were related to race and similar categories (61.8%), sexual orientation (20%), religion (13.3%), and gender identity (2.2%). There were an additional 346 victims in 211 multiple bias-based hate crimes. Perhaps what is most disturbing about the data is that it is not representative of all law enforcement agencies throughout the country. Data was available from only 15,138 out of 18,625 agencies in the United States (Federal Bureau of Investigation Crime Data Explorer, 2021); thus, the rate of hate crimes is higher than reported and is increasing with each passing day.

How Did We Get Here?

The question on everyone's mind is, how is this happening today? How did domestic terrorist organizations with myriad hate-filled philosophies grow to the point they pose one of the greatest threats to our national security (Department of Homeland Security, 2020; McGarrity, 2019; Walters and Chang, 2021)? The answer is not complicated; however, it is multifaceted. In the following sections we will review the three primary factors that led to our current state: the prioritization of law enforcement, the influence of social media, and cognitive openings in those vulnerable to indoctrination.

New Prioritization in Law Enforcement Following the 9/11 Attacks

The attacks of 9/11 took all eyes off this potential risk and directed them toward foreign terrorist organizations, especially Al Qaida and the Islamic Stats in Iraq and Syria (ISIS), which allowed white supremacy groups to grow in membership and potential for violence (Walters & Chang, 2021). In the wake of failures of the security community following 9/11, there was a firm commitment to the ideas of "never forget" and "never again." The DHS was created to address these fears and focus multiple law enforcement agencies on a common goal: to prevent another 9/11 from happening. The United States law enforcement and counter-terrorism community was directed to focus on the Middle East and de-prioritize focus on the likes of Timothy McVeigh. As with a fire that has been reduced to embers, our focus moved to other concerns. Who would have thought the Ku Klux Klan (KKK), Nazism, and an isolationist policy of American First would ignite once again?

While the embers continued to smolder, the 9/11 attacks led the FBI to transform from a more "intelligence-driven, threat-based, national security and law enforcement agency" toward addressing foreign terrorist organizations (FTOs) (Federal Bureau of Investigation, 2021b). The agency also created hundreds of Joint Terrorism Task Forces throughout the U.S. These task forces were a partnership between the FBI and local law enforcement agencies. Regional fusion sites were created to help provide intelligence information to the federal government. Together, they were better equipped to deal with the threat posed by foreign terrorists.

Though the FBI transformed significantly post-9/11, the most significant show of determination to fight FTOs was President Bush's creation of the DHS. As stated in a document titled *Department of Homeland Security* (Bush, 2002):

> The President—using the maximum legal authority available to him—created the Office of Homeland Security and the Homeland Security Council in the weeks following the attack on America as an immediate step to secure the homeland. Since then, the government has strengthened aviation and border security, stockpiled more medicines to defend against bio-terrorism, improved information

> sharing among our intelligence agencies, and deployed more resources and personnel to protect our critical infrastructure.
>
> (p. 4)

Meanwhile, the embers of white supremacy were restoked online and we found ourselves on December 4, 2021, watching live news feeds of the neo-Nazi group Patriot Front marching from the Lincoln Memorial toward the Capitol Building. Their message was eerily similar to Hitler's message to reclaim Germany, as the Patriot Front was marching with a battle cry of reclaiming America (Silverman, 2021). To credit the FBI, the agency is aware of the threat posed by domestic terrorists and has adjusted accordingly to dedicate the necessary resources to the greatest threats. According to an article in the *Indo-Canadian Voice*, "Remembering 9/11: Events 20 Years Ago Moved Many to Serve" (2021), FBI Executive Director Jill Sanborn acknowledged the acts of violence posed by domestic terrorist organizations motivated by hatred for non-white, non-heterosexual US citizens.

Social Media and Extremist Thoughts: Gateway to Radicalization

First popularized by the Columbine attackers and the creation of their basement tapes, the idea of not only killing others but presenting these killings as a pathway to encourage and inspire others to continue in their footsteps arose as a pattern in the United States. Most disconcerting is the fact that social media has provided a forum not only for future shooters to post their rants and collect injustices but also to host dozens of hate groups (Frederick, 2019). Researchers who have studied the relationship between the social media phenomenon and suicide and mass shootings refer to this as media contagion (Pescara-Kovach and Raleigh, 2017; Towers et al., 2015). As Pescara-Kovach and Raleigh (2017) state:

> Behavior is learned from the environment through the lens of social context. No direct experience is needed for an individual to pick up a mass shooting-related term (e.g., trench coat mafia) heard at school or a new behavior (e.g., using high-powered weapons from the thirty-second floor of a high rise) described in the media.
>
> (p. 36)

The growth of social media has led to some positive new technologies, services, and ways of connecting with the world, but it brings certain challenges. Two primary social media-related challenges are indoctrination and the contagion effect. In terms of indoctrination, leaders of hate groups are tech savvy to the extent they use traditional social media platforms (Flanagan et al., 2019; Pescara-Kovach et al., 2020) to promote their hate-filled agendas and encourage violence.

Media contagion often turns deadly (Pescara-Kovach and Raleigh, 2017), leading to copycat shootings among at-risk individuals. The tragic shooting at Oxford High School in 2020 is an example of extensive news coverage and social media interaction contributing to contagion. The incident claimed four innocent lives, injured many, and acted as a catalyst for others. As with most school shootings, the events that transpired at Oxford received media attention at the local, national, and international levels. The coverage ranged from a description of the day's events to a full investigation into the shooter's childhood history. In effect, the shooter's name was stated over and over and over, making it a household name and gaining him the notoriety he likely craved.

The week after the Oxford shooting was one of fear and confusion as school leaders across the US dealt with threats from students within their own districts (Nathanson and Meckler, 2021). Most threats were communicated via social media. Given the potentially deadly nature of the threats, some schools switched to virtual classes while others were canceled entirely. Michigan, Ohio, Texas, Washington, DC, and other states were hit with these threats and the possibility of a copycat incident. Media contagion and resulting copycat incidents demonstrate the power of the media. Without it, there would be no knowledge of such incidents and therefore no likelihood of another tragedy.

Media is also used to share frustrations and gain sympathizers among struggling individuals. The attacker in Christchurch, New Zealand made his thoughts clear via previous social media posts, the music playing in his vehicle on the way to the first mosque, and his manifesto. Like many before him, the shooter was an "injustice collector" who learned of the societal "injustices" through various forms of media. Several phrases and symbols associated with the shooter were immediately recognized as hate verbiage (Pescara-Kovach et al., 2020) including, but not limited to, the statement on his weapon that read "We must secure the existence of our people and a future for white children" (Southern Poverty Law Center, 2019), a widely used white supremacist slogan. Also written on the weapon was, "Here's [your] migration compact." Within the shooter's manifesto was reference to immigrants whom he referred to as "foreign invaders" (Southern Poverty Law Center, 2019). The manifesto speaks of revenge toward "foreign invaders" whom he blames for thousands of deaths.

Similar ideology and use of technology is evident among the perpetrators of violence at the 2015 Unite the Right rally (Heim, 2017), Charleston church massacre (Hawes, 2019), the El Paso Walmart (Hernandez and Dewey, 2021), and others. Each made social media posts or comments before their attacks placing blame on those of other races or ethnic backgrounds. According to survivors, the Charleston church shooter stated, "Y'all raping our women and taking over the world" (Shapiro, 2017), whereas attendees at the Unite the Right rally chanted, "Jews will not replace us!" (United States Department of Justice, 2019), and the El Paso shooter's social media history showed an alignment with the Great Replacement philosophy as well as warning of an invasion by non-whites.

The power of media is demonstrated in the proliferation of the neo-Nazi mindset that has crossed generations. Today's white supremacists look at Timothy McVeigh as they do Adolf Hitler: both serve as heroes. The 1995 domestic terrorist attack on the Alfred P. Murrah Building in Oklahoma City, Oklahoma, remains the deadliest act of its kind in US history. The Oklahoma City bombing was initially thought to be an act perpetrated by a foreign terrorist organization. It was difficult for many Americans to process that the monster who killed 168 people, including small children, was homegrown. The FBI (n.d.) states:

> Coming on the heels of the World Trade Center bombing in New York two years earlier, the media and many Americans immediately assumed that the attack was the handiwork of Middle Eastern terrorists.
>
> (Federal Bureau of Investigation, n.d.)

Given the years that have passed, most would have thought McVeigh forgotten or at least unnoticed by today's white supremacists. However, a recent study by the FBI uncovered multiple references to McVeigh by youth with the same views (Levine et al., 2020). Brandon Russell, who both killed his roommates and law enforcement officers, was found to have a framed photo of McVeigh on his wall. Jeremy Christian, also born and raised in the US, went on a slashing rampage after posting a month prior, "May all the Gods Bless Timothy McVeigh—a TRUE PATRIOT!" (Morlin, 2017).

Not only does media serve to spread the neo-Nazi mindset, perhaps more disconcerting is the way domestic hate groups use media to recruit others by exploiting the current political climate and encouraging violence against those who are Black, LGBT, female, Muslim, Jewish or who otherwise do not fit their definition of what it means to be American. As stated in a 2021 *The Washington Post* article:

> "victims of all incidents in recent years represent a broad cross-section of American society, including Blacks, Jews, immigrants, LGBTQ individuals, Asians and other people of color who have been attacked by right-wing extremists wielding vehicles, guns, knives and fists."
>
> (O'Harrow et al., 2021, para. 7)

Cognitive Openings and Identity Fusion

In addition to social media influences, the notion of a cognitive opening (Wiktorowicz, 2005) provides an additional factor that plays a role in the rise of white supremacy. Cognitive openings provide an entry point for someone who feels repressed, discriminated against, deprived of resources, and generally isolated to be open to and fascinated with alternative ideologies. It is common for those who gravitate toward white supremacist beliefs to be drawn in and influenced by charismatic, outspoken leaders (Horgan, 2008; Pressman, 2009; Sinai, 2005, 2012; Travis, 2008). Those to whom they gravitate echo their thoughts and beliefs, which then allows the leader to easily exploit the opening (Neumann and Rodgers, 2007) by shifting the blame to a particular group (Moghaddam, 2005).

Cognitive openings might lead to identity fusion, a process by which an individual loses their sense of self and instead becomes one with a radicalized group (Swann and Buhrmeister, 2015). It makes sense then that those who feel persecuted and alienated are easily transformed into hateful white supremacists. Gill et al. (2014) and Malthaner and Lindekilde (2015) support the idea that isolated youth fall victim to radicalization far more easily than those who have social and emotional connections to others. If we look at factors presented by Van Brunt and Murphy (2016), as presented in Table 1.1, it is easy to grasp how some are so easily radicalized.

Examples of cognitive openings leading to identity fusion and related violence are Abdul Razak Ali Artan (Dobuzinskis, 2017), who referenced the ISIS and lone wolf attacks before running his car into students at The Ohio State University and attempting to stab his victims. Omar Mateen (Barry et al., 2016) killed 49 people at a nightclub in Florida citing alliance to ISIS leader Abu Bakr al Baghdadi. Louis Beam (Kolenovsky, 2021) is considered a voice of anti-government hatred and white supremacy, inspiring others to firebombing attacks of Jewish centers.

Know the Domestic Enemy

One purpose of this chapter is to introduce you to terms used throughout the book. We will review the importance of understanding the terms terrorism, domestic terrorist organizations, alt-right, extreme/far/radical right, hate group, neo-Nazi, racist skinhead, white nationalism, white separatism, and white supremacy. We hope increased familiarity with these terms will provide readers with a foundation of understanding for the rest of the book.

Table 1.1 Risk Factors for Susceptibility to Radicalization (Van Brunt and Murphy, 2016)

Dogmatic	*Connects with subcultures*	*Victims of bullying*
Injustice Collectors	Seeks connections with others	Sympathy for violent doctrines
Failures at work/ dating	Frustration with social climate	Low self-esteem
Hopelessness	Frustration with political climate	Willingness to consider violence

Alternative-Right (Commonly Known as Alt-Right)

The alt-right is a hate-filled, loosely affiliated group of individuals who possess extreme racist, white supremacist, and antisemitic views (Southern Poverty Law Center, n.d.). The alt-right is more conservative than the Republican Party and despises liberal beliefs and politics. They are known to attack via social media those who do not adhere to their views, often using mainstream platforms until they are silenced, at which point they move to the dark web.

Domestic Terrorism

The FBI derives its definition of domestic terrorism from the Homeland Security Act. Specifically, according to the definition quoted below, domestic terrorism involves an act that:

- Is dangerous to human life or potentially destructive of critical infrastructure or key resources; and
- Is a violation of the criminal laws of the United States or any State or other subdivision of the United States, and

Appears to be intended to:

- Intimidate or coerce a civilian population;
- Influence the policy of a government by intimidation or coercion; or
- Affect the conduct of a government by mass destruction, assassination, or kidnapping.

(Federal Bureau of Investigation/Department of Homeland Security, 2021, p. 4)

Domestic Extremism Movements

These are groups or individuals who try to get others to adopt their views by using violence or force (Anti-Defamation League, n.d.).

Extreme/Far/Radical Right

Both the "patriot" movement and the white supremacist movement can be considered within this category whose descriptors (i.e., extreme, far, and radical) lend clarity to the deep conviction they have to their causes. The patriot mindset represents primarily anti-mainstream government, militia-type views.

Hate Crimes

Hate crimes consist of criminal activity directed at an individual or a particular group based on the target(s)' race/color, national origin, religion, sexual orientation, gender/sex, gender identity, or disability (United States Department of Justice, n.d.). The largest-scale hate crimes were those committed and commanded by Hitler against anyone of Jewish descent or not fitting his vision of a "pure" human being. Hitler viewed Jews as less than human individuals who sought to take over the world and therefore should be eradicated. Further, he deemed impure anyone struggling with substance use issues or physical or mental illnesses, as well as other groups such as homosexuals and gypsies (Friedman, 1990). He forced them into sterilization, torture, starvation, and ultimately death (Venezia, 2011). Hitler is revered among white supremacists.

Neo-Nazis

As indicated in their moniker, neo-Nazis share Hitler's hateful beliefs regarding those of Jewish descent and others they deem inferior (Southern Poverty Law Center, n.d.). These groups exist both outside and within our nation and pose a risk to many.

Racist Skinheads

This group falls under the neo-Nazi description with the added distinction of visible outward signs such as body-covering tattoos, shaved heads, shared rituals, and racist-themed music.

Terrorism

Terrorism is defined as an attempted or previously planned violent act toward particular people or property with the purpose to frighten or convince others to adopt religious, social, or ideological causes (28 Code of Federal Relations Section. 0.85), Acts of terrorism are significantly violent, as they often include high-powered weapons, explosives, targeted and/or mass shootings, vehicle ramming, and other potentially deadly means.

White Nationalism

Although this is a softer sounding term that white supremacists have used to try to hide extremist views, nationalism and supremacy are one and the same in that they both view whites as superior to all others and, as such, believe that a white nation must prevail.

White Supremacy

According to *Defining Extremism: A Glossary of White Supremacist Terms, Movements and Philosophies*, those adhering to a white supremacist belief system stand by one or more of the following philosophies:

1) whites should have dominance over people of other backgrounds, especially where they might co-exist; 2) whites should live by themselves in a whites-only society; 3) white people have their own "culture" that is superior to other cultures; 4) white people are genetically superior to other people. As a full-fledged ideology, white supremacy is far more encompassing than simple racism or bigotry. Most white supremacists today further believe that the white race is in danger of extinction, owing to a rising "flood" of non-whites, who are controlled and manipulated (Anti-Defamation League, n.d., para 20).

Traditional White Supremacy

White supremacy is not a new phenomenon. Unfortunately, this type of hate has been woven into the fabric of our existence for decades. This belief system centers around disdain and opposition to granting equal rights to Black people (Anti-Defamation League, n.d.). The most notorious traditional white supremacist group is the KKK (Southern Poverty Law Center, n.d.).

Moving Forward

Reminiscent of the World War II era, it is imperative that educators, law enforcement, researchers, and other key stakeholders understand key definitions and descriptions, not only of the groups themselves, but also their hate-filled philosophies. The greater the understanding of the depth of white supremacy and related hate crimes, the greater the likelihood we can work toward creating a safer nation. As President Biden stated in the National Strategy for Countering Domestic Terrorism (2021):

> We cannot ignore this threat or wish it away. Preventing domestic terrorism and reducing the factors that fuel it demand a multifaceted response across the Federal Government and beyond. That includes working with our critical partners in state, local, tribal, and territorial governments and in civil society, the private sector, academia, and local communities, as well as with our allies and foreign partners. We have to take both short- term steps to counter the very real threats of today and longer-term measures to diminish the emerging threats of tomorrow.
>
> (p. 2)

Our goal is to provide you with knowledge and guidance toward helping you identify, assess, prevent, and mitigate hate crimes committed by white supremacists, whether they are acting alone or as part of a domestic terrorist organization. White supremacists have demonstrated their capacity for violence. They are here. They are dangerous. They are the wolf at the door. Understand that we can intervene but only if we recognize that wolf and what path it took to get here.

Forthcoming chapters offer a broad understanding of the extreme right and a discussion of where these individuals appear most commonly in society. Furthermore, we will examine the historical underpinnings of the extreme right and provide greater detail on the reasons why the hate movement has resurged and gained ground both in the US and abroad.

Keep the Conversation Going

- What factors do you see contributing most the growth of white supremacy in the United States? Is this phenomenon limited to the US?
- What groups are missing from this chapter that also experience the negative effects of white supremacy?
- While covered in more detail in Chapter 6, discuss the initial summary of cognitive openings as it relates to radicalization?
- In your mind, can a white supremist or nationalist agenda exists without violence or threat to other marginalized groups?

References

28 Code of Federal Regulations. Section 85.

Anti-Defamation League. (n.d.). Defining Extremism: A Glossary of White Supremacist Terms, Movements and Philosophies. https://www.adl.org/education/resources/glossary-terms/defining-extremism-white-supremacy.

Barry, D., Kovaleski, S., Blinder, A., and Mashal, M. (2016). 'Always Agitated. Always Mad': Omar Mateen, According to Those Who Knew Him. Retrieved on January 21, 2022 from www.nytimes.com/2016/06/19/us/omar-mateen-gunman-orlando-shooting.html.

Biden, J. (2021). Executive Office of the President. *National Strategy for Combating Domestic Terrorism.*

Bush, G.W. (2002). The Department of Homeland Security. www.dhs.gov/xlibrary/assets/book.pdf.

Department of Homeland Security. (2020). *Homeland Threat Assessment.* www.dhs.gov/sites/default/files/publications/2020_10_06_homeland-threat-assessment.pdf.

Dobuzinskis, A. (2017). Perpetrator of 2016 attack at Ohio State acted alone: FBI. Retrieved on January 21, 2022 from www.reuters.com/article/us-ohio-university-attack/perpetrator-of-2016-attack-at-ohio-state-acted-alone-fbi-idUSKBN1DT2WF.

Federal Bureau of Investigation. (n.d.). History: Oklahoma City Bombing. www.fbi.gov/history/famous-cases/oklahoma-city-bombing.

Federal Bureau of Investigation.. (2021). Remembering 911. Retrieved December 29, 2021, at www.fbi.gov/news/stories/911-moved-many-to-serve-090921.

Federal Bureau of Investigation Crime Data Explorer. (2021, October). https://crime-data-explorer.fr.cloud.gov/pages/explorer/crime/hate-crime.

Federal Bureau of Investigation/Department of Homeland Security. (2021). *Strategic Intelligence Assessment and Data on Domestic Terrorism.* Published by the FBI and DHS.

Flanagan, N., Acee, J., and Schubiner, L. (2019). *Confronting White Nationalism in Schools: A Toolkit.* Western States Center.

Frederick, E. (2019). 'Dark pools' of hate flourish online. Here are four controversial ways to fight them: A new study maps the "ecology" of online hate groups across platforms. Retrieved on January 21, 2022 from www.science.org/content/article/dark-pools-hate-flourish-online-here-are-4-controversial-ways-fight-them.

Friedman, I. (1990). *The other victims: first-person stories of non-Jews persecuted by the Nazis*. Boston, MA: Houghton Mifflin.

Gera, V. (2020, January 26). Auschwitz survivors warn of rising anti-Semitism 75 years on. Associated Press.

Gill, P., Horgan, J., and Deckert, P. (2014). Bombing alone: Tracing the motivation and antecedent behaviors of lone actor terrorists, *Journal of Forensic Sciences*, 59, 425–435.

Hankes, K. and Janik, R. (2021). *The Year in Hate and Extremism*. Report by the Southern Poverty Law Center. 1–64.

Hawes, J.B. (2019). *Grace Will Lead Us Home: The Charleston Church Massacre and the Hard Inspire Journey to Forgiveness*. New York: St. Martin's Press.

Heim, J. (2017, August 14). Recounting a day of rage, hate, violence and death. *The Washington Post*. www.washingtonpost.com/graphics/2017/local/charlottesville-timeline.

Hernandez, A.L. and Dewey, J. (ed.). (2021). *El Paso's Darkest Day*. Independently published.

Horgan J. (2008). From profiles to pathways and roots to routes: Perspectives from psychology on radicalization into terrorism. *Ann Am Acad Poli Soc Sci.*, 618, 80–94.

Indo-Canadian Voice. (2021, September 9). Remembering 9/11: Events 20 years ago moved many to serve in FBI. https://voiceonline.com/remembering-9-11-events-20-years-ago-moved-many-to-serve-in-fbi.

Kolenovsky, E. (2021). Lone Wolves Connected Online: A History of Modern White Supremacy. Retrieved on January 21, 2022 from www.nytimes.com/2021/01/26/us/louis-beam-white-supremacy-internet.html.

Levine, M., Margolin, J., Courts, J., and Hosenball. (2020). Nation's Deadliest Domestic Terrorist Inspiring New Generation of Hate-Filled 'Monsters,' FBI Records Show. ABC News, Retrieved from https://abcnews.go.com/US/nations-deadliest-domestic-terrorist-inspiring-generation-hate-filled/story?id=73431262.

Malthaner, S. and Lindekilde, L. (2015). *Analyzing Pathways of Lone-Actor Radicalization: Relational Approach*. Online www.orfaleacenter.ucsb.edu/sites/secure.lsit.ucsb.edu.

McGarrity, M.C. (2019). Confronting the Rise of Domestic Terrorism in the Homeland: Federal Bureau of Investigation (FBI) Statement for the Record. Retrieved November 17, 2019 from www.fbi.gov/news/testimony/confronting-the-rise-of-domestic-terrorism-in-the-homeland.

Moghaddam, F.M. (2005). The staircase to terrorism: A psychological exploration. *American Psychologist*, 60, 161–169.

Morlin, B. (2017, June 27). McVeigh Worship: The New Extremist Trend. Southern Poverty Law Center. www.splcenter.org/hatewatch/2017/06/27/mcveigh-worship-new-extremist-trend.

Nathanson and Meckler. (2021, December 20). School threats and social media hoaxes are forcing closures, time-consuming investigations. *The Washington Post*. www.washingtonpost.com/education/2021/12/20/school-threats-oxford-shooting-tiktok.

Neumann, P. and Rodgers, B. (2007). *Recruitment and Mobilisation for the Islamist Militant Movement in Europe*. International Centre for the Study of Radicalisation and Political Violence. Retrieved from http://icsr.info/wpcontent/uploads/2012/10/1234516791ICSREUResearch Report_Proof1.pdf (accessed September 6, 2017).

O'Harrow Jr., R., Ba Tran, A., and Hawkins, D. (2021, April 12). The Rise of Domestic Extremism in America, *The Washington Post*. www.washingtonpost.com/investigations/interactive/2021/domesticterrorism-data.

Pescara-Kovach, L. and Raleigh, M.J. (2017). The Contagion Effect as it Relates to Public Mass Shootings and Suicides. *Journal of Behavioral Intervention Teams*, 5, 35–45.

Pescara-Kovach, Van Brunt, B., and Murphy, A. (2020). Terrorist in Training: The Role of Social Media and the Rise of Terrorism through Nationalistic White Agenda. *The Journal of Campus Behavioral Intervention*, 8, 1–11.

Pressman, D.E. (2009). *Risk Assessment Decisions for Violent Political Extremism*. (Her Majesty the Queen in Right of Canada, Ottawa).

Shapiro. (2017, April 10). Key moments in Charleston church shooting case as Dylann Roof pleads guilty to state charges. ABCNews. https://abcnews.go.com/US/key-moments-charleston-church-shooting-case-dylann-roof/story?id=46701033.

Silverman, E. (2021). A white supremacist march in D.C. was pushed by a fake Twitter account, experts say. *The Washington Post*. www.washingtonpost.com/dc-md-va/2021/12/06/white-supremacist-dc-march-patriot-front.

Sinai, J. (2005). A conceptual framework for resolving terrorism's root causes. In *The Root Causes of Terrorism: Myths, Reality and Ways Forward*. T. Bjorgo, ed. London: Routledge.

Sinai, J. (2012). *Radicalisation into extremism and terrorism. Intelligencer J U.S. Intell Stud.*, 19, Summer/Fall.

Southern Poverty Law Center: Ku Klux Klan (n.d.). Retrieved on January 21, 2022, from www.splcenter.org/fighting-hate/extremist-files/ideology/ku-klux-klan.

Southern Poverty Law Center. (2019). *The Intelligence Report: The Year in Hate and Racism*, 166, 1–73.

Southern Poverty Law Center. (2020). *The Year in Hate and Extremism*.

Swann, W.B. and Buhrmester, M.D. (2015). Identity Fusion. In *Current Directions in Psychological Science*, 52–57.

Towers, S., Gomez-Leviano, A., Khan, M., Mubavi, A., and Castillo-Chavez, C. (2015). Contagion in Mass Killings and School Shootings. *PLoS ONE*, 10(7): e0117259. doi:10.1371/journal.pone.0117259.

Travis, A. (2008). MI5 report challenges views on terrorism in Britain. *The Guardian*, August 20.

Trujillo, C. (2020). Remembrance Of The 75th Anniversary Of The Liberation Of Auschwitz. Retrieved on January 21, 2022 from https://usoas.usmission.gov/remembrance-of-the-75th-anniversary-of-the-liberation-of-auschwitz.

United Nations Meetings Coverage and Press Releases. (2019). Secretary General Calls Cyberterrorism Using Social Media, Dark Web, 'New Frontier' in Security Counsel Ministerial Debate.

United States Department of Justice (n.d.). Learn About Hate Crimes. www.justice.gov/hatecrimes/learn-about-hate-crimes/chart.

United States Department of Justice. (2019). United States Attorney's Office Western District of Virginia. Three Members of California-Based White

Supremacist Group Sentenced on Riots Charges Related to August 2017 "Unite the Right" Rally in Charlottesville.

Van Brunt, B. and Murphy, A. (2016). Radicalization Risk Rubric: An Exploration of the Risk Factors, Protective Factors & Mobilization Related to College Student Radicalization and Extremism. *J. Gender and Violence*, 3, 78–88.

Venezia, S. (2011). *Inside the Gas Chambers – Eight Months in the Sonderkommando of Auschwitz*. Medford, MA: Polity Books.

Walters, J. and Chang, A. (2021, September 8). Far-Right Terror Poses Bigger Threat to U.S. Than Islamist Extremism Post-9/11. www.theguardian.com/us-news/2021/sep/08/post-911-domestic-terror.

Wiktorowicz, Q. (2005). *Radical Islam rising: Muslim extremism in the West*. Lanham, MD: Rowman and Littlefield Publishers, Inc.

2 The Religious Influences of White Supremacy in the United States[1]

Box 2.1 Key Take-aways

1 White supremacy grew from a US history steeped in the African slave trade supported by many of the Christian faith, particularly in the southern US.
2 Images of God and Christ, central to the Christian faith, are frequently seen through a lens of whiteness despite clear, historical evidence that Christ was not Caucasian. This systemic view of God and Christ as white and holy while sin and the devil are depicted as black and evil creates strong, historical images that contribute to the perception of white in a position of power and good.
3 While Jim Crow laws, segregation and antisemitism all have strong historical roots in the US and were addressed in the Civil Rights Act, the recent Trump presidency and the rise of other far-right politicians further enflamed the issues at hand and contributed to a rise in racial violence.

The Reverend Martin Luther King Jr. famously cited the 11th hour of Sunday mornings as the most segregated hour in Christian America (Prince, 2016). This was true long before the 1960s and, sadly, rings as true today as it did 60 years ago. Segregation in our institutions of faith, politics, and social justice demands a critical analysis and shift. White American Christianity has a long track record of promoting white superiority. As many denominations remain primarily white dominated (Lipka, 2020), they maintain the message of white supremacy within the confines of religion, a message that began with slavery and continues to be reinforced in critical issues such as limited financial opportunities, housing inequity, and attacks on "mixed-race" marriages.

DOI: 10.4324/9781003199656-2

Slavery's Southern Roots

Slavers emotionally and physically abused Black people. They raped them, created inhumane work expectations and left a lasting indoctrination that the Black American is less than, a fraction the worth of a white American. To the modern reader, it would seem implausible that those supporting slavery worshipped in church on Sunday morning and espoused the beliefs of the Biblical New Testament (Gjelten, 2020). Although at odds with the very core doctrines of the Christian faith, congregants and church leadership were intimately involved in the growth and nurturance of the slave culture and the propagation of the idea of Black people as inferior to white people. And while many might scoff at the connection between the German Nazi Party and modern-day American white supremacist movements, the historical connection remains fact.

White supremacy has its roots within the scope of religion within the United States (Howard et al., 2021). We can find this in references to slavery within the texts of both the Christian Old and New Testaments and in the teachings of those who preach its word. At the heart of the historically racist conversation on religion and slavery was James Henley Thornwell, a religious leader in pre-Civil War South Carolina, notorious for advancing racist, white supremacist views. Thornwell was a powerful force among white evangelicals and his message was woven throughout the fabric of the southern evangelical churches (Gjelten, 2020). Thornwell is an exemplar of the promotion of racism, yet the racist behaviors of the evangelical church began long before. As stated in Reed (1994) regarding the historical actions of the church,

> Tragically, white evangelicals did not merely look the other way as African Americans were denied full equality and participation in American life. They were among the most fiery champions of slavery and later segregation—all the while invoking God's name and quoting the Bible to justify their misdeeds
>
> (p. 236).

Reed describes the behaviors of those like Thornwell who regularly referred to Ephesians 6:5, "Slaves, obey your masters, with fear and trembling and a sincerity of heart." Thornwell's teachings conveyed support of slavery, not only because of his racist beliefs but also because he believed southern businesses were more profitable if they relied on slavery. Within a matter of years, Thornwell's presence reached a national level, carrying with it the white supremacist beliefs of his congregation and spreading hate speech wherever he went (Gjelten, 2020). His words resonated with many white evangelicals. Although slavery has long been abolished, white supremacy within the church has proliferated and led to vicious attacks on Black Americans and their allies.

Racism and the Freedom Rider Attack

> "On Mother's Day, May 14, 1961, a Greyhound bus carrying Freedom Riders arrived at the Anniston, Alabama, bus station...Led by Ku Klux Klan leader William Chappell, a mob of 50 men armed with pipes, chains, and bats, smashed windows, slashed tires, and dented the sides of the Riders' bus. Once the attack subsided, police pretended to escort the crippled bus to safety, but instead abandoned it at the Anniston city limits. Soon after the police departed, another armed white mob surrounded the bus and began breaking windows...When a member of the mob tossed a firebomb through a broken bus window, others in the mob attempted to trap the passengers inside the burning vehicle by barricading the door. They fled when the fuel tank began to explode. The Riders were able to escape the ensuing flames and smoke through the bus windows and main door, only to be attacked and beaten by the mob outside."
>
> (A History of Racial Justice, n.d., para. 2 and 3)

Many perpetrators of this racist brutality were self-identified church-going Christians (Gjelten, 2020). In fact, Henry Lyon, Jr., a pastor who led a congregation of approximately 3,000 people, advanced bigoted and racist sentiments in a speech less than a month after the attack on the Freedom Riders. Lyon caused significant damage in his role; however, he was not the only individual in such a position to culture these attacks and fight the desegregation movement. The south, despite laying claim to thousands upon thousands of self-proclaimed evangelical Christians, was a central gathering place of racism and white supremacy (Dupont in Gjelten, 2020). This hatred, cloaked in religious doctrine and rhetoric, spread across the nation and continues to wreak havoc in the lives of Black, Jewish, Muslim, and other non-Anglo-Saxon individuals.

The Colors of Christianity

White supremacist ideology is not present solely in interpretations of the Bible and related sermons; it is also evident in the colors used to depict specific religious celebrations, rituals, and symbols (United Church of Christ, 2021). White American Christianity has created a largely intentional misunderstanding in color representations. According to Christianity.com, "White refers to holiness, light, purity, redemption, and the righteousness of Jesus Christ," whereas black symbolizes "sin, darkness, death, and catastrophe" (Kalu, 2019). The greatest color divide within Christianity is seen between that of black and white. The aspirational and the base, good and evil, Christ and Satan; this is the conflict of white versus black. This color symbolism has provided fodder for microaggressions, those unintended messages that continue to further insult and marginalize groups of people. For example, phrases related to evil might be referred to as black soul, dark deed, or other related actions of misfortune or transgressions (Bastide, 1967). At the other end of the spectrum, white can bring about more feelings of positivity, enlightenment, joy, peace, and actions taken against evil. Brooks (2020) furthers this argument, referencing religious rituals that use white to represent purity and black to represent corruption. Further, this is evident in the white clothes of baptism and the black clothes of funeral attire.

The Whiteness of God

White Americans tend to view God as a white male, an idea that was demonstrated as early as Michelangelo's "Creation of Adam" (Jackson et al., 2018). Historians have long argued that the illustration of God as a white man is a form of empowerment directed at the white man and a form of disempowerment of the Black population. During his enslavement, Frederick Douglass hoped that his master finding Christianity would lead to more humane and kind treatment, alongside the possibility of emancipation. However, according to Douglass, his former master's involvement in Christianity had the opposite effect, resulting in his becoming more cruel and hateful (Luo, 2020). This drive to disempower the Black population through the means of Christianity can be directly seen in Luke 12:47: "He that knoweth his master's will, and doeth it not, shall be beaten with many stripes" (Luo, 2020, para. 1). Equating God with the concept of a white man in turn creates an anti-Black mindset (Howard and Sommers, 2019). This concept was driven in full force immediately after the American Civil War, when full citizenship was granted to Black people. According to Roberts et al., (2020) many whites feared Black retribution, and there was a desire to unify whiteness and pacify Blacks away from militancy. To this end, images of an all-forgiving and white savior were increasingly prevalent. This contributed to the conceptualization of God as a white man of power (Roberts et al., 2020). "Most Christians have the perception of God as unknowable and perhaps diverse in appearance but have the assumption rooted in their religious ideologies that God is masculine, youthful and white" (Jackson et al., 2018). Furthermore, it is important to note that most American Christians, regardless of their own race, depict God as a white man with omniscience.

Christians see Jesus as not only the son of God but also as God in human form, and this man is also depicted as white (Roberts et al., 2020) without evidence of any non-white external traits. Even though Christ was a brown-skinned, Middle Eastern Jew, he is often depicted as a savior with light skin and eyes and light-colored hair (Pindi and De La Garza, 2018). This choice further prioritizes the white imagery of Jesus and contributes to concepts used to defend a white supremacy.

In the Christian faith, Jesus is the holy son, believed to be the most powerful leader on earth, chosen to guide and lead his followers. Congregations are taught it is sinful to speak negatively about or doubt the power of Jesus. The depiction of him as white and pure is an intentional message that contributes to the ideology supporting the greatest goodness and power in individuals who fit this appearance. Despite numerous geographical and biological truths that contradict the idea of Jesus having been a powerful white man, many American Christians still insist upon his whiteness (Howard et al., 2021).

Cultural and Political Influences on Religious Thought

During Reconstruction, the time directly after the Civil War, Blacks were granted full citizenship and attempts were made to redress some of the wrongs of slavery. This caused a backlash, and in many states steps were taken to limit the rights of Black individuals. They could not marry outside of their own race or reside on certain streets. For example, in 1914, Texas had many towns where Blacks were forbidden to live. There was a Jim Crow curfew that meant Blacks could not exit their homes after 10 pm. Segregation also occurred in parks, hospitals, prisons, orphanages, and schools (Chafe, 2001; Packard, 2002). These conditions ensured that Black individuals had to comply with their oppression or face severe repercussions. These repercussions not only kept the Black population down but lifted the white population up, in that now whites had ordinances to support their blatant disrespect and disregard for the Black population. It was a white person's right to be free and a Black person's place to be oppressed, and this mindset was protected by law.

World War II created some major changes regarding the notion of white supremacy. Jim Crowe laws were still in place, with racial segregation serving as a driving force in the country. As a result, Black men in the military were also segregated. Positions given to them were considered of lesser value such as cooking and grave digging. During the initial part of the war, Black men were not given the opportunity to participate in combat. However, as time passed and casualties among white soldiers mounted, this was disregarded and these men were placed in the front lines (University of Southern California, 2020). The UN was in shock about the treatment of Black soldiers and the segregation between Blacks and whites in the United States. In 1948 President Harry Truman took action to promote racial equality by urging Congress to abolish the poll tax, bring back fair voting standards, and end unfair transportation segregation policies. Truman also ordered the integration of the armed forces (Chafe, 2001; Packard, 2002). Truman believed that the United States owed it to all citizens to provide them with the same quality of life. Further he felt that it was the federal government's obligation to protect individual liberties and provide equal protection under the law for every person regardless of race (Goldstein, 2014).

In 1950 the NAACP challenged the concept of "separate but equal." Black parents grew tired of overcrowded and poorly kept schools and sued to get their children into white schools. In these cases, federal courts initially upheld segregation, and in response an appeal was made. In Topeka, Kansas, Oliver Brown petitioned for his daughter to attend a segregated school. On May 17, 1954, the Supreme Court decided on these cases, grouped as Brown v. Board of Education. They ruled that racial segregation of children, even in schools of equal quality, was harmful to minority children (Chafe, 2001; Packard, 2002) and was in direct violation of the Equal Protection Clause of the Constitution.

The court examined this harm by identifying the effect of racial segregation on Black children. In doing so, they relied on scientific statements of psychologists of the time. These findings showed that segregation and discrimination damage the personality of all children, but in different ways and with different impacts for white and Black children. Furthermore, it was noted that this creates a sense of social class differences within children's development (Onwuachi-Willig, 2019).

This concept of the identification of differences in race and social class would not disappear with the racial integration of public schools. Children do not simply forget that they belong to different social classes or races. This ruling allowed for Black students to receive the same education as white students; however, this did not eliminate racism. Rather, it further pointed out differences among social classes and races. Children were easily able to identify these differences, and whites were able to further reinforce their sense of superiority. Although Brown v. Board of Education had the intention of desegregating schools and allowing for equal learning opportunities, it had the effect of furthering white supremacist ideology. Brown v. Board of Education failed to clarify that while segregation allowed for feelings of inferiority in a generation of Black children, this same segregation created a sense of white supremacy in white children. This has furthered the harm of discrimination, even when learners have received an education under the same roof (Onwuachi-Willig, 2019).

In 1963, in response to resistance to desegregation, President John F. Kennedy asked Congress to enact a comprehensive bill of civil rights. After Kennedy's assassination, President Lyndon Johnson pressed this issue even harder, and the Civil Rights Act of 1964 was passed. This prohibited discrimination based on color, race, sex, religion, or national origin. The act also prohibited discrimination in places of public accommodations and federally funded programs. It strengthened voting rights and reinforced school desegregation (United States Department of Labor, n.d.). In addition, the Voting Rights Act of 1965, enacted by Johnson, put an end to literacy tests, which had at this point prevented many people from registering to vote (Johnson, 2021).

"Lost Cause" Confederate Sympathizing

The hate mindset is evident among supporters of the "Lost Cause" mentality regarding the Civil War. According to the Southern Poverty Law Center (2019), many in the south believe that the Civil War was fought to the southern lifestyle from Northern aggression. In short, adherents of the Lost Cause mentality argue the Civil War was not about slavery but about states' rights, despite historical writings and documents that make it clear that the South seceded in order to preserve the system of slavery and the largely free labor it provided (Levine, 2005). The myths and half-truths surrounding the Old South are the basis for the frequent refrain of "heritage, not hate." Lost Cause supporters actively wish for, and often work toward, a return to antebellum times—when slavery was still legal.

Slavery and Jim Crow scarred the nation, but this is of no importance to Lost Cause adherents who hold strongly that the South—in all its white supremacist glory—will rise again. Rather than a swastika, they fly the so-called Confederate flag (even though it historically was never the national flag of the Confederacy). Rather than read *Mein Kampf*, they read Lyon Gardiner Tyler's 1935 tract *A Confederate Catechism*, reprinted as recently as 2014 and freely available online. This tract denies that the South fought for slavery or tried to overthrow the US government; for example, in response to the question "Was slavery the cause of secession or the war?" Tyler writes in part "Both from the standpoint of the Constitution and sound statesmanship it was not slavery, but the vindictive, intemperate anti-slavery movement that was at the bottom of all the troubles" (2014, p. 5).

Two of the biggest supporters of the Lost Cause mythos include the United Daughters of the Confederacy (UDC) and the Sons of Confederate Veterans (SCV). Much to their disappointment, statues and other symbols commemorating the Confederacy are being removed with increasing frequency, schools named after Confederate generals are being renamed with some regularity, and many textbooks have stopped publishing the Lost Cause as part of their curriculum. Like other white supremacist groups that have reduced their physical footprint under the bright light of public scrutiny, so too have supporters of the cause moved their presence largely online. We will explore in detail within Chapter 3 the use of the internet by hate groups.

The UDC incorporated in 1919 and established 7 objectives, two of which are "To protect, preserve and mark the places made historic by Confederate valor" and "To collect and preserve the material for a truthful history of the War Between the States" (United Daughters of the Confederacy , n.d.). As such, the UDC was financially responsible for the construction of many of the monuments to the Confederacy throughout the nation that we are still reckoning with today. While they continue to have chapters and divisions in 14 states (including California, New Jersey, and Utah) and two physical libraries (ironically located on Arthur Ashe Boulevard in Richmond), it is online where they have the most significant presence. They answer inquires, publish a journal, give awards to students who do school projects based on the Confederacy, and manage scholarships.

The male counterpart of the UDC, the SCV, also counts among its efforts funding and establishing monuments celebrating the Confederacy. However, their rhetoric is much more radically aligned with Lost Cause mentality than that of the UDC. While overtly claiming to be a non-political organization, the opening line of their descriptive webpage declares that "The citizen-soldiers who fought for the Confederacy personified the best qualities of America." Denying the role of slavery, it goes on to state "The preservation of liberty and freedom was the motivating factor in the South's decision to fight the Second American Revolution" (Sons of Confederate Veterans, n.d., c).

The SCV was incorporated in 1896, and its constitution has changed little since. It references the Magna Carta and Great Charter of England, and cites white supremacist "Anglo-Saxon rights and personal liberties transmitted to us"; it refers to the "War for Southern Independence" and the descendants of Confederate veterans as holding a "glorious heritage of valor, chivalry, and honor which we now hold and venerate" (Sons of Confederate Veterans, n.d., b).

Box 2.2 The Great Replacement

Modern day white supremacists, such as the Proud Boys, focus on the concept of the Great Replacement; that through minority growth and immigration, populations of white, European descent are being replaced. Those who believe this theory feel that the media and politicians are seeking to destroy the white Western way of life (Davey & Ebner, 2019). The ideas of the Great Replacement have impelled white supremacists to violence. In 2019 in El Paso, a mass shooting took place in which the motivation was to cause violence in retaliation and create division between European individuals and what the shooter identified as "invaders" (Pescara-Kovach et al., 2020).

Christianity Today

White supremacy has lost favor in any kind of direct messaging from most pulpits and white evangelicals have declared racism a sin. Southern Baptists have apologized for their role in American Slavery. However, this is belied by their 2019 annual convention being opened with the use of a gavel owned by the founder of their seminary—a slaveholding white supremacist (Butler, 2021). As the white evangelical movement has become more and more aligned with conservative politics, many white Christians turn a blind eye to, or even support, racism and racist policies in service of other, larger goals related to immigration concerns, anti-abortion messages, and a more conservative agenda that benefits whiteness and supports white leadership (Butler, 2021). Given this tie to conservative politics, the white evangelical community fully embraced Donald Trump and his white nationalist policies.

During the 2020 presidential race, Donald Trump was questioned about his failure to condemn white supremacists. Rather than answering this directly, he avoided the question and began several rants about violence approaching the United States of America, mostly coming from the left (McCammon, 2020). The debate moderator pressed on and addressed the issue of militia groups and white supremacists adding to the violence that Trump had attributed to the left. Trump insisted he wanted peace but failed to condemn or show disapproval of this violence coming from white supremacist groups. Upon being asked repeatedly to condemn white supremacist groups like the Proud Boys, Trump responded "Proud Boys, stand back and stand by. But I'll tell you what: somebody's got to do something about antifa and the left" (McCammon, 2020). This statement acted as a catalyst for the Proud Boys and encouraged white supremacists to further violence in the name of defending the right-wing mission. One need only look at the events of January 6, 2020, during which several white supremacist symbols such as the Confederate flag, Proud Boys gear, 1776 memorabilia, and the Kekistan flag (see Chapter 4) were blatantly on display.

We can also look to Trump in the spread of Asian hate in response to the COVID-19 pandemic. When speaking about COVID-19, Trump referred to it as a Chinese-caused illness, regularly calling it the "China virus." Many saw this as an opportunity to promote anti-Asian hostility. White Americans told those of Asian backgrounds to go back to their own country, integrated racial slurs directed toward Asians into their vocabulary, or sometimes completely avoided Asians all together.

Although Trump is out of office, his words continue to weave through the nation, and many remain loyal to this day, believing the election was stolen. This belief is what led to the insurrection at the US Capitol on January 6th. White supremacists were among those in the violent, unruly crowd, breaching security and threatening the safety of those in office.

When There is One, There are More

Trump was not the first member of the GOP to use racist and white supremacist language, but he brought it to the forefront and made it more acceptable in some circles. We cannot assume that with Trump out of office, white supremacy within politics will go away. In elections at local and national levels, openly white supremacist candidates are running and winning.

In a recent school board election just outside of Seattle, long-time PTA member Sara Cole, who was supported by community leaders and educators, lost to a member of the "Three Percenters," a far-right militia with a vengeance against the federal government. (Allum, 2022). The victor is a proud Three Percenter who did not hide her alliance to the militia during the election. She is a proud white nationalist with a visible red, white, and blue Three Percenter neck tattoo (2022).

Proud Boys and Oath Keepers, two recognized white supremacist groups are being represented in national-level elections. The Anti-Defamation League is now tracking over 100 elections involving what they deem "problematic candidates." (Anti-Defamation League, 2022). Like those winning local elections, some have ties to white supremacist organizations and are known to attend rallies, post with extremist group leaders, praise the violence of January 6, 2021, and oppose immigration. Some of these individuals are already in office and seeking re-election, including Wendy Rogers, an Arizona State Senator, who praises white supremacist leaders and speaks on neo-Nazi streaming media platforms and Rep. Marjorie Taylor Greene of Georgia, a QAnon supporter who has used racial slurs and antisemitic tropes.

Moving Forward

What began and proliferated in religion and politics has to be stopped. If hate can brew and fester as part of our past and current national climate, so can peace. We cannot stand by and allow hate to prevail, and we stand with our readers in solidarity toward fighting extremism.

Though a controversial figure given his initial support for the Third Reich, Martin Niemöller, a German theologian and Lutheran pastor, frequently shared the following quote.

> First they came for the socialists, and I did not speak out—because I was not a socialist. Then they came for the trade unionists, and I did not speak out— because I was not a trade unionist. Then they came for the Jews, and I did not speak out—because I was not a Jew. Then they came for me—and there was no one left to speak for me
>
> (United States Holocaust Memorial Museum, 2012)

In the next chapter, we will review the importance of intersecting identities among the targets of white supremacy and how the lean into that power of connection and the power of allies committed to pushing back against the tenets of the white supremacist movement.

Keep the Conversation Going

- Is housing inequity an issue in your city? If so, what impact is it having on marginalized groups?
- Are there parts of the Bible currently taken out of context by white supremacists?
- What role did mental health professionals play in desegregation?
- Do you feel there would be less anti-Asian disparaging under different presidential leadership than Trump?
- What can Christian leaders do to promote acceptance of all races and cultures within their congregations?

Note

1 Dr. Edward Janak and Candice Seiple contributed to this chapter, adding significant content on "lost cause" Confederate sympathizing and the racist roots of religion, respectively.

References

A History of Racial Injustice. (n.d.). May 14, 1961 – On this Day, Freedom Riders Attacked in Anniston, Alabama. https://calendar.eji.org/racial-injustice/may/14.

Allum, H. (2022, January 8). A Rural Washington school board race shows how far-right extremists are shifting to local power. *The Seattle Times*. www.seattletimes.com/nation-world/a-rural-washington-school-board-race-shows-how-far-right-extremists-are-shifting-to-local-power.

Angulano, D. (2022, February 3). California county on track to be run by militia-aligned group. *The Guardian*. www.theguardian.com/us-news/2022/feb/03/california-county-controlled-by-militia-group.

Anti-Defamation League. (2022, January 25). *Extremism on the ballot*. www.adl.org/blog/extremism-on-the-ballot-in-2022.

Bastide, R. (1967). Color, Racism, and Christianity. *Daedalus*, 96(2), 312–327. www.jstor.org/stable/20027040.

Brooks, J. (2020). *Mormonism and white supremacy: American religion and the problem of racial innocence*. Oxford: Oxford University Press.

Butler, A. (2021). *White Evangelical Racism*. Chapel Hill, NC: The University of North Carolina Press.

Chafe, W. (2001). *Remembering Jim Crow: African Americans Tell about Life in the Segregated South*. New York: The New Press, 2001.

Davey, J. and Ebner, J. (2019, July 7). The 'Great Replacement': The Violent Consequences of Mainstreamed Extremism. Institute for Strategic Dialogue. Retrieved December 20, 2021, from www.isdglobal.org/wp-content/uploads/2019/07/The-Great-Replacement-The-Violent-Consequences-of-Mainstreamed-Extremism-by-ISD.pdf.

Gjelten, T. (2020, July 1). White supremacist ideas have historical roots in U.S. Christianity. NPR. Retrieved November 2, 2021, from www.npr.org/2020/07/01/883115867/white-supremacist-ideas-have-historical-roots-in-u-s-christianity.

Goldstein, J. (2014, July). The Presence of the Past: Confronting the Nazi State and Jim Crow. Humanity in Action. Retrieved December 20, 2021, from www.humanityinaction.org/knowledge_detail/the-presence-of-the-past-confronting-the-nazi-state-and-jim-crow.

Howard, S. and Sommers, S.R. (2019). White religious iconography increases anti-black attitudes. *Psychology of Religion and Spirituality*, 11(4), 382–391. https://doi.org/10.1037/rel0000144.

Howard, S., Vine, K.T., and Kennedy, K.C. (2021). "jesus was a white man too!": The relationship between beliefs about jesus' race, racial attitudes, and ideologies that maintain racial hierarchies. *Psychology of Religion and Spirituality*. https://doi.org/10.1037/rel0000374.

Jackson, J.C., Hester, N., and Gray, K. (2018). The faces of god in america: Revealing religious diversity across people and politics. *PLOS ONE*, 13(6). https://doi.org/10.1371/journal.pone.0198745.

Johnson, C. (2021, August 26). How the Voting Rights Act came to be and how it's changed. NPR. Retrieved November 17, 2021, from www.npr.org/2021/08/26/1026457264/1965-voting-rights-act-supreme-court-john-lewis.

Kalu, M. (2019, December 9). Is there any significance to colors in the Bible? Christianity.com. Retrieved December 28, 2021, from www.christianity.com/wiki/bible/is-there-any-significance-to-colors-in-the-bible.html.

Levine, B. (2005) *Half Slave and Half Free: The Roots of the Civil War*. New York: Hill and Wang.

Lipka, M. (2020, May 30). The most and least racially diverse U.S. religious groups. Pew Research Center. Retrieved November 2, 2021, from www.pewresearch.org/fact-tank/2015/07/27/the-most-and-least-racially-diverse-u-s-religious-groups.

Luo, M. (2020, September 2). American christianity's white-supremacy problem. *The New Yorker*. Retrieved January 12, 2022, from www.newyorker.com/books/under-review/american-christianitys-white-supremacy-problem.

McCammon, S. (2020, September 30). From debate stage, trump declines to denounce white supremacy. NPR. Retrieved December 19, 2021, from www.npr.org/2020/09/30/918483794/from-debate-stage-trump-declines-to-denounce-white-supremacy.

Onwuachi-Willig, A. (2019). Reconceptualizing the Harms of Discrimination: How Brown V. Board of Education Helped to Further White Supremacy. *Virginia Law Review*, 105(2), 343–369.

Packard, J. (2002). *American Nightmare: The History of Jim Crow*. New York: St. Martin's Press.

Pescara-Kovach, Van Brunt, B., and Murphy, A. (2020). Terrorist in Training: The Role of Social Media and the Rise of Terrorism through Nationalistic White Agenda. *The Journal of Campus Behavioral Intervention*, 8, 1–11.

Pindi, G.N. and De La Garza, A.T. (2018). "The colonial jesus." *Interrogating the Communicative Power of Whiteness*, 218–238. https://doi.org/10.4324/9780203730003-12.

Prince, Z. (2016, June 15). 11 O'Clock on Sundays is Still the Most Segregated Hour in America. *The Louisiana Weekly*. www.louisianaweekly.com/eleven-oclock-on-sundays-is-still-the-most-segregated-hour-in-america.

Reed, R. (1994). *Politically Incorrect: The Emerging Faith Factor in American Politics*. Dallas, TX: Word Publishers.

Roberts, S. O., Weisman, K., Lane, J. D., Williams, A., Camp, N. P., Wang, M., Robison, M., Sanchez, K., and Griffiths, C. (2020). *God as a white man: A psychological barrier to conceptualizing black people and women as leadership worthy. Journal of Personality and Social Psychology*, 119(6), 1290–1315. https://doi.org/10.1037/pspi0000233.

Sons of Confederate Veterans. (n.d., a). The Constitution of the Sons of Confederate Veterans. Sons of Confederate Veterans Forms and Documents. https://scv.org/forms-and-documents/scv-constitution.

Sons of Confederate Veterans. (n.d., b). What is the Sons of Confederate Veterans ? Sons of Confederate Veterans. https://scv.org/what-is-the-scv.

Southern Poverty Law Center. (February21, 2019). Whose Hate? Public Symbols of the Confederacy. www.splcenter.org/20190201/whose-heritage-public-symbols-confederacy.

Tyler, L.G. (2014). A Confederate Catechism. The Confederate Reprint Company. Retrieved from https://confederatereprint.com/samples/Confederate_Catechism_sample.pdf.

United Church of Christ. (2021, January 22). Liturgical colors and the seasons of the church year. United Church of Christ. Retrieved December 19, 2021, from www.ucc.org/worship-way/worship_liturgies_liturgical-colors.

United Daughters of the Confederacy. (n.d.). History of the UDC. United Daughters of the Confederacy. https://hqudc.org/history-of-the-united-daughters-of-the-confederacy.

United States Department of Labor. (n.d.). Legal highlight: The civil rights act of 1964. United States Department of Labor. Retrieved November 17, 2021, from www.dol.gov/agencies/oasam/civil-rights-center/statutes/civil-rights-act-of-1964.

United States Holocaust Memorial Museum. (2012). "*Martin Niemöller: "First they came for the socialists...*". Holocaust Encyclopedia. Retrieved on January 21, 2022 from https://encyclopedia.ushmm.org/content/en/article/martin-niemoeller-first-they-came-for-the-socialists.

University of Southern California. (2020, March 19). Brief history of Jim Crow Laws. Online International LLM Degree Program. Retrieved December 19, 2021, from https://onlinellm.usc.edu/a-brief-history-of-jim-crow-laws.

3 The Intersecting Identities of Primary Targets

BIPOC, Muslims, Jews, AAPI, Women, LGBTQ+

Box 3.1 Key Take-aways

1. A central approach to addressing the rise in white supremacy is found in the shared pain and targeting of groups by the movement and the collaborative efforts among these groups to push back together.
2. While those who have been oppressed must be instrumental in the dissembling of those oppression, those white allies have an equally important part to play in addressing change from within a historically racist system.
3. The manifesto from the June 15, 2015, mass shooting that took place at Emanuel African Methodist Episcopal Church in Charleston, South Carolina is included in the chapter. This manifesto provides a clear outline of how white supremacists target different groups. While a disturbing writing, with many racial slurs, it was included to provide a direct example of the true nature of the problem and how hate is spread widely by those involved in this movement.
4. The role of the US government in addressing many of these historic and systemic issues through the Civil Rights Act of 1968 is discussed.

Our Many Selves

When we define ourselves, we often refer to our gender expression, sexual orientation, race, and ethnicity. Think of a common introduction or even a profile page on a dating site. One can hop on to look for "matches" regarding likes and dislikes as well as some of the identifiers listed above. Seems simple enough for some. Yet others have lived a lifetime in fear of revealing one or more defining characteristics, knowing there are white supremacists among us who have nothing but nefarious intentions. Those who might fall into multiple minoritized groups often have even more reason to fear. The term minoritized, introduced by Yasmin Gunaratnum in 2003, provides a social constructionist approach

DOI: 10.4324/9781003199656-3

to understanding that people are actively minoritized by others rather than naturally existing as a minority, as the terms racial minorities or ethnic minorities imply. White supremacists tend to have a deep hatred for individuals and target those who fit within one minority, so one can imagine the dangers posed for those who possess characteristics aligned with more than one.

Kimberlé Crenshaw (2017) is credited with coining the term intersectionality in 1989, to describe how race, class, gender, and other characteristics intersect and overlap with one another. In the same way understanding the connective overlap related to race and gender both being factors in the systemic oppression of Black woman, intersectionality provides a useful model for appreciating how the white supremacist movement not only targets people based on skin color but more broadly assaults a collection of traits, difference, politics, philosophies, cultures, and religious beliefs. While rarely expressed so eloquently at their gatherings, this hatred toward various groups provides a pathway to unravel their movement as with the downfall of Rome, whose expansive network of roads became its ultimate downfall by providing a pathway for its enemies to mobilize more quickly.

Box 3.2 Terminology

Before continuing, let's be sure we are on the same page regarding the meaning of key terms. Gender expression refers to the way we show our gender to others, typically via our clothing, hairstyle, activities, or even mannerisms (GLSEN, n.d.). Though often confused as having the same meaning, sexual orientation is something psychologists agree is not a conscious choice (American Psychological Association, 2011). Sexual orientation involves sexual attraction. That is, sexual orientation is based upon the gender or genders that spark our sexual desire. According to genome.gov, race is a term used to group together individuals with similar skin color and facial features. Contemporary views on race suggest race is not a biological construct but rather a social construct. Those who share similar beliefs, norms, and practices (e.g., same language, same religion) because of a shared history and cultural inheritance are of the same ethnicity.

One way to thwart white supremacy is to bring together the groups on whom the white supremacist targets their hatred. By leaning into our commonalities and gathering our resources, we become more efficient and effective in our mobilization to push back against their escalation of hatred and violence. As school children gather to fight a common bully, the gathering of those targeted creates a *gestalt*, an organized whole that is perceived as more than the sum of its parts. To this end, let us understand the some of the groups targeted by the white supremacist to better learn how we can all work together to counteract their violent philosophy.

As is often the case, authors are friends with other scholars who are kind enough to offer critique and review of chapters as they are in development. Dr. Poppy Fitch is one such friendly scholar, and during our personal correspondence (2022), she shared the following regarding the preceding paragraph. We were tempted to work the concept into the existing writing more subtly or change the text to lessen her concerns, yet Fitch says this so clearly, we felt her words should stand on their own and the lesson here highlights both the nature of unintended microaggressions and, if we might be so bold, an example of how to address them.

> I'm having an interesting reaction to the previous paragraph. Should we consider if it is the responsibility of targeted groups to counteract the target, or is it the responsibility of those with similar identities to push against white supremacist hate and extremism? I'm thinking: "White people, come get your people." I think it is appropriate for us to start thinking of the ways that we are responsible for speaking up, holding accountable, and calling out/in when we see issues within our families and communities.
>
> (Fitch, 2022)

This microaggression, one of those subtle, unintended messages that conveys a negative message to a minoritized group, is addressed here and hopefully serves as a teachable moment. There is something problematic in the implication that those targeted have the responsibility to come together and solve this problem because of their shared pain. This is a conversation in advocacy, with allies taking this message up and not expecting those who have been harmed to be solely responsible for the solution. White people, come get your people. This is not a problem to be solved solely by those who have been targeted by this hatred.

Box 3.3 Limitations

When writing this chapter, we attempted to cast a wide, inclusive net over all of those affected by the hatred and pain grown and dissemination by the white supremacist movement. Without question, other groups have been very directly and powerfully impacted by this hatred, including those with physical or mental disabilities and those faithful in other religions such as the Sikhi, Jains, Buddhists, and Sufi Muslims. We do not want to appear to diminish the effect of white supremacy on these other groups; however, space and time constraints prevented a detailed discussion of some groups.

BIPOC (Black, Indigenous and People of Color)

As white supremacists define themselves, they declare first the whiteness of their skin as a feature to be desired and one that is superior to that of others. The rise of white supremacist rhetoric was illuminated more fully during the Trump presidency and as a countermovement to the Black Lives Matter (BLM) movement (Whitaker, 2020) and related protests that unfolded in the spring and summer of 2020 following the murders of George Floyd, Ahmaud Arbury, Breonna Taylor, Rayshard Brooks, Jacob Blake, and Daniel Prude (Ortiz, 2020). But it began centuries ago.

It is easy to recognize this mindset of white superiority in such theories as the "Great Replacement" (Camus, 2012; English translation, 2018). The great replacement began as a philosophy held by Albert Camus who believed that immigration into France and other nations would end national purity. Today, white supremacists across the globe use the philosophy as their justification for acts of hate against those without "pure" roots within their nation. A term used by Camus that summarizes this perspective simply is "genocide by substitution" (Bullens, n.d., para. 6).

The great replacement is not the only philosophy that degrades BIPOC people. On June 17, 2015, a mass shooting took place at Emanuel African Methodist Episcopal Church in Charleston, South Carolina. The attacker left a manifesto describing his reasons for the attack. The manifesto sums up the major talking points of the movement well. A larger section of the manifesto is quoted below. As a content warning, the language is coarse and filled with spelling errors and makes use of racial slurs:

> I was not raised in a racist home or environment. Living in the South, almost every White person has a small amount of racial awareness, simply because of the numbers of negroes in this part of the country. But it is a superficial awareness. Growing up, in school, the White and black kids would make racial jokes toward each other, but all they were jokes. Me and White friends would sometimes would watch things that would make us think that "blacks were the real racists" and other elementary thoughts like this, but there was no real understanding behind it.
>
> The event that truly awakened me was the Trayvon Martin case. I kept hearing and seeing his name, and eventually I decided to look him up. I read the Wikipedia article and right away I was unable to understand what the big deal was. It was obvious that Zimmerman was in the right. But more importantly this prompted me to type in the words "black on White crime" into Google, and I have never been the same since that day. The first website I came to was the Council of Conservative Citizens. There were pages upon pages of these brutal black on White murders. I was in disbelief. At this moment I realized that something was very wrong. How could the

news be blowing up the Trayvon Martin case while hundreds of these black on White murders got ignored?

From this point I researched deeper and found out what was happening in Europe. I saw that the same things were happening in England and France, and in all the other Western European countries. Again I found myself in disbelief. As an American we are taught to accept living in the melting pot, and black and other minorities have just as much right to be here as we do, since we are all immigrants. But Europe is the homeland of White people, and in many ways the situation is even worse there. From here I found out about the Jewish problem and other issues facing our race, and I can say today that I am completely racially aware.

Blacks

I think it is fitting to start off with the group I have the most reallife experience with, and the group that is the biggest problem for Americans.

Niggers are stupid and violent. At the same time they have the capacity to be very slick. Black people view everything through a racial lense (sic). Thats what racial awareness is, its viewing everything that happens through a racial lense (sic). They are always thinking about the fact that they are black. This is part of the reason they get offended so easily, and think that some thing (sic) are intended to be racist toward them, even when a White person wouldn't (sic) be thinking about race. The other reason is the Jewish agitation of the black race. Black people are racially aware almost from birth, but White people on average dont (sic) think about race in their daily lives. And this is our problem. We need to and have to. Say you were to witness a dog being beat by a man. You are almost surely going to eel (sic) very sorry for that dog. But then say you were to witness a dog biting a man. You will most likely not feel the same pity you felt for the dog for the man. Why? Because dogs are lower than Men. This same analogy applies to black and White relations. Even today, blacks are subconsciously viewed by White people are lower beings. They are held to a lower standard in general. This is why they are able to get away with things like obnoxious behavior in public. Because it is expected of them. Modern history classes instill a subconscious White superiority complex in Whites and an inferiority complex in lacks. This White superiority complex that comes from learning of how we dominated other peoples (sic) is also part of the problem I have just mentioned. But of course I dont (sic) deny that we are in fact superior. I wish with a passion that niggers were treated terribly throughout history by Whites, that every White person had an ancestor who owned slaves, that segregation was an evil an oppressive institution, and so on. Because if it was all it true, it would make it so much easier for me to accept our current situation. But it isn't true. None of it is. We are told to accept what is happening to us because of ancestors wrong doing, but it is all based on historical lies, exaggerations and myths. I have tried endlessly to think of reasons we deserve this, and I have only came (sic) back more irritated because there are no reasons.

Only a fourth to a third of people in the South owned even one slave. Yet every White person is treated as if they had a slave owning ancestor. This applies to in the states where slavery never existed, as well as people whose families immigrated after slavery was abolished. I have read hundreds of slaves (sic) narratives from my state. And almost all of them were positive. One sticks out in my mind where an old ex-slave recounted how the day his mistress died was one of the saddest days of his life. And in many of these narratives the slaves told of how their masters didnt (sic) even allowing (sic) whipping on his plantation.

Segregation was not a bad thing. It was a defensive measure. Segregation did not exist to hold back negroes. It existed to protect us from them. And I mean that in multiple ways. Not only did it protect us from having to interact with them, and from being physically harmed by them, but it protected us from being brought down to their level. Integration has done nothing but bring Whites down to level of brute animals. The best example of this is obviously our school system.

Now White parents are forced to move to the suburbs to send their children to "good schools". But what constitutes a "good school"? The fact is that how good a school is considered directly corresponds to how White it is. I hate with a passion the whole idea of the suburbs. To me it represents nothing but scared White people running. Running because they are too weak, scared, and brainwashed to fight. Why should we have to flee the cities we created for the security of the suburbs? Why are the suburbs secure in the first place? Because they are White. The pathetic part is that these White people dont (sic) even admit to themselves why they are moving. They tell themselves it is for better schools or simply to live in a nicer neighborhood. But it is honestly just a way to escape niggers and other minorities.

But what about the White people that are left behind? What about the White children who, because of school zoning laws, are forced to go to a school that is 90 percent black? Do we really think that that White kid will be able to go one day without being picked on for being White, or called a "white boy"? And who is fighting for him? Who is fighting for these White people forced by economic circumstances to live among negroes? No one, but someone has to.

Here I would also like to touch on the idea of a Norhtwest Front. I think this idea is beyond stupid. Why should I for example, give up the beauty and history of my state to go to the Norhthwest (sic) To me the whole idea just parralells (sic) the concept of White people running to the suburbs. The whole idea is pathetic and just another way to run from the problem without facing it.

Some people feel as though the South is beyond saving, that we have too many blacks here. To this I say look at history. The South had a higher ratio of blacks when we were holding them as slaves. Look at South Africa, and how such a small minority held the black in apartheid for years and years. Speaking of South Africa, if anyone thinks that think will eventually just change for the better, consider how in South Africa they have affirmative action for the black population that makes up 80 percent of the population.

It is far from being too late for America or Europe. I believe that even if we made up only 30 percent of the population we could take it back completely. But by no means should we wait any longer to take drastic action.

Anyone who thinks that White and black people look as different as we do on the outside, but are somehow magically the same on the inside, is delusional. How could our faces, skin, hair, and body structure all be different, but our brains be exactly the same? This is the nonsense we are led to believe.

Negroes have lower Iqs (sic), lower impulse control, and higher testosterone levels in generals. These three things alone are a recipe for violent behavior. If a scientist publishes a paper on the differences between the races in Western Europe or Americans, he can expect to lose his job. There are personality traits within human families, and within different breeds of cats or dogs, so why not within the races?

A horse and a donkey can breed and make a mule, but they are still two completely different animals. Just because we can breed with the other races doesnt (sic) make us the same.

In a modern history class it is always emphasized that, when talking about "bad" things Whites have done in history, they were White. But when we lern (sic) about the numerous, almost countless wonderful things Whites have done, it is never pointed out that these people were White. Yet when we learn about anything important done by a black person in history, it is always pointed out repeatedly that they were black. For example when we learn about how George Washington carver was the first nigger smart enough to open a peanut.

On another subject I want to say this. Many White people feel as though they dont (sic) have a unique culture. The reason for this is that White culture is world culture. I dont (sic) mean that our culture is made up of other cultures, I mean that our culture has been adopted by everyone in the world. This makes us feel as though our culture isnt (sic) special or unique. Say for example that every business man I the world wore a kimono, that every skyscraper was in

> the shape of a pagoda, that every door was a sliding one, and that everyone ate every meal with chopsticks. This would probably make a Japanese man feel as though he had no unique traditional culture.
>
> I have noticed a great disdain for race mixing White women within the White nationalists community, bordering on insanity it (sic). These women are victims, and they can be saved. Stop.

Roof's manifesto was clearly racist. As if the verbiage is not clear enough, he refers to the Council of Conservative Citizens (CCC), an organization with its roots in the 1950s and 1960s formed for the sole purpose of battling desegregation. Fast forward to today and the CCC has within its Statement of Principles that they "oppose all efforts to mix the races of mankind" (Southern Poverty Law Center, n.d.). Roof also speaks highly of slavery and indicates that slaves had enjoyable experiences despite what we all know today about that shameful part of history.

It is important to understand how the concept of whites as superior came to be. It is easy to assume that Caucasians were referred to as white since the beginning of time, but this is far from accurate. According to Roediger's "Historical Foundations of Race" (n.d.), Europeans used the terms, white, slave, and race in the 1500s, but it was not until the United States was developing that the terms took on the meanings they have today. In fact, before the mid-1600s, the English men never labeled themselves "white," but instead used the term as a moniker for wealthy English women whose skin remained white because they did not have to partake in outdoor labor (Roediger, n.d.). Believe it or not, this was a period in which Englishmen were insulted if they were called white, as it implied weakness or incompetence for outdoor work.

Colonists embraced the term to distinguish themselves from those they referred to as the "savage" Indian race and from Blacks whom they considered less than human. Colonists soon weaponized to torture and enslave others. And so began our nation's long history of racism that continues today. We can see its continuation in a wide range of contexts extended beyond slavery. Words like "lynching" and "whipping" should never be associated with the treatment of any human being. These terms describe acts committed by racist slave owners against the innocent Black people they enslaved. And today the words are expressed in the rhetoric and acts of white supremacists as evident in the torture of James Byrd, Jr. (Chapter 7, case 15).

James Byrd, Jr was a trusting man. He was the kind of man who did not hesitate to hop into a truck with friends to catch a ride. It likely never crossed his mind that doing so would result in one of the most violent anti-Black hate crimes in our nation's history. On June 7, 1998, Byrd hopped into a truck with three men from his hometown of Jasper, Texas. He considered the driver to be a friend and thought that together he and the others in the truck would spend some time together relaxing or having some drinks. Nothing could be farther from the truth. Unbeknownst to Byrd, he was riding with a group of individuals who hated him because of the color of his skin (Goodwyn, 2019). He did not notice that one of the men wore his white supremacy with pride in the form of tattoos, including a Black man hanging from a noose, "Aryan Pride," and an array of Nazi symbols.

What transpired on the last evening of James Byrd's life was violent beyond belief. He was driven into the woods where he was urinated upon and beaten with a baseball bat (Goodwyn, 2019). In addition, his face was spray painted (*Chicago Tribune*, 1998). Once the men beat him nearly lifeless, they chained his ankles to the back of the truck and dragged him, face down, for approximately three miles. He did not die until about halfway through the journey. Byrd's badly torn body was then removed from the truck, and the perpetrators placed several of his bodily remains in front of a known Black church. This was a racially motivated hate crime without a doubt, as the men were known white supremacists. However, men who think like the perpetrators who killed James Byrd have existed not only in small towns, but also in scientific laboratories.

Box 3.4 Scientific Racism

Scientific racism is an ideology based on Darwin's idea of natural selection, Mendel's law of inheritance, and the manipulation of advances in genetic research (Eugenics and Scientific Racism Fact Sheet, n.d.). Scientific racism is blatantly clear when we dig into the actual practices involved. In the world of genetics, we see scientific racism hiding under the guise of "eugenics," which claims that an ethical means to eradicate illness and diseases is by selective "breeding" via careful manipulations of genetics and heredity (National Human Genome Research Institute, n.d.).

James Marion Sims is lauded as the "father of modern gynecology" (Holland, 2018). Sims' legacy is a dark and devious one, as he chose only Black female slaves as his subjects. To those who defend Sims's claim that he was providing surgical intervention and medical care to women who otherwise would not have otherwise had the treatment. Those who see Sims as a medical marvel must understand that his inventions were torture for the innocent Black women. The procedures he conducted involved experimental surgical tools and various methods of cutting and stitching of the vaginal and other reproductive areas. And we must understand that Sims did this to women without anesthesia (Holland, 2018). The women had no choice but to do what a white man commanded them to do. Sims was not just a doctor, but a slave owner who had free rein to mutilate innocent women because of the color of their skin. But torturous research within our nation's history does not end there.

One of the most notorious acts of hate in the name of science is the 1932 study initially deemed the "Tuskegee study of untreated syphilis in the Negro male."

> The study initially involved 600 Black men – 399 with syphilis, 201 who did not have the disease. Participants' informed consent was not collected.
>
> Researchers told the men they were being treated for "bad blood," a local term used to describe several ailments, including syphilis, anemia, and fatigue. In exchange for taking part in the study, the men received free medical exams,
>
> free meals, and burial insurance.
>
> (Centers for Disease Control and Prevention, n.d., para.1)

Not only were the individuals experimented upon targeted due to the color of their skin, but they were also deceived in ways that led to tragedies beyond measure, all of which were preventable. As was determined in 1943, Penicillin is an effective treatment for syphilis, yet the Tuskegee participants were not privy to this information, nor provided the treatment. Had it not been for an article in the Associated Press (Heller, 1972), the study would have gone on indefinitely, which is unconscionable given the high number of innocent men who died because of untreated syphilis and their innocent wives, partners, and children who were infected with the bacteria. It was as though, by nature of their race, they were viewed as dispensable. But the suffering did not end with the article. A panel was selected to review the ethics or lack thereof involved in the study. Despite knowing of the sickness, death, and deceit imposed upon the men, the panel concluded that the men were willful participants who were treated ethically by the racist researchers. In truth, the Tuskegee experiment paralleled what took place in Nazi Germany, and the acts were not only criminal; they were monstrous.

Box 3.5 Eugenics

Eugenics, the brainchild of Charles' Darwin's cousin, Francis Galton, is nothing but involuntary sterilization, unethical experimentation, segregation, prohibition of marriages, and social exclusion. Galton described his new scientific strategy as something that could control lower intellectual ability and flawed social skills he deemed related to race (Aubert-Marson, 2009). Galton convinced many across the world that marriage and procreation outside of the white race led to inferior human beings. Although Darwin and Galton are thought to be the genetic and medical sources of the eugenics movement, and World War II historians speak heavily of its use by Nazis, our nation's hands are not clean. Heinous crimes have been committed against innocent Black men and women.

In the United States, as in many countries, it is easy to view the eugenics movement as part of an isolated and long, distant history. However, in 2020 Project South shared a letter from a healthcare worker to several national and Atlanta area officials describing "vile, unacceptable acts against detained immigrants." In the letter, the healthcare worker/author discusses the atrocities taking place at a for-profit detention facility:

> ...this complaint raises red flags regarding the rate at which hysterectomies are performed on immigrant women under ICE[1] custody at ICDC[2]. This complaint also documents hazardous and reckless actions taken by ICDC management such as allowing employees to work while they are symptomatic awaiting COVID-19 test results and hiding information from employees and detained immigrants about who has tested positive for COVID-19. In addition, this complaint documents ICDC's disregard for public health guidelines set by the Centers for Disease Control and Prevention by maintaining unsanitary conditions and continuously allowing transfers of detained immigrants, even those who have tested positive for COVID-19, and punishing immigrants with solitary confinement when they speak out against these injustices.
>
> (p. 2)

As recently as September 2020, the healthcare worker's sentiments, as summarized by Project South's Institute for the Elimination of Poverty and Genocide, show that innocent women are being sterilized and socially excluded, which echoes the atrocities of Hitler and his followers and demonstrates just how little has changed from the days when slaves and other innocents were viewed as undeserving of humanity.

Box 3.6 Racism in Housing

The history of physical and medical violence was intensified by politics. The US government has also had a role in furthering racist policies beyond slavery. For instance, *redlining* involved blocking Black home seekers from gaining access to home loans. Unbeknownst to potential home buyers, many of whom were Black, government agencies created maps of various geographic locations with red lines dividing those who should be granted loans from those who should not. Several organizations, including the Federal Housing Administration (FHA), the Homeowners Loan Corporation, and the GI Bill, worked under the premise that living among or near Black communities devalued property (Faber, 2020). This led to what Rothstein deems, a "white noose" of wealth encircling communities in poverty (Rothstein, 2017, p. 201). Redlining is far more than a historical artifact. Rather, its impact remains. Most Americans gain the bulk of their wealth and net worth in the value of their homes. Homes that today are valued at $300,000 to $400,000 were purchased decades ago at more affordable prices via VA or

FHA loans that were denied to prospective Black buyers who were well equipped to pay their mortgages. Instead, redlining resulted in forcing Black families out of areas that continued to gain in wealth and possess greater wealth even today (Rothstein, 2017).

Muslim Americans

Another group often targeted by white supremacists is those who follow the teaching of Islam. The root of this hatred is more pronounced in European countries and dates all the way to the crusades. Following the attacks on 9/11 in the United States, hatred increased toward those from the Middle East, which translated to anti-Muslim sentiment writ large.

On July 22, 2011, a massacre took place starting in Oslo, Norway and ending on the island of Utøya (Chapter 7: Case 44) Eight innocent people were killed in Oslo, and 69 youths were gunned down in Utøya. Before the attack, the perpetrator purportedly posted a 12-minute video and wrote a 1500-page manifesto. His motive, as stated in the video, was to prevent the Islamization of Europe (Botelho et al., 2011). The terrorist killer desired a war against Muslims because, he claimed that, without it, Europe would be overtaken by Muslims by 2050 (Botelho et al, 2011; Pidd, 2012).

The policies and statements of former-president Trump added fuel to the fire and provided justification to white supremacist groups. By extension, Trump's vow to block Muslims from entering the United States, combined with travel bans on several Muslim countries, led to a documented increase in hate crimes against Muslims in the United States. According to the Muslim Advocates group in Washington, DC, "[Trump's] anti-Muslim politics led to real violence and hate against Muslims" (Waheed, in Abdalla, 2021).

On March 15, 2019 a total of 51 people were killed and 49 injured in Christchurch, New Zealand (Chapter 7: Case 78). The shooter targeted two mosques at a time when he knew they would be in morning prayer. Like the Norwegian attacker, the Christchurch attacker wrote a manifesto in which he spewed hatred of unwelcome intruders who needed to be subjected to retaliation and violence because they were inhabiting European territory (Pescara-Kovach, Van Brunt, and Murphy, 2020). There is no question that the gunman chose mosques, as he knew they would be filled with those practicing the Muslim faith.

Jewish Americans

The targeting of Jewish people has been on the rise in the United States again in recent years. White supremacist thought puts forth the idea of Jews being in control of the banks and media with strong influences throughout US culture.

One of the more prominent antisemitic groups is the National Anarchist Movement (NAM), which stands for racial separatism. Members of NAM were present at the January 6, 2021, attack at the Capitol, which indicates they remain a source of hate (Neilson and McFall-Johnsen, 2021). Such a mindset encourages violence. One of the most disturbing attacks on those of Jewish descent took place at the Tree of Life Synagogue in Pittsburgh, Pennsylvania, on October 27, 2018 (Chapter 7: Case 77). The worship services were cut short when a gunman entered the synagogue, yelling antisemitic slurs while firing an AR-15 assault rifle, killing 11 innocent Jews (Green, 2019).

Less than a year later, on April 27, 2019, the Poway Synagogue in Poway, California, was the site of yet another antisemitic attack (Chapter 7: Case 81). Like the Tree of Life perpetrator, the Poway perpetrator was a white male filled with antisemitic views, as was evident when he called 9–1-1 as he was leaving the synagogue, stating "I just shot up a synagogue...because Jewish people are destroying the white race" (Watson and Spagat, 2020). In December 2019 there was an attack on a kosher market in Jersey City, New Jersey, in which three innocent civilians and a police officer lost their lives (Chapter 7: Case 87). In addition, a forced entry into a rabbi's Hannukah celebration in Monsey, New York, resulted in five individuals stabbed by a perpetrator armed with a knife (Chapter 7: Case 88).

Women

Patriarchal and misogynist sentiment has been co-mingled with white supremacy by the likes of conservative talk show radio host Rush Limbaugh and his infamous use of the term "feminazis" and the anti-feminist, derogatory speech and actions on the US political scene during the 2016 election. When women are accepted in the white supremacist movement, it is often conditioned on their willingness to behave in so-called "appropriate gender roles" and align their thoughts to subjugated positions. According to the "IntelBrief: Women in White Supremacist Online Ecosystems," white supremacist ideology sees traditional gender roles as part of the natural order and that liberal outside forces are purposely corrupting this order (The Soufan Center, 2020).

Among white supremacist groups, the alt-right shares a commonality with incels (involuntary celibates) and men's rights activists (ADL, n.d.). That is, each has a disdain for women and believes they should be able to have sex with any woman at any time. In fact, the hatred of women among white supremacists has turned violent and is so common that this list of white supremacists who have been charged with domestic are living proof of misogynist hatred:

- Richard Poplowski murdered three police officers who responded to a call from his mother after he threatened her (Wildmoon, 2009; Chapter 7: Case 34).
- JT Ready killed his girlfriend, her son, and her boyfriend before killing himself (Schwartz, 2012; Chapter 7: Case 47).
- William Fears IV choked his girlfriend to the point she feared for her life (Barrouquere, 2018; Chapter 7, case 71).
- Matthew Heimbach attacked his wife and choked his mistress' husband (Walters, 2018; Chapter 7: Case 74).

Hatred of women is evident in the actions of white supremacists beyond domestic and partner violence. On March 16, 2021 Robert Aaron Long directed his anger at massage parlors in metropolitan Atlanta, Georgia, that he had visited in the past. Long was a self-proclaimed sex and pornography addict, and at the end of his shooting spree, eight people of Asian descent were dead, including six women (Chapter 7: Case 96). Upon speaking to police, Long professed a desire to eliminate the temptation of the massage parlors (Craig et al., 2021).

The LGBTQ+ Population

Those whose sexual orientation does not match the heteronormative model are seen as divergent and deviant by the white supremacist movement. A report by the Southern Poverty Law Center (2019) indicated a 43% increase in anti-LGBT hate groups in 2019 over 2018. This was the largest increase among all types of hate groups that particular year. The number is not diminishing.

Our nation has a long history of anti-LGBT hate. Attacks dating as far back as the 1960s range from individual shootings, stabbings, drownings, and beatings to arson fires and bombings of gay bars. Today's anti-LGBT white supremacists share similar beliefs with Hitler's regime. As stated by Friedman (n.d.):

> Homosexuals were often given the choice of sterilization, castration, or incarceration in a concentration camp. This treatment was "because of a law passed in 1871, under paragraph 175 of the German penal code, making homosexuality a criminal offense.5 Under the Nazis, thousands of persons were persecuted and punished on the charge of homosexuality. Many were sent to concentration camps, where they had to wear a pink triangle *(Rosa Windel)*.
>
> (para. 11)

Though not the only gay man to die a horrific death at the hands of hate, the death of Matthew Shepard (Chapter 7: Case 16) opened many people's eyes to the daily reality and risks to those who identify as LGBT.

On October 7, 1999 Shepard, a small-statured, peaceful 21-year-old University of Wyoming student, was found tied to a fence, beaten so badly the cyclist who found him initially thought he was a scarecrow (Matthew Shepard Foundation, n.d.). Shepard was unresponsive, having been gravely injured and exposed to the cold for 18 hours. The assault was not the result of an altercation; instead, Shepard was targeted for one reason: he was gay. Shepard succumbed to his injuries five days later, surrounded by family and friends. Matthew Shepard was not the first person to die in an anti-LGBT attack, but his death reminds us that we must do all we can to identify those with a tendency to engage in such acts of violence against the innocent. Shepard's death, coupled with the death of James Byrd, Jr (Chapter 7, Case 15), led to the passing of the Matthew Shepard and James Byrd, Jr. Hate Crimes Prevention Act of 2009.

Asian Americans and Pacific Islanders

As we speak, two serious threats, COVID-19 and white supremacy, seem to be on a collision course with innocent people. Rumors are running rampant regarding vaccine safety and effectiveness, safe treatments, and the origin of the virus. Of all populations within our nation, Asian Americans are most affected by COVID-19 rumors.

The rise in hatred began in 2020, shortly after the World Health Organization released a statement regarding a novel coronavirus originating in Wuhan, China, specifically, in the Huanan Wholesale Seafood Market. The rumor that patient zero ate an infected bat at a dirty outdoor market was then spun into a false narrative that Asian Americans consume unclean animals, leading to death and disease within the US. This belief has led to racial slurs and worse. As stated in Pescara-Kovach and Dagostino-Kalniz (2020):

> Hate is threatening safety and security on a parallel path with COVID-19. It seems the more media hype and false information that circulates... the more violence we are seeing at a time when we should be unified against a common enemy, COVID-19.
>
> (p. 4)

A recent Pew Research survey (Ruiz et al., 2021) found that post-COVID origination, a much higher percentage of Asian adults feel there has been a greater increase in violence directed at them. Eighty-one percent of Asian adults and 56% of the general public feel that violence toward their own group is rising. Tragically, 32% of Asian adults live in fear of being physically attacked or threatened (2021).

Dr. Fitch's comments above speak volumes when it comes to the maltreatment of Asian Americans and the response of white people. By extension, a previous Pew Survey determined that the majority of those surveyed have witnessed a range of discrimination directed toward Asian Americans in our nation (Ruiz et al., 2021). The number is somewhat shocking: 71% are seeing this, but the question is, what is being done? How do we stop it when we see it, and if we don't, are we part of the problem? Hate groups are increasing swiftly and it takes all of us to thwart their actions. We need to work to protect all of those affected by white supremacist views, especially those who identify with more than one of the targeted groups. This brings us to intersectionality.

Intersectionality, Hatred, and Violence

The issue of intersectionality arises in some of the most disturbing hate crimes in our nation. It is important to recognize those who, by nature of identifying with more than one marginalized group, are at greatest risk of being harmed or killed at the hands of those with white supremacist views and motives. Though not all intersections will be covered, two clear examples are provided.

Black LGBT Americans

According to Mahowald (2021), "2021 is on track to become the deadliest year in history for violence against Black transgender individuals, at least 16 of whom have been killed by in hate incidents as of this April" (para. 1). Eliel Cruz states (in Kesslen, 2019), homophobia and racism combine as intersections of violence, which lend themselves to increased hate crimes by those experiencing both. Further, according to the National Coalition of Anti-Violence Programs, known for its work in anti-LGBT violence prevention, "transgender women of color are particularly at risk…22 of the 52 LGBT hate-motivated homicide victims (42 percent) in 2017 were trans women of color" (Kesslen, 2019, para 6).

Muslim American Women

Recent research conducted by Alimahomed-Wilson (2017) combined interviews of 40 Muslim American women, a review of civil rights policies, and an examination of hate crimes data. In the interviews alone, Alimahomed-Wilson indicated that 85% of those she interviewed were verbally threatened or assaulted in public, and 25% indicated they were victims of physical violence. These are but a few statistics, yet it is clear, regardless of one's information source, that post-9/11 America has not been pleasant for many Muslim Americans who often live in fear of what will be said or done to them.

Federal Laws Against Hate Crimes

The United States Department of Justice (USDOJ) has been involved in hate crimes legislation since the introduction of the Civil Rights Act of 1968. However, many recent hate crimes, though terrorizing to the victims, do not fit within federal hate crime laws because the laws are specific to certain actions and particular groups of individuals. The following are the current federal laws related to hate crimes:

- The Matthew Shepard (Chapter 7, case 16), and James Byrd, Jr. (Chapter 7, case 15), Hate Crimes Prevention Act of 2009
- Criminal Interference with Right to Fair Housing
- Damage to Religious Property, Church Arson Prevention Act
- Violent Interference with Federally Protected Rights

As stated on the USDOJ website, "Federal laws protect against *certain* crimes motivated by race, color, national origin, religion, sexual orientation, gender, gender identity, and disability" (United States Department of Justice, 2021). The term "certain" being included in the definition is disconcerting, as it opens the opportunity for domestic terrorists who commit acts of hate to dodge prosecution and related charges. Many laws and statutes rest within local territories and states, with variations as to what constitutes a hate crime in each state or region.

The USDOJ provides a table on its website that lists seven potential bases for hate crimes: race/color, national origin, religion, sexual orientation, gender/sex, gender identity, and disability. Perhaps unsurprisingly, the reality of the situation rests in the political ideology and will of state officials. It seems logical that one would find the strictest hate crime laws in liberal/moderate states and the least strict in conservative states.

According to Laguardia (2020), our nation is lacking a statute that can be successfully applied to terrorism, including what some might see as small acts of terrorism. Also lacking is an unwillingness to designate those in the extreme far right as domestic terror groups. Many white perpetrators of domestic terrorism have not been charged with hate crimes, but their actions are minimized as resulting from being "disgruntled" and the race, religious, or cultural background of the victims are deemed coincidental (Ray, 2021). White male shooters like Dylann Roof at the church in Charleston and Patrick Crusius in El Paso were charged with hate crimes because they had clearly targeted Black Americans and Latinos, but this is not always the case when white nationalist or white supremacist motives lead to the terror. Whether it is loyalty to "fellow Americans" or the weak or nonexistent nature of potential charges, it seems that some domestic terrorists avoid being labeled and charged as such.

Moving Forward

Given the vulnerability of marginalized individuals, how do we work together to ensure we safeguard their well-being? Part of this work involves the acknowledgment that those allies in the white community have a responsibility to stand with and for those targeted by white supremacist groups. This involves a commitment to understanding how their hatred and behaviors affect all of society and the importance of a coordinated, multifaceted response to keep everyone safe, regardless of whether they have been targeted or not. The next chapter provides a summary of common symbolism used by white supremacists to express connection to one another and enlist new members.

Keep the Conversation Going

- Why is race a social rather than biological construct? Who benefits from incorrectly claiming it is biological?
- What can you do in your current role to dispel myths among minoritized groups?
- What phrases in Dylann Roof's manifesto represent a mindset analogous to the "Great Replacement" theory?
- Black Americans have expressed COVID-19 vaccine hesitancy due to a mistrust of researchers. Given the history of research in the US, what led to the hesitancy and how can we work to improve their trust?
- What are some ways allies can work together to develop school or university policies geared toward fighting white supremacy?

Notes

1 Immigration and Customs Enforcement.
2 Irwin County Detention Center.

References

Abdalla, J. (2021, September 9). 'Under the prism': Muslim-Americans reflect on life post 9/11. Al Jazeera. www.aljazeera.com/news/2021/9/9/under-the-prism-muslim-americans-reflect-on-life-post-9.

Alimahomed-Wilson, S. (2017). Invisible violence: Gender, Islamophobia, and the hidden assault on U.S. Muslim women. *Women, Gender, and Families of Color*, 5(1): 73–97.

American Psychological Association. (2011, December). Sexual orientation and gender identity. www.apa.org/topics/lgbtq/sexual-orientation.

Anti-Defamation League's Center on Extremism. (n.d.). When Women are the Enemy: The Intersection of Misogyny and White Supremacy. www.adl.org/media/11707/download.

Aubert-Marson, D. (2009). Sir Francis Galton: the father of eugenics. *Med Sci (Paris)*, Jun-Jul, 25(6–7): 641–645. French. https://pubmed.ncbi.nlm.nih.gov/19602363.

Barrouquere, B. (2018, January 23). Cops say Richard Spencer supporter William Fears IV choked girlfriend days before Florida shooting. Southern Poverty Law Center. www.splcenter.org/hatewatch/2018/01/23/cops-say-richard-spencer-supporter-william-fears-iv-choked-girlfriend-days-florida-shooting.

Botelho, G., Carter, C.J., Shoichet, C., and Stang, F. (2011, July 24). Purported manifesto, video from Norway terror suspect detail war plan, CNN. www.cnn.com/2011/WORLD/europe/07/24/norway.terror.manifesto/index.html.

Bullens, R. (n.d.). How France's 'great replacement' theory conquered the global far right. France 24. www.france24.com/en/europe/20211108-how-the-french-great-replacement-theory-conquered-the-far-right.

Camus, R. (2018). *You Will Not Replace Us.* Chez L'auteur.

Centers for Disease Control and Prevention. (n.d.). The United States Public Health Service Syphilis at Tuskegee: The Tuskegee Timeline. www.cdc.gov/tuskegee/timeline.htm.

Chicago Tribune. (1998, June 25). Dragging Victim's Face Reportedly Spray Painted. www.chicagotribune.com/news/ct-xpm-1998-06-25-9806250327-story.html.

Craig, T., Pulliam Bailey, S., Firozi, P., and Witte, G. (2021, March 17). Suspect charged with killing 8 in Atlanta-area shootings that targeted Asian run spas. *The Washington Post.* www.washingtonpost.com/national/shooting-in-atlanta/2021/03/17/a4027d46-8758-11eb-8a67-f314e5fcf88d_story.html.

Crenshaw, Kimberlé W. (2017). "On Intersectionality: Essential Writings". *Books.* 255. https://scholarship.law.columbia.edu/books/255.

Faber, J.W. (2020). We Built This: Consequences of New Deal Era Intervention in America's Racial Geography. *American Sociological Review*, 85, 739–775.

Fitch, P. (2022). *Personal Communication.*

Friedman, I.R. (n.d.). The Other Victims of the Nazis. www.socialstudies.org/sites/default/files/publications/se/5906/590606.html.

GLSEN. (n.d.). *Gender Terminology: Discussion Guide.* www.glsen.org/sites/default/files/Gender%20Terminology%20Guide.pdf.

Goodwyn, W. (2019, April 24). Texas Executes Man Convicted In 1998 Murder of James Byrd Jr. *National Public Radio.* www.npr.org/2019/04/24/716647585/texas-to-execute-man-convicted-in-dragging-death-of-james-byrd-jr.

Green, E. (2019). America Has Already Forgotten the Tree of Life Shooting. Retrieved on February 4, 2020 from www.theatlantic.com/politics/archive/2019/10/tree-life-and-legacy-pittsburghs-synagogue-attack/600946.

Gunaratnum, Y. (2003) *Researching Race and Ethnicity.* Thousand Oaks, CA: Sage Publications.

Heller, J. (1972, July 26). Syphilis Victims in U.S. Study Went Untreated for 40 Years. Associated Press, published in *The New York Times.* www.nytimes.com/1972/07/26/archives/syphilis-victims-in-us-study-went-untreated-for-40-years-syphilis.html.

Holland, D. (2018, December 4). The 'Father of Modern Gynecology' performed shocking experiments on enslaved women. *History newsletter.* www.history.com/news/the-father-of-modern-gynecology-performed-shocking-experiments-on-slaves.

Kesslen, B. (2019, January 30). LGBTQ people of color face 'compounded violence,' advocates say. NBC News. www.nbcnews.com/feature/nbc-out/lgbtq-people-color-face-compounded-violence-advocates-say-n964891.

Laguardia, F. (2020). Considering a Domestic Terrorism Statute and Its Alternatives. *Northwestern University Law Review*, 114. https://scholarlycommons.law.northwestern.edu/nulr/vol114/iss4/4.

Mahowald, L. (2021, July 13). Black LGBT Individuals Experience Heightened Levels of Discrimination. Center for American Progress. www.americanprogress.org/article/black-lgbtq-individuals-experience-heightened-levels-discrimination.

Matthew Shepard Foundation. (n.d.). Our Story. www.matthewshepard.org/about-us/our-story/.

National Human Genome Research Institute. (n.d.). Eugenics and Scientific Racism Fact Sheet. www.genome.gov/about-genomics/fact-sheets/Eugenics-and-Scientific-Racism.

Neilson, S. and McFall-Johnsen, M. (2021). Several groups of extremists stormed the Capitol on Wednesday. Here are some of the most notable individuals, symbols, and groups. *Business Insider*. www.businessinsider.com/hate-symbols-and-extremist-groups-at-the-us-capitol-siege-2021-1.

Ortiz, J. (2020). 'It's nothing but pain': The latest on the cases of violence against Black people that sparked America's racial reckoning. Retrieved on January 11, 2022 from www.usatoday.com/story/news/nation/2020/09/09/george-floyd-breonna-taylor-jacob-blake-what-we-know/5753696002/.

Pescara-Kovach, L. and Dagostino-Kalniz, V. (2020, March 31). COVID-19 and White Supremacy: When Fiction Kills. Tip of the Week, published in *NaBITA Newsletter*.

Pescara-Kovach, L., Van Brunt, B., and Murphy, A. (2020). Terrorist in Training: The Role of Social Media and the Rise of Terrorism through Nationalistic White Agenda. *Journal of Campus Behavioral Intervention (J-BIT)*.

Pidd, H. (2012). *Breivik: I shot Utøya victims because EU law made it hard to make bombs. The Guardian*. Retrieved on Oct. 2, 2015, from www.theguardian.com/world/2012/apr/19/anders-behringbreivik-utoya-victims.

Project South. (2020, September 14). Letter from the Institute for the Elimination of Poverty and Genocide to the United States Inspector General, Officer for Civil Rights and Civil Liberties, Acting Director of Atlanta ICE Field Office, Warden of the Irwin County Detention Center. Re: Lack of Medical Care, Unsafe Work Practices, and Absence of Adequate Protection Against COVID-19 for Detained Immigrants and Employees Alike at the Irwin County Detention Center.

Ray, R. (2021). Why is it so hard for America to designate domestic terrorism and hate crimes? Retrieved on January 21, 2022 from www.brookings.edu/blog/how-we-rise/2021/03/18/why-is-it-so-hard-for-america-to-designate-domestic-terrorism-and-hate-crimes.

Roediger, D.R. (n.d.) Foundations of Race. National Museum of African American History and Culture.. https://nmaahc.si.edu/learn/talking-about-race/topics/historical-foundations-race.

Rothstein, R. (2017). *The Color of Law: A Forgotten History of How Our Government Segregated America*. New York: Liveright.

Ruiz, N., Edwards, K., and Hugo-Lopez, M. (2021). One-third of Asian Americans fear threats, physical attacks and most say violence against them is rising. Retrieved on January 21, 2022 from www.pewresearch.org/fact-tank/2021/04/21/one-third-of-asian-americans-fear-threats-physical-attacks-and-most-say-violence-against-them-is-rising.

Schwartz, D. (2012). Militia leader suspected in Arizona murder-suicide. Reuters. www.reuters.com/article/us-usa-arizona-shooting/militia-leader-suspected-in-arizona-murder-suicide-idUSBRE8420RD20120503.

The Soufan Center. (2020). IntelBrief: Women in White Supremacist Online Ecosystems. Retrieved on January 21, 2022 from https://thesoufancenter.org/intelbrief-women-in-white-supremacist-online-ecosystems.

Southern Poverty Law Center. (n.d.). Council of Conservative Citizens. www.splcenter.org/fighting-hate/extremist-files/group/council-conservative-citizens.

Southern Poverty Law Center. (2019). The Year in Hate and Extremism. www.splcenter.org/sites/default/files/yih_2020_final.pdf.

United States Department of Justice. (2021). *Laws and Policies*. Retrieved on January 21, 2022 from www.justice.gov/hatecrimes/laws-and-policies.

Waheed, S. (2019, September 9), 'Under the prism': Muslim-Americans reflect on life post 9/11. Al Jazeera. www.aljazeera.com/news/2021/9/9/under-the-prism-muslim-americans-reflect-on-life-post-9.

Walters, J. (2018, March 4). Prominent US neo-Nazi arrested on domestic violence charge. *The Guardian*. www.theguardian.com/world/2018/mar/14/matthew-heimbach-neo-nazi-white-nationalism-arrest-domestic-violence.

Watson, J. and Spagat, E. (2020). Gunman told 911 'I just shot up a synagogue' after attack in Poway near San Diego. Retrieved on January 21, 2022 from www.desertsun.com/story/news/2019/05/10/gunman-poway-told-911-i-just-shot-up-synagogue/1162870001.

Whitaker, C.J. (2020, October). The Secret Power of White Supremacy — and How Anti-Racists Can Take It Back. *Politico*. www.politico.com/news/magazine/2020/10/29/knighthood-white-supremacy-433569.

Wildmoon, K.C. (2009, April 9). Police shooting suspect may have been a white supremacist. CNN, www.cnn.com/2009/CRIME/04/09/pa.shooting.suspect/index.html.

4 Know Thine Enemy

Language and Symbols of Hate

Box 4.1 Key Take-aways

1. White supremacists make use of a unique language and symbols to communicate with each other, recruit new members, and attempt to place fear in the hearts of those who they view as different and less than themselves.
2. The chapter provides an overview of these symbols and language in six categories, including numbers, gestures, phrases and acronyms, symbols, and concepts. These provide the reader a foundation of understanding and many of these examples will be referenced throughout the book.

What comes to mind when you hear the word, "defend?" At face value, defend is an innocuous term. As a transitive verb, Webster defines it as, (a) "to drive danger or attack away," or (b) "to maintain or support in the face of argument or hostile criticism." As an intransitive verb, it is defined as "to take action against attack or challenge" (Mirriam-Webster, Retrieved from www.merriam-webster.com/dictionary/defend). You might envision the mother who puts herself between her child and a bear or the way a good friend steps in when another is being insulted. These examples align with the transitive verb meanings and are a typical aspect of our daily lives. Yet the intransitive verb use of "defend" has become the go to explanation for white supremacists who also lean on the term "protect" to justify increasingly violent attacks.

"Defend," "protect," and "patriot" seem to be the words of the white supremacists as they justify their actions against immigrants, BIPOC, constitutional violations, democracy, Asian-Americans, and anyone who does not fit their "preserve the white race at all costs" mindset. We need to recognize this language and the insight it gives us into their philosophy. We must also learn the terms and symbols that are only recognized by those who subscribe to white supremacist views. Failing to identify and understand the message behind these symbols can leave us vulnerable.

DOI: 10.4324/9781003199656-4

Groups have rallied around symbols throughout history to signal their connection to certain ideas and beliefs. Many communities use language, symbols, and gestures to express a sense of bonding, community, and a shared sense of purpose. While dwelling on the hate-filled and racist symbols used by white supremacists is not recommended, having a knowledge of the symbols used within this group allows those opposing their viewpoints to place themselves in better vantage point to intercept communications, apply countermeasures and thwart a potential violent attack.

Given the increase in white supremacist organizations and threats, it is key to be situationally aware of our surroundings. Situational awareness saves lives. Think of the Capitol riot and the potential life-saving benefits to those responding if they could have readily identified those who posed a threat and those who were there to stop the violence and protect the Capitol. What follows in this chapter is a list of symbols commonly used within the world of white supremacy (Allyn, 2019).

At the time of writing, The Anti-Defamation League (ADL) maintains a continuous database of hate symbols used by white supremacist groups (Anti-Defamation League, 2021a). The ADL makes available a downloadable PDF version of this guide for reference for law enforcement and those who work to identify and thwart those who push forward their agenda. The ADL also maintains an updated list of antisemitic incidents (Anti-Defamation League, 2021b).

While the ADL database is an ideal starting place for reviewing the various symbols associated with this movement, this chapter provides a brief overview of the major categories of symbols to aid the reader in understanding how these symbols are used to intimidate others and strengthen the connection among those in the white supremacist groups. The categories are detailed in Table 4.1.

Numbers

White Supremacists are drawn to the use of numbers (Palmer, 2008). Those in closed communities and tight-knit groups often use numbers to identify fellow members. An example of this would be the Hells Angels using the number 81 (H=8, A=1). One reason for this can be found in David Lane's racist document 88 *Precepts* in which precepts number 11 reads, "Truth requires little explanation. Therefore, beware of verbose doctrines. The great principles are revealed in brevity". Of course, another way to view this statement is the encouragement of blind obedience, akin to the mindless chanting of "Let's go Brandon" first made popular at a NASCAR race in October of 2020, that has come to mean "F*ck Joe Biden" (Long, 2021).

Table 4.1 Categories of Hate Symbols

Category	*Description*
Numbers	Numbers are used to communicate coded alphabetic references (A=1, B=2, C=3…), references to phonetic pronunciations (hate and eight), and the number of words in certain key phrases central to the movement.
Gestures	Hand and arm gestures range from finger gestures symbolizing letters (like W and P for white power) and the Nazi salute.
Phrases and Acronyms	There are several phrases used in the white supremacist movement (e.g., Blut und Ehre, which is German for blood and honor) and acronyms used to represent these phrases (e.g., FGRN representing the Klan's chant For God, Race and Nation).
Symbols	Symbols like the Swastika, dual lightning bolts, and the KKK robes are iconic representations of the white supremacist movement. The Nazis also appropriated ancient runes and use them as code.
Concepts	Concepts include references to writings in the movement (e.g., the day of the rope from The Turner Diaries) and the use of fire and torches as a course of action to rally around.

III

The Roman numeral III when displayed on a flag represents the "Three Percenters." The Three Percenters are part of the United States militia movement. The phrase signifies their belief that only 3% of those who fought the British in the Revolutionary War were Americans.

1776 Logo on Clothing or Other Items

1776 and the American Revolution serve as a symbol of future revolution in protest of Donald Trump's failed re-election and other events warranting an uprising.

Fourteen Words/14

Near the end of the 88 *precepts* is the fourteen-word phrase "We must secure the existence of our people and a future for white children". This phrase has become a popular white supremacist slogan and has been adopted by several who committed violence including as the Tree of Life shooter in Pittsburgh and the Christchurch shooter (McClure, 2021; Smith and Scolforo, 2021).

18

Adolf Hitler. The simplest of alphanumeric codes involves swapping the letters of the alphabet for corresponding numbers. So, a=1, b=2, c=3 and so on. The use of the number 18 symbolizes the A in Adolf (a=1) and the H in Hitler (h=8).

88

Heil Hitler. The use of the number 88 symbolizes the H in Heil (a=8) and the H in Hitler (h=8).

28

Blood and Honor. The use of the number 28 symbolizes the B in blood (b=2) and the H in honor (h=8). Blood and Honor was the motto of the Hitler Youth.

H8

Hate. This is a leetspeak version of the word hate. Leetspeak originated from the punk and/or computer hacking/gaming subculture. This occurs when a letter of the alphabet is used in place of a number and/or when a number is pronounced phonetically to make a word. One of the most popular examples of leetspeak is 1337, as the 1 resembles an L, the 33s resemble EE, and the 7 a T (spelling LEET).

4/20

This is Adolf Hilter's birthday. This is also a common reference to marijuana that began in 1971 from San Rafael, CA teens who would smoke marijuana at 4:20 each day.

5 Words

"I have nothing to say" is the advice white supremacists suggest using when responding to questions by law enforcement.

Gestures

Gestures of the hands, fingers and arms are often used to signify affiliation with a group or as a greeting to members within a group. Many recognize the common use of hand gestures within the gang community and to identify allegiance and territory. Gestures are another way closed

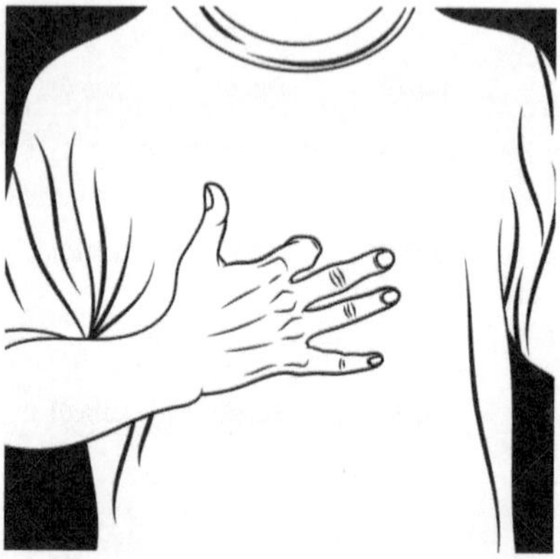

Figure 4.1 Aryan circle hand gesture

communities communicate with each other and differentiate their customs and thinking from other groups.

Aryan Circle

This gesture is made by placing the hand palm down against the chest with the pointer finger bent in. This leaves the thumb signifying number 1 (1=A) and the middle, ring and little finger as the number 3 (3=C). Together this represents AC or the Aryan circle, one of the largest white supremacist prison gangs in the United States. Another way of making this gesture is holding up the palm flat against the chest with the ring finger bent, also representing the 1 and 3 or A and C.

Hitler Salute

This movement consists of a raised, outstretched right arm with the palm facing down. In Nazi Germany, this gesture was often accompanied by the phrase "Sieg Heil" or "Heil Hitler."

"OKAY"

A hand gesture that mimics the common circle with the pointer finger and the thumb with the remaining three fingers up. The three fingers represent a W and the finger and thumb represent a P for white power. The gesture was originally used by those on the political right to troll (i.e., the process of intentionally trying to instigate conflict or arguments, often in an online environment) liberals. It is important to judge this symbol carefully and within the context of where, when, and how it was made, as it a common gesture well beyond white supremacist circles.

Figure 4.2 "OKAY" hand gesture

Figure 4.3 White power hand gesture

White Power

This is made by holding up three fingers on the right hand, which creates a "W," and joining the index finger and thumb on the left hand to create a "P."

Phrases

Phrases are used to indicate membership within a group and to communicate an understanding of the underlying beliefs within the group itself. Phrases are used both verbally and in a written form to communicate a deeper connection to white supremacist beliefs and teachings.

ACAB

This is an acronym that stands for "all cops are bastards" and is commonly used by racist skinheads.

AKIA

This klansmen declaration signifies "a Klansman I am."

Anudda Shoah

This is an antisemitic phrase used to troll and trigger Jews. The phrase utilizes the Hebrew term for Holocaust, Shoa, and implies Jews bring up the Holocaust when confronted by anything they do not like.

Atomwaffen Division

Atomwaffen is the German word for atomic weapons and represents a neo-Nazi group that was created in 2016. The group's logo includes a radiation warning symbol.

AYAK

This is a Ku Klux Klan phrase for "are you a Klansman?"

Blut und Ehre

This is a German phrase that translates to "blood and honor." This phrase was used by the Nazi Party during World War II as a Hitler

Figure 4.4 Atomwaffen symbol

Youth Slogan. It has been adopted by many white supremacist groups.

FGRN

This phrase meaning "for God, race, and a nation" is commonly used by the Ku Klux Klan.

GTKRWN

Antisemitic white supremacists use this term to signify "gas the kikes, race war now."

Kek

Kek has become a way white supremacists determine if someone with whom they are interacting understands their lingo. Kek is the god in a semi-ironic religion created by white nationalists. Kek, whether written or spoken, indicates their loyalty to this all-powerful fictional god.

OFOF

This phrase stands for "one front, one family" and is the slogan for the white supremacist group Volksfront.

RAHOWA

When the letters are separated into RA-HO-WA the phrase can be more easily understood as abbreviation for the phrase "racial holy war." The term was originally created and used by the Creativity Movement as an inspirational call to action.

Sieg Heil

This German phrase means "hail victory" and was used by the Nazi Party. It is often paired with the Hitler salute and is one of the most widely used and recognizable phrases used to signify connection to the white supremacist movement.

Soup Bois

Soup Bois is a phrase used by those with the Boogaloo philosophy. It is code for law enforcement who are hated and frequently targeted by Boogaloos.

Specialty Soup Bois

Specialty Soup Bois is an elaboration upon Soup Bois. "Specialty" has been added as an identifier of Federal officers. The logic of the term rests in the various letters used by federal agencies: CIA, FBI, ATF, DHS, which Boogaloos view as a type of alphabet soup; hence, the term specialty soup.

Three Percenters

As described above related to the Roman numeral III, the Three Percenters are part of the United States militia movement. The phrase signifies their belief that only 3% of those who fought the British in the Revolutionary War were Americans.

Work Brings Freedom

This phrase is the English translation of a phrase that was posted outside of the Auschwitz concentration camp.

Symbols

Arrow Cross/Cross Star

This symbol was used during World War II by a Hungarian fascist political party, and is now used by a number of white supremacist and neo-Nazi groups.

Burning Cross

Burning crosses have often been used as a symbol of terror by the Ku Klux Klan.

Confederate Flag

As with the iron cross, the confederate flag should be assessed contextually, as it is used by many to represent southern pride or references to the civil war confederacy. Notwithstanding, the flag carries with it powerful negative connotations.

Iron Cross

This is a famous German military medal that should be assessed contextually, as it is used in many non-racist situations. The iron cross has become a common white supremacist symbol.

Figure 4.5 Iron cross

Figure 4.6 Kekistani flag

Kekistani Flag

The Kekistani flag is a symbol of the fictional nation of Kekistani (Neiwert, 2017). The flag resembles the Nazi flag, but the Swastika is replaced by the letter, K and the red that symbolized Germany is replaced by frog green. Kekistan is a fictional location that is said to be the birthplace of Kek, the all-powerful god currently depicted by Pepe the Frog.

Ku Klux Klan Robes

Perhaps the most recognizable symbol of the white supremacist movement, the hooded Klansman with their burning cross is among the most hate-filled, horrific symbols of the white supremacist movement. While not believed to have national organization any longer, each Klan has different meanings regarding the colors and stripes on the robes.

Figure 4.7 Ku Klux Klan robes

Noose

A symbol of lynching and terror, the noose is a powerful image used to intimidate or harass African Americans. It also refences to *The Turner Diaries*, a 1978 novel revolving around a violent uprising against the federal government that led to an eventual race war. In the novel, the "day of the rope" is when race traitors were publicly hanged in the streets of Los Angeles. Interestingly, the book was an inspiration behind the Oklahoma City bombings (Chapter 7: case 13).

Pepe the Frog

Pepe is an internet image (or meme) used in several contexts usually related to trolling. It is used frequently on alt-right websites as a symbol of hate (Anti-Defamation League, 2021a; Gomez, 2016). According to the

Figure 4.8 Pepe the Frog

Figure 4.9 Red, white, and blue lion

ADL, Pepe the Frog is the embodiment of "Kek," a chaotic, god-like deity who has granted power to white supremacists and Donald Trump alike. It is not uncommon to see Pepe the Frog with a Donald Trump hairdo.

Red, White, and Blue Lion

The tri-colored lion is often found on flags as a symbol of the VDAR website known for its xenophobia and racist philosophy.

Sieg, previously known as Sowilo Rune

The ancient rune of the sun, the Sowilo rune was converted into an Armanen rune, which was then doubled for the SS/Lightning bolts above.

Figure 4.10 Sowilo rune

Figure 4.11 Double sieg

Double Sieg, SS, or Lightning Bolts

Sieg translates into "victory" and became a symbol for Hitler's elite soldiers, the Nazi Schutzstaffel (SS), Hitler's protection squad that included Gestapo agents, Waffen SS soldiers, and concentration camp guards.

Swastika

Originally, a symbol of divinity and spirituality in Hinduism, Buddhism, and Jainism, it was co-opted by the Nazi Party in Germany. It has since become the single most recognizable and prominent hate symbol in Western culture.

Tyr/Tiwaz Rune

The tyr rune (whose Proto-Germanic name is tiwaz) is an upward facing arrow recently seen on members of Junge Revolution and Junge Tat,

Figure 4.12 Tyr rune

Figure 4.13 QAnon snake

German and English hate groups. The symbol represents war and taking action and has historically been worn by the Hitler Youth and Sturmabteilung groups (Buchner, 2021).

Uppercase Q

White supremacists typically use a twisted serpent, often in red, white, and blue, shaped like an uppercase Q to signify loyalty to "Q," an anonymous figure who has led thousands to believe that wealthy democrats worship Satan and kidnap and kill innocent children in effort to remain immortal, as part of the QAnon conspiracy.

Valknot

This is a Nordic symbol consisting of three interlocking triangles. The valknot does not have white supremacist roots but has been used by

Figure 4.14 Valknot

white supremacists as is evident by its presence in the January 6th, 2021, insurrection.

Concepts

Bowl Cut

The bowl cut concept indicates loyalty to Dylann Roof, the Charleston, SC shooter (Chapter 7: case 54).

Day of the Rope

This phrase comes from the racist book, *The Turner Diaries*, written by neo-Nazi William Pierce. See noose above. The hangman's noose was used during the January 6th, 2021, attacks on the United States Capitol alongside other white supremacist imagery.

Generation Identity (GI)

This concept highlights one example of an attempt to mask the growing movement of a nationalistic, isolationist white agenda. GI refers to a quest to preserve the white race from the impact of mass migration (Pescara-Kovach et al., 2020).

"Great Replacement" or Replacement Theory

This concept or philosophy arose from Renaud Camus' book of the same title. The notion is that white supremacists must take action to protect their nations or they will soon be overtaken by immigrants or those from other races or cultures.

Figure 4.15 Bowl cut

Figure 4.16 Pit bull

Pit Bull

These dogs are a favorite among white supremacists as they are often viewed as being vicious, strong, and aggressive fighters. For those who have owned or spent time with pit bulls, they understand the dogs, like any dogs, reflect how they are raised and handled. Nonetheless, the image of the pit bull has been taken by white supremacists as a symbol of their movement.

Torches and Fire

Fire was often used in Nazi Party Rallies during World War II. Torchlight parades occurred on January 30th, 1933, as Adolf Hitler became the chancellor of Germany. Further, in the 1934 Nazi Party Rally in Nuremberg, the torchbearers formed a massive human swastika. Torches were used as a central messaging device during the rally in Charlottesville, VA in August 2017. (Murphy, 2017).

Moving Forward

This chapter provides a useful foundation for those looking to better understand the language and symbols used by this movement to communicate with each other, recruit new members, and build a stronger alliance. In the next chapter, we will explore the role of social media in expanding and escalating the rise of the white supremacist movement.

Keep the Conversation Going

- How might a school or campus administrator train faculty and staff on ways to identify the various numbers, symbols, and concepts used by white supremacists?

- Looking back to the January 6, 2021, attack on the Capitol, do you recall seeing any of the numbers, symbols, and concepts among those present?
- How do outward gestures and symbols benefit white supremacist groups?
- Would it be beneficial for allies of those targeted by white supremacists to wear symbols that identified themselves as against white supremacy? If so, what could some of the symbols look like?
- Can you think of a literary work/book that embodies a philosophy that runs counter to the "Great Replacement?" What is it titled and how is it the antithesis of the "Great Replacement?"

References

Allyn, B. (2019, September 26). The 'OK' Hand Gesture Is Now Listed as A Symbol of Hate. NPR. www.npr.org/2019/09/26/764728163/the-ok-hand-gesture-is-now-listed-as-a-symbol-of-hate.

Anti-Defamation League. (2018). New Hate and Old: The Changing Face of American White Supremacy. Retrieved on December 17, 2021 from www.adl.org/media/11894/download.

Anti-Defamation League. (2021a). Hate on Display: Hate Symbols Database. Retrieved on December 17, 2021 from www.adl.org/hate-symbols.

Anti-Defamation League. (2021b). Tracker of Anti-Semitic Incidents. Retrieved on December 17, 2021 from www.adl.org/education-and-resources/resource-knowledge-base/adl-tracker-of-antisemitic-incidents.

Gomez, L. (2016). Pepe the frog is a hate symbol, officially. Here's why. Retrieved on December 17, 2021 from www.sandiegouniontribune.com/opinion/the-conversation/sd-pepe-the-frog-officially-a-hate-symbol-says-20160928-htmlstory.html.

Buchner, V.T. (2021, January 29). Nazis in Germany and Switzerland: JUNGE TAT AND JUNGE REVOLUTION. *Belltower News*. www.belltower.news/nazis-in-germany-and-switzerland-junge-tat-and-junge-revolution-111101.

Long, C. (2021). How 'Let's go Brandon' became code for insulting Joe Biden. Retrieved on December 17, 2021 from https://apnews.com/article/lets-go-brandon-what-does-it-mean-republicans-joe-biden-ab13db212067928455a3dba07756a160.

McClure, T. (2021). Christchurch mosque shooter claims guilty plea obtained under duress, expected to appeal. Retrieved on December 17, 2021 from www.theguardian.com/world/2021/nov/08/christchurch-mosque-shooter-claims-guilty-plea-obtained-under-duress-expected-to-appeal.

Murphy, P. (2017). White nationalists use tiki torches to light up Charlottesville march. Retrieved on December 17, 2021 from www.cnn.com/2017/08/12/us/white-nationalists-tiki-torch-march-trnd/index.html.

Neiwert, D. (2017). What the Kek: Explaining the White Supremacy 'Diety' Behind Their 'Meme Magic.' Southern Poverty Law Center. www.splcenter.org/hatewatch/2017/05/08/what-kek-explaining-alt-right-deity-behind-their-meme-magic.

Palmer, B. (2008). Why white supremist love the numbers. Retrieved on December 17, 2021 from https://slate.com/news-and-politics/2008/10/14-and-88-why-white-supremacists-love-the-numbers.html.

Pescara-Kovach, Van Brunt, B., and Murphy, A. (2020). Terrorist in Training: The Role of Social Media and the Rise of Terrorism through Nationalistic White Agenda. *The Journal of Campus Behavioral Intervention*, 8, 1–11.

Smith, P. and Scolforo, M. (2021). 3 years after Pittsburgh synagogue attack, trial still ahead. Retrieved on December 17, 2021 from https://whyy.org/articles/3-years-after-pittsburgh-synagogue-attack-trial-still-ahead.

5 Social Media and the Growth of Hate Speech and Exposure[1]

Box 5.1 Key Take-aways

1. Stormfront.org., Micetrap, and Thor Steiner are some of the largest online sites to promote white supremacy and host open extremist forums. Other mainstream sites (e.g., Society6, Zazzle, Redbubble, and Amazon) allow artist created materials, décor, and literature that overlaps with white supremacist images such as those found in Norse mythology.
2. It is likely Society6 and the other mainstream sites are unaware of what is being sold on their sites, but Stormfront.org and its counterparts exist for the sole purpose of promoting white supremacy.
3. Mainstream social media sites such as Facebook, TikTok, Instagram, YouTube, and Twitter struggle with managing white supremacist agendas, discussions, and recruitment.
4. Bespoke chat sites such as Discord, Gab, and Telegram remain places where white supremacist content is discussed and shared, despite efforts to reduce access to such material.

A young man gets bullied at school. When he gets home, rather than get comfort or advice from his parents, he seeks the wisdom of Iliza, the house's artificial intelligence (AI) program, equivalent to a Siri or Alexa. Iliza explains to the young man where his law enforcement officer mother keeps her gun and what the digital code is to unlock it. It encourages him to take the gun to school and kill his bullies to defend himself. He brings the gun but decides against using it at the last minute and instead calls his mother. On the drive home, he explains everything; in a panic, she destroys all the smart devices in their home. These events were watched by over 1.5 million viewers in an early episode of the 2020 television show *neXt*. (Requa and Ficarra, 2020). Viewers who tuned in were likely to look around their homes and reconsider if they really needed a linked device listening in every room. Most would sympathize with the mother

DOI: 10.4324/9781003199656-5

for removing all access to Iliza in order to protect her son. However, few (if any) viewers made the connection that they are essentially placing their children in similar harms' way; instead of being goaded into violence by a rogue AI, the children are being targeted by a variety of extremist groups across social media platforms. By allowing their children to walk around with unfettered and unmonitored access to social media platforms on every device they own, parents are surreptitiously participating in their children's recruitment.

Social media has changed the nature of both threat assessment and the risk of violent extremism. It gives us the opportunity, through such tools as the VRAW-2 (Van Brunt, 2016), to analyze posts and comments that might otherwise have gone unsaid publicly. Further, these online posts and comments afford us the ability to report threats to law enforcement agencies, school or work personnel, and even the Department of Homeland Security through the See Something, Say Something campaign. On the flip side, social media has become a forum for white supremacists to share ideologies, spread propaganda, and encourage acts of terrorism. The content is at times disguised via words, symbols, and gestures as seen in Chapter 4, which give the groups a sense of confidence of going unnoticed. There are also the intangible effects, involving philosophies, rally cries, and attempts to radicalize. While multi-billion-dollar sites claim they are working very hard to address the white supremacy interaction and promotion on their sites, they can and should be doing more to address and put an end to the promotion of hate and violence.

While most social media platforms promote neutrality or serve as a positive force, Neil Postman cautioned that:

> "To be unaware that a technology comes equipped with a program for social change, to maintain that technology is neutral, to make the assumption that technology is always a friend to culture is, at this late hour, stupidity plain and simple."
>
> (Postman, 2006, 157)

White supremacist content is not hidden beneath the surface, unavailable to potentially violent youth or adults. There are tens of thousands of social media accounts on mainstream sites and neo-Nazi merchandise is available for purchase on Amazon and other mainstream retailers. Like many in our nation, white supremacists communicate and shop on the internet.

According to Pescara-Kovach et al. (2020), "social media is playing a role in the contagion of a hate mindset and related violence" (p. 8). A 2021 study conducted by SafeHome.org (n.d.) examined the number of hate groups operating per state and the number of Twitter followers of each group. If we look at those groups with the most online followers, we see that The Federation for American Immigration Reform, an anti-immigrant hate group, has close to 73,000 followers, the Bill Keller Ministries, with a hatred of

Muslims and all non-Christian religions, has nearly 66,000 followers, followed by Anti-Muslim groups ACT for America and Jihad Watch that have over 58,000 and over 56,000 followers, respectively (SafeHome.org, Most Popular Hate Groups Table).

While the type of messaging and communication taking place via social networking sites and the Dark web can at times seem innocuous at face value, it is strategic in its approach. Take for example *Stormfront*, which was introduced in 1995 and remains notorious for being the first online site with a clear white supremacist agenda (Southern Poverty Law Center, n.d.). Despite a flood of news articles in 2017 to 2018 with such titles as "Oldest White Supremacy Site, Stormfront.org, Shut Down" (Reeves, 2017) and a January 2017 article in *The Washington Times* (Blake, 2017) stating it had been shut down, as you can see in Figure 5.1, any shutdown did not last. Figure 5.1 is a screenshot of a post from January 6, 2021, a testament to the tenacity of hate groups and their ability to use free speech and technology to continue to spew hatred, encourage violence, and recruit members. Stormfront has once again been shut down, but white supremacist groups are skilled at remaining alive on social media. If the group follows their insidious history, they have or will appear in another online location.

Stormfront is but one example. Today, white supremacy groups can be found hiding in plain sight on both mainstream online shopping sites and media (Tech Transparency Project, 2022) and within the dark web.

Within chapter 2, there was discussion of the Lost Cause mythos. The United Daughters of the Confederacy and the Sons of Confederate Veterans, as well as the League of the South, date far back in our history, yet have since embraced modern technology in furthering their cause. The League of the South, which is the most radical and overtly political of the three organizations, has a significant online presence. Visitors to their website can spend hours combing through a maze of hyperlinks, each increasingly feeding anti-American sentiment. Their "news" page includes a variety of links to old statements and presidential addresses. Clothing sold on their online store is referred to as "uniforms". The media page branches out with links to multiple YouTube videos including a "Buy Southern" advertising campaign and a particularly distasteful brief commercial filmed at the Emmett Till memorial. In

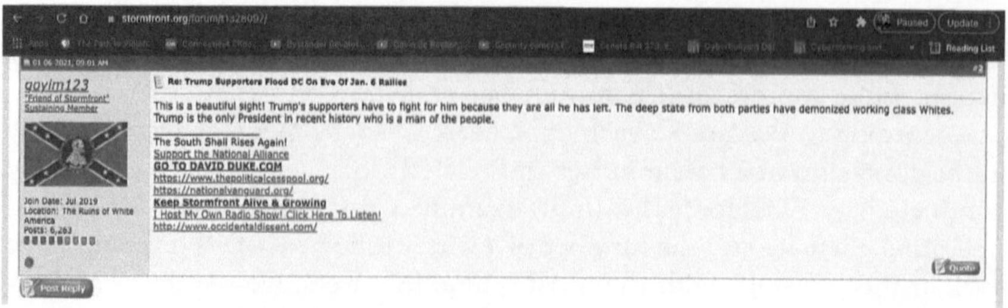

Figure 5.1 Stormfront screenshot from January 6, 2021

terms of favored publications, the group has one site featuring twelve articles furthering their cause—including one citing Sinn Fein as an exemplar. They are very active on social media, with the Twitter hashtag "#secedeactivism." On their "Find Your Tribe!" page, there are links to local chapters, many of which have their own website and/or Facebook accounts, while others have YouTube, Gab, and VK pages as well. At the least, they have an email account hosted by ProtonMail, an end-to-end encrypted email server hosted in Switzerland (League of the South, n.d.). This just one example of the myriad resources and websites provided by white supremacist organizations.

In the following sections, we will examine a range of online sites and how they are used by white supremacists, starting with online shopping, followed by mainstream sites like Facebook, Twitter, Instagram and TikTok, and ending with activity on the dark web.

Online Shopping for Hate

Micetrap

Online shopping is a hotbed for white supremacist merchandise. One such shopping site was launched in 1996 by Steven J. Weigand under the name Whitepride.com. Over time, the site was renamed *Micetrap* and it offered a plethora of neo-Nazi regalia. This site is an open door into white supremacist views and a host of related social media sites. As is clear in Figure 5.2, Weigand and his white supremacy counterparts were also found on a radio station, a blog site, Facebook, and Twitter.

Weigand shut down Micetrap in 2017. His statement about the closing acknowledged that closing the site would not put an end the violence, but

Figure 5.2 Micetrap screenshot

that he did not want to be involved or associated with it (Bellano, 2017, para. 5). However, Micetrap lives on despite that, with numerous t-shirts with the image of Adolf Hitler as well as a link to a self-proclaimed "Pro-White Music" site for the "Resistance" (see Figure 5.3).

Thor Steinar

Dubai is a destination for the wealthy, owing to its vast collection of designer stores and glorious high-rise buildings. One can purchase handbags and fashion right off the runway. A lesser-known fact about Dubai is its connection to retailer Thor Steinar, founded in 2002 and manufactured by MediaTex, who has since sold the rights to Dubai-based International Brands General Trading. Its alignment to neo-Nazi sentiment is evident in one of their bestselling logos, which is a combination of the sowilo rune and tiwaz rune (see Chapter 4). Together, the symbols create a well-known Nazi symbol now used by neo-Nazis worldwide. Thor Steiner has an international presence and consumers need only visit their website to order neo-Nazi merchandise and have white supremacist clothing at their fingertips.

Society6, Zazzle, and Redbubble

Society6 is a popular online retailer of "home decor and lifestyle goods," as described on its Facebook page. While the site offers pastel hued,

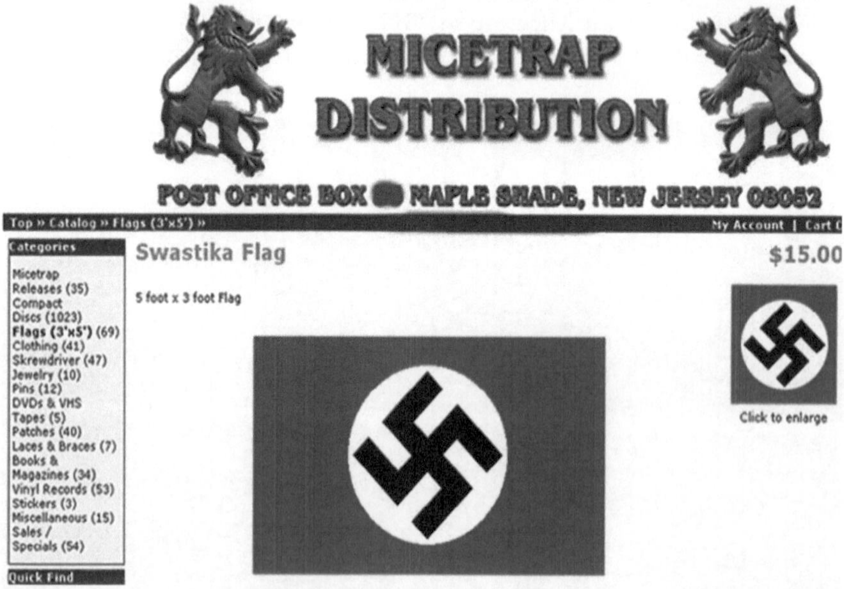

Figure 5.3 Micetrap screenshot

neutral décor and every day useful items, there is a side of Society6 we stumbled upon when doing a simple image search for "sowilo rune." We found white supremacist décor at Society6, as well as clothing and décor at seemingly benign sites such as Zazzle, Redbubble, and Etsy. Currently Zazzle's home page is a soft pink with a modern office set up in prominent view. The words "Prints Charming" and "Home is where your art is" disguise something the company might be blissfully unaware of, as a few clicks away there lurks white supremacist merchandise with symbols likely unrecognized by the powers-that-be. Redbubble is a place independent artists can create and sell their own designs. It seems there is little concern about the type of self-expression and design available for purchase on Redbubble. Various rune designs and Valkyrie wings rise to the surface on t-shirts and hoodies. While it is possible the artists sell the merchandise as related to Norse mythology, we know from Chapter 4 that these symbols have been adopted by white supremacist groups and displayed proudly. Not so subtle designs are available as well, such as stickers with the "OK" symbol and shirts with the double lightning bolts of the white supremacist movement.

Amazon

Online retail giant Amazon is not immune to the sale of hate merchandise. At the time of writing, numerous rune symbols are available on merchandise currently available on Amazon. As with the retailers, the runes can be dismissed as related to Norse mythology, which was the origin of many of the symbols. However, it is a well-established fact that these symbols are widely used by white supremacists (adl.org). The most disturbing item on Amazon is Hitler's *Mein Kampf*, which is available in several formats, including a Kindle edition. Although a 2020 article released by The Guardian indicated that Amazon had succumbed to the pressure of Holocaust education campaigns and banned the sale of *Mein Kampf*, within days, Amazon was directly selling the book, while maintaining the ban only for secondhand sellers (Waterson, 2020). In terms of white supremacist symbols, there is a vast array of Pepe the Frog merchandise, one of the most prominent symbols of white supremacy.

Mainstream Social Networking Sites

Mainstream social media has proven to be a hotbed for online communication among various white supremacy groups. The January 6th attack on the Capitol would not have happened at such a large scale if it occurred before the advent of mainstream social media sites. Those who spread hate have become savvy in targeting for recruitment those with similar views. As stated by Clark Estes (2021):

> Over the years, these groups used an evolving set of organizing techniques to spread extremist messages to larger and more mainstream groups of people online. They found ways to game the algorithmic feeds of Facebook, Twitter, and YouTube, so that their new audiences didn't necessarily know they were being radicalized. And there's reason to believe this is only the beginning, since these platforms tend to amplify provocative content.
>
> (para. 7)

Facebook (owned by Meta Productions, Inc.)

Facebook uses its algorithm to determine what groups to recommend its users. Although Mark Zuckerberg claims to have dedicated significant resources to prohibiting the platform's use by hate groups, recent information from former Facebook employees discovered the effort fell short because there was a disconnect between researchers and executives. In fact, Facebook seems to struggle with being able to track hate speech across the globe due, in part, to the vast number of users of the social media platform (Chappell, 2021). Most disturbing is the fact that influential Facebook users are given carte blanche to post anything and everything regardless of its message. By extension, special privileges are granted via a system called XCheck (Chappell).

Perhaps this explains why Facebook has been a popular site among hate groups; they know they have a safe place to post their hateful speech and conspiracy theories and work to radicalize the vulnerable. The Anti-Defamation League (ADL) (2021) made disturbing finds in its examination of white supremacist content. Two examples of openly hateful anti-Muslim groups are "Islam is not a religion" and "Islam is a cult," whose content labels Muslims as "pedophiles," "racists," "terrorists," "retarded," and a host of derogatory terms (Anti-Defamation League, 2021). As of November 17, 2021, when the ADL released its report, the sites remained widely accessible. This is just the tip of the iceberg.

David Patrick Underwood, a 53-year-old Federal security guard, was a man who protected others, yet had no protection from white supremacists. The day of his death, Officer Underwood had been placed at the Federal Building and Courthouse in Oakland, California, owing to protests occurring over the death of George Floyd. Officer Underwood died after being struck by bullets in the neck and torso, at the hands of members of Boogaloo Bois in a drive-by shooting (Chapter 7: Case 93). Boogaloo as a concept is an amalgamation of hate perspectives, with a special hatred of government officials and law enforcement officers. Boogaloo refers to a civil war, which they are actively preparing for in our nation. Facebook is a welcoming site to those with Boogaloo ideals. Members are often white supremacists, conspiracy theorists, and militia, and they are communicating freely on one of the most widely used social media platforms.

Officer Underwood's sister has since filed a lawsuit against Meta, Inc. In the court complaint document, his sister's reasoning can be found within allegation I. 13, which states:

> The shooting was not a random act of violence. It was the culmination of an extremist plot hatched and planned on Facebook by two men who Meta connected through Facebook's groups infrastructure and its use of algorithms designed and intended to increase user engagement and, correspondingly, Meta's profits.
>
> (Angela Underwood Jacobs v. Meta Inc., 2022)

The lawsuit contains information regarding Facebook's role in Officer Underwood's death. Specifically, there exists a multi-group network on Facebook that shares the Boogaloo mindset. Within the network are BoojieBastards: The Armory, BoojieBastards: Intelligence and Surveillance, and /K/alifornia Komando (Angela Underwood Jacobs v. Meta Inc., 2022). The day before the shooting, a member of one of the groups encouraged violence against federal officers. He did so using phrases common among Boogaloo members. One such phrase is, "specialty soup boys," which is a term referring to federal law enforcement officers. The individual using this term shared a YouTube video showing a brutal attack on law enforcement and encouraged others to engage in such violence. The soon-to-be gunman commented on the post, expressing he was ready to do what was encouraged – attack federal law enforcement. The originator of the post and the commenter met up to do just that; they worked together as driver and shooter to kill Officer Underwood for no reason other than he was a "specialty soup boy."

Time will tell if the lawsuit against Meta will be won in court. In the meantime, we need to realize when there's one, there are many, and Facebook joins them all together.

TikTok

TikTok is doing what it can to address white supremacy. Glancing at its community guidelines, the rules are specific and clear (www.tiktok.com/community-guidelines?lang=en). In fact, the top two categories, violent extremism and hateful behavior, target white supremacists. However, the site has grown too large to effectively monitor, with one billion people using the platform every month (TikTok, 2021).

For those unfamiliar with TikTok, the platform was initially introduced in 2017 under the name Music.ly before being renamed TikTok. The app allows any type of brief video clip to be shared worldwide via a user account. One can find content related to cooking, makeup, dancing, comedy, and other benign topics as well as a great deal of political content, conspiracy theories, and false information sharing. TikTok has created algorithms that lead to targeted, user-specific advertising, to ensure its users have content related to their interests. This is known as the "For You Page" and it gets more and more user-specific over time. The more a user watches or comments on a particularly themed video, the more that user will receive similar content.

TikTok has been a source of comfort for many during the pandemic. Those on lockdown learned new recipes, dances, and home décor ideas. Unfortunately, while these positive TikTok videos were circulating, other users were spreading hate. According to *Hatescape: An In-Depth Analysis of Extremism and Hate Speech on TikTok* (O'Connor, 2021), TikTok is used to deny that the Holocaust occurred, claim genocides are myths, and encourage extremism and terrorist activity. It is a place for conspiracy theories to spread and for the dissemination of content that denies the Holocaust and violent events like genocides ever happened.

According to Little (2021), the Three Percenters far-right militia is one group that uses TikTok to promote their message and recruit new members. By taking advantage of a loophole in TikTok's attempt to block the search for their group, they evade detection by using other acronyms (Little, 2021). According to the ADL, the Three Percenters militia abides by the false belief that freedom was achieved by a brave 3% of colonists who battled the British in the Revolutionary War. Those affiliated with today's Three Percenters identify with the historical 3% but view the U. S. government as the enemy. Easily identified by others with similar views, the Three Percenters self-identify through the use of the roman number three ("III") (Anti-Defamation League, n.d.). The Three Percenters, like the Boogaloo groups, are prepared to fight for the freedom they believe we are denied.

Unlike the casual way non-politically motivated entities use TikTok, hate groups like the Three Percenters use the platform with clear goals in mind. Little (2021) provides examples of TikTok videos available prior to the January 6th attack on the Capitol encouraging violence. These video clips have such captions as "January 6 (sic) Let's do this my brothers and sisters," "So who all is going to be with me on January 6th," and "When Tyranny becomes law. Rebellion becomes duty."

According to O'Connor (2021), TikTok's abuse by white supremacists runs deep. In a recent examination of 1,030 videos posted to TikTok over a three-month period, the Institute for Strategic Dialogue discovered 312 videos supporting white supremacy philosophies, such as the white genocide conspiracy and the Great Replacement (O'Connor, 2021). They found 246 TikTok videos singing the praises of Adolf Hitler and other well-known historical hate figures. The support and adulation of the Christchurch shooter was evident in an additional 30 videos, with three of them depicting the attacks in the form of a video game and 13 using the shooter's own previously posted statements. In terms of antisemitism on TikTok, in O'Connor's sample, 26 videos denied the existence of the Holocaust.

TikTok has recently made efforts to remove accounts linked to white supremacist views, but the news is not promising. As of the release of *Hatescape: An In-Depth Analysis of Extremism and Hate Speech on TikTok* (O'Connor, 2021), only 18.5% of the 1,030 identified videos have been removed from the platform, leaving 81.5% still active. The report found several instructional and tutorial videos related to the manufacturing of 3D weapons, including where and how to purchase the materials. Also found were videos supporting the use of explosive devices and weapons as well as information on building firearms (O'Connor).

Instagram

Instagram devotes large portions of their terms of service and community guidelines to addressing hate speech. They elaborate upon their definition of hate speech as well as their now stricter actions against those engaging in hate speech, including algorithms in its Direct Messages features, which will lead to blocking and permanently shutting down the originating account. The new feature debuted several months ago, yet recent research conducted by the ADL delves into the somewhat ineffective "stricter actions."

In their research, a targeted search for the term "Atomwaffen" uncovered a number of posts (Guynn & Carless, 2021). Atomwaffen Division is not a small band of individuals claiming to be anti-government; instead, they are a designated terrorist organization that has perpetrated violence and is planning more. But the accounts and communication does not end with Atomwaffen Division. The ADL researchers discovered 200 posts openly displaying Swastikas and other easily identified white supremacist content (Guynn and Carless, 2019). Like Facebook, Instagram needs to do more.

Twitter

At its formation, Twitter was dedicated to providing open communication in a mostly unmonitored space (Twitter, 2009). This openness allowed hateful and abusive content to thrive on the platform. Twitter is working to change this environment and the latest update to its hateful content policy (https://help.twitter.com/en/rules-and-policies/hateful-conduct-policy) has led to a crackdown on hate speech, with Twitter taking action on over a million accounts and removing 3.8 million tweets in the second half of 2020, up 77% over the first half of the year (https://time.com/6080324/twitter-hate-speech-penalties/). This has not eliminated hate speech on Twitter but is a move in the right direction.

Unfortunately, white supremacists have learned to work within the rules. In her study analyzing the alt-right leadership on Twitter, Gallaher (2021) found three major themes in their tweets. First, they are attempting to normalize their racial politics, positing that white people are oppressed because of their race just like other racial and ethnic minorities. Second, they couch their misogyny in the ideas of women needing to be protected and serve important roles in the home. This aligns them with evangelicals and other social conservatives. Finally, there is a focus on Europe as the white homeland, particularly when discussing Middle Eastern and African immigrants. White supremacists, particularly those in power within the movement, are savvy to how they are getting their message out. On these mainstream sites, they are trying to appeal to those that might not seek them out but are susceptible to their ideas.

YouTube

Google, which owns YouTube, seems to be doing the most to eliminate extremist content online. Within their policy on content violations, the company strictly prohibits accounts or posts linked to foreign terror organizations. In terms of domestic terror and extremist content, the company indicates they consider it hateful, violent, or graphic content that will be flagged and reviewed to determine if it violates community guidelines. This strong response to violence and the promotion thereof gives us hope that mainstream media is taking action. While this is progress, the groups often have a tenacity that leads them to seek out other platforms.

Dedicated Platforms

Discord and Gab

Some groups work to avoid being discovered, staying off mainstream social media sites and using dedicated platforms. Atomwaffen Division utilizes Discord, which allows users to engage via speaking, chatting, and sharing videos at no cost. Discord has proven to be a haven for hate groups. Research by ProPublica discovered 250,000 chats by members of Atomwaffen Division within a six-month period (Thompson et al., 2018). Discord is not the only platform used by hate groups.

When a platform becomes hostile to their ideas, or is shut down because of them, hate groups leave in search of a safer place on the web. We saw this after the 2019 El Paso shooting in which a lone gunman walked into a Walmart and gunned down innocent people. He had posted his manifesto on 8chan, which then lost its internet provider. Owing to the shutdown, many white supremacist groups moved to a site within Zeronet, an alternative to the dark web. Others switched to 4chan or Gab.

Gab is unlike mainstream social media in that they do not even attempt to fight white supremacy. Gab is defiant and encourages freedom and independence. As with mainstream platforms, there are sponsored ads; the current most prominent is an ad for Peace of Mind, an ammunition retailer, with the words "Build up a supply of ammo automatically...So it's there when you need it most." The perpetrator of the Tree of Life shooting utilized both Gab and IMGUR (a site that allows image posting and creativity). Posts captured prior to the shooting read, "Daily Reminder: Diversity means chasing down the last white person" and "HIAS likes to bring invaders in that kill our people. I can't sit by and watch my people get slaughtered. I'm going in," which were posted on Gab and IMGUR, respectively.

Gab's company philosophy is clearly conveyed in their statement, "The more journalists demonize companies like Gab and 8chan, the more you accelerate us towards the inevitable and decentralized future" (in Paul, 2019). Whether it is a chan site, Gab, or Discord, the communication continues, and warrants a deeper understanding of how to address it to potentially thwart violence.

Telegram

Telegram, created by a pioneer of technology in Russia, goes to great measures to protect its users' content. Like Gab and Discord, its users can communicate a multitude of ways. Telegram is a messenger app that delivers a promise of encrypting user content. White supremacists are free to post whatever they desire. Many refer to Telegram as the white supremacist platform. The Counter Extremism Project (2019) provided a glimpse into Telegram within its research. They found a channel/account that posted "Firebomb your local synagogue" with 295 followers. Other channels celebrated the injuries and fatalities from the Midland-Odessa shooting, in which a gunman shot multiple people from a vehicle, killing eight and injuring 25 others, with one specific channel having close to 1,500 followers. This is not the entirety of it, as there were numerous white supremacist channels with thousands of followers praising specific shooters. While we cannot dig deep enough into the dark web to uncover all encrypted sites, we encourage you to familiarize yourself with mainstream sites. As we've stated, the power to address the issue rests with us.

Moving Forward

When he was considering the impact of television back in 1985, Neil Postman argued that it was nothing short of revolutionary. His argument is twice as relevant when considering social media:

> Introduce speed-of-light transmission of images and you make a cultural revolution. Without a vote. Without polemics. Without

> guerrilla resistance. Here is ideology, pure if not serene. Here is ideology without words, and all the more powerful for their absence.
>
> (2006, 157–158)

Social media's revolutionary impact is a double-edged sword. It provides an unprecedented way to connect with others across the world, sometimes in positive ways. For example, Stevie Berberick documents how YouTube became a positive force for young male trans vloggers, a place to find support and community. While the trans community is often silenced in mainstream outlets or tokenized by the cult of celebrity, YouTube is a place for real conversations with "transgender people outside of celebrity." Popular culture, and social media specifically, "teaches us about sexual identity" and "such lessons can intensify stigma and shame of those outside the binary." However, "independent popular culture productions…can help audiences to unlearn such rigid acceptance of the gender binary" (Berberick, 2020, xvii).

Unfortunately, social media also provides a platform for hate groups and others to fling abuse and recruit converts to their cause. Social media platforms and internet providers must take responsibility to monitor and remove this content. Admittedly, hate groups and their members use sophisticated messaging and dedicated sites to fly under the radar of this monitoring. There is no simple solution, but we must begin by learning and watching for these techniques. Nick Couldry and Ulisses A. Mejias explain that in today's world, social media is too ubiquitous to simply tell people "just stay offline." Instead, they offer a set of recommendations, many of which are relevant to this chapter when applied in the context of hate. First, people should recognize that no website, whether shopping, user generated content, or commercial, is ever neutral. Second, people should limit their online exposure only to sites that serve immediate purpose in their lives. Third, media literacy should be infused in schools starting in kindergarten and repeated at every level through university. Just as we would not send children out in public without teaching them how to navigate their world safely, so too should children (and their parents) be taught to navigate the online world. Fourth, we should encourage websites that serve nefarious purposes to be held accountable for the outcomes of their information (Couldry and Mejias, 2019, 197–205).

Finally, Couldry and Mejias recommend developing a freely available crowd-sourced database of detestable websites that can serve several purposes. It will allow the public to reframe core arguments used by hate groups and refute them. It can restore some sense of dignity of life of those being attacked. It will name those who sponsor hate publicly and protect vulnerable populations. Ultimately, the first line of defense against social media that preaches hate is refusing to be silent about it (Couldry and Mejias, 2019, 210).

Continuing the Conversation

- Given the loopholes that white supremacists have been able to get through, what do you suggest is a way for major social media companies to safeguard their vulnerable users?
- We raise the point that no website or media is ever neutral. Do you agree? Why do you think that is the case?
- What social media platforms would you add to a potential "detestable sites" database if you were in control of creating it for public use?
- Should sites like Telegram be monitored closely and/or shut down? If so, do you feel doing so would violate the right to free speech?

Note

1 For this chapter, we once again reached out to Dr. Edward Janak.

References

Angela Underwood Jacobs v. Meta Inc. Superior Court of the State of California for The County of Alameda. www.documentcloud.org/documents/21174499-underwood-v-meta-complaint1047326228.

Anti-Defamation League. (n.d.). Three Percenters. www.adl.org/resources/glossary-terms/three-percenters.

Anti-Defamation League. (2021, December 9). Instagram Hosting White, Accelerationist Content.

Bellano, (2017, August 22). Cherry Hill Man Shuts Down Business Selling White Supremacist Merchandise. Patch.com. https://patch.com/new-jersey/cherryhill/cherry-hill-man-shuts-down-business-selling-white-supremacist-merchandise.

Berberick, S. (2020). *Reframing Sex: Unlearning the Gender Binary with Trans Masculine YouTube Vloggers*. Lexington Books.

Blake, A. (2017, August 26). Stormfront, Internet's Longest-Running White Supremacist Site, Goes Offline. *The Washington Times*. www.washingtontimes.com/news/2017/aug/26/stormfront-internets-longest-running-white-suprema.

Chappell, B. (2021, October 25). The Facebook Papers: What You Need to Know About the Trove of Insider Documents. National Public Radio. www.npr.org/2021/10/25/1049015366/the-facebook-papers-what-you-need-to-know.

Couldry, N. and Mejias, U.A. (2019). *The Costs of Connection: How Data is Colonizing Human Life and Appropriating it for Capitalism*. Stanford University Press.

Counter Extremism Project. (2019). Extremist Content Online: Last Edition of ISIS Magazine Youth of the Caliphate Released. www.counterextremism.com/press/extremist-content-online-last-edition-isis-magazine-youth-caliphate-released.

Estes, A. (2021). How neo-Nazis used the internet to instigate a right-wing extremist crisis. *Vox*. www.vox.com/recode/22256387/facebook-telegram-qanon-proud-boys-alt-right-hate-groups.

Gallaher, C. (2021). Mainstreaming white supremacy: a twitter analysis of the American 'Alt-Right'. *Gender, Place & Culture*, 28(2), 224–252, doi:10.1080/0966369X.2019.1710472.

Guynn, J. and Carless, W. (2021, December 9). White Supremacy, Nazi Ideology Still a Big. Problem for Instagram. *USA Today*. https://news.yahoo.com/instagram-still-big-problem-nazis-000825918.html.

League of the South. (n.d.). Find Your Tribe! League of the South State Chapters. https://leagueofthesouth.com/state-chapters.

Little, O. (2021). Far Right Militias are Using Tik Tok to Organize and Recruit New Followers. *Media Matters*.

O'Connor, C. (2021). *Hatescape: An In-Depth Analysis of Hate Speech and Extremism on TikTok*. Institute for Strategic Dialogue.

Paul, K. (2019, August 8). 8chan: ex-users of far-right site flock to new homes across internet. *The Guardian*. www.theguardian.com/us-news/2019/aug/08/8chan-shutdown-users-social-media.

Pescara-Kovach, L, Van Brunt, B., and Murphy, A. (2020). Terrorist in Training: The Role of Social Media and the Rise of Terrorism through Nationalistic White Agenda. *Journal of Campus Behavioral Intervention*, 8 , 39–49.

Postman, N. (2006). *Amusing Ourselves to Death: Public Discourse in the Age of Show Business* (20th Anniversary Edition). Penguin Press.

Reeves, J. (2017, August 28). Oldest White Supremacist Site, Stormfront.org, Shut Down. Associated Press.

Requa, J. (writer), Ficarra, G. (writer), and Clements, K. (director). (October 13, 2020). File #2 (season 1, episode 2). In John Requa (Executive Producer), neXt. Manny Coto Productions/Zaftig Films.

Safehome.org. Team. (n.d.). Hate on Social Media. www.safehome.org/resources/hate-on-social-media.

Satkalmi, R. and Miller, J. (2019). Opinion: We Work for the NYPD. This is What We've Learned About Terrorism. *The New York Times*. www.nytimes.com/2019/09/11/opinion/nypd-domestic-terrorism.html.

Southern Poverty Law Center. (n.d.). Stormfront. www.splcenter.org/fighting-hate/extremist-files/group/stormfront.

Tech Transparency Project. (2022, January 4). A Year After Capitol Riot, Facebook Remains an Extremist Breeding Ground. www.techtransparencyproject.org/articles/year-after-capitol-riot-facebook-remains-extremist-breeding-ground.

Thompson, A.C. (2018, February 23). Inside Atomwaffen as It Celebrates a Member for Allegedly Killing a Gay Jewish College Student. *ProPublica*. www.propublica.org/article/atomwaffen-division-inside-white-hate-group.

TikTok. (2021, September 27). Press Release. https://newsroom.tiktok.com/en-us/1-billion-people-on-tiktok.

Twitter. (2009). The Twitter Rules. https://web.archive.org/web/20090118211301/http://twitter.zendesk.com/forums/26257/entries/18311.

Van Brunt, B. (2016). Assessing threat in written communications, social media, and creative writing. *J Gender Violence*, 3, 78–88.

Waterson, J. (2020, March 16). Amazon bans sale of most editions of Adolf Hitler's Mein Kampf. *The Guardian*. www.theguardian.com/technology/2020/mar/16/amazon-bans-sale-of-most-editions-of-adolf-hitlers-mein-kampf.

6 The Lost and Looking

Box 6.1 Key Take-a-ways

1. Those who turn to white supremacy often carry with them a personal grievance or injustice that motivates their exploration in this space.
2. These individuals often have a life in disarray, lacking connection or opportunities for growth and positive relationships. This void creates a cognitive opening for the potential for radicalization by extremists offering friendship, support, and shared experiences.
3. The process of radicalization moves across hardened viewpoint, freefall, cognitive opening, need for group affiliation, connection to extremist thoughts, and justification for violent actions.

Why do people go down this path of extremist violence? What motivates someone to separate from their everyday life and see violent action as an option? While a complex issue in terms of the exact alchemy, the straightforward answer is a pervasive sense of hopelessness, isolation, and ultimately a calculus whose result is that their life is not worth continuing in its current state. They are convinced they are trapped by a world they cannot align with. They perceive themselves eternally cast in the role of outsider and want the unrelenting pain to stop. The allure of making a difference and going out in a blaze of glory offers them a meaning for their life that has remained disconnected and illusive.

Although many people may feel marginalized, treated unfairly, and discriminated against, only a few express these frustrations through violence. Likewise, there are many who are hopeless, isolated, and suicidal that do not engage in extremist violence and instead looking for a personal escape from their chronic pain and despair. However, a few in these vulnerable conditions who are exposed to extremist ideology

DOI: 10.4324/9781003199656-6

are then radicalized toward violence, having been offered a solution to their pain, loss of meaning in their life, and outsider status.

It is worth mentioning that radical thoughts and ideas are not, in and of themselves, dangerous. They may be unpopular or outright misogynistic or racist, but those that hold them do not always, or even often, incite violence as a solution. But for some, their radical thoughts and ideas transform and embrace violence and intimidation as reasonable actions to reach their political, religious, or ideological goals. Understanding this transition is the focus of this chapter.

Hardened Point of View or Free Fall?

This is the old question about which came first, the chicken or the egg. Do the negative life circumstances and experiences that lead to an outsider status make the individual more susceptible to seeing violence as an answer to an unhappy life or is their life made unhappy by holding an inflexible way of looking at a particular issue? Let's start with understanding the hardened point of view and free fall that can lead to violence.

A ***hardened point of view*** reflects a set way of thinking that can escalate toward action. There is a difficulty accepting alternative explanations for events and will fit the facts to their worldview or ignore them if they cannot. They engage in harmful debate with others and increasingly look for ways to widen their impact and solidify their viewpoint. This escalates to include a quality of obsession and a spiralling negative impact to other aspects of their work, school, social relationships, and family. They seek opportunity to troll and create demonstrations to push this view on others. They not only hold a hardened point of view, but this becomes a defining characteristic of their entire person. When limits are set by their workplace, school, or the police, they move quickly past these, feeling justified in their actions because of their locked perspective.

Free fall describes an individual in descent. They have multiple challenges in life such as failing supports, mental illness flair ups, and a general sense of hopelessness. The free fall becomes more concerning as multiple, chronic problems intersect, eventually creating an inability to function and a lack of hope that things will improve. They have trouble integrating with their community, school, social circle, peer group, and/or work. The sense of free fall is increased with the addition of negative events like chronic unemployment, the death of a loved one, financial hardship, difficulty adjusting to a new life circumstance such as failure and dismissal from an academic program or internship, the sudden loss of a job, or blocked upward mobility based on their personal characteristics such as race, ethnicity, religious beliefs, or appearance (Bhui et al., 2012; Schmid, 2013; Travis, 2008). These events occur suddenly or in quick succession and act like the catalyst in a chemical reaction, speeding up the escalation toward violence.

Free fall, or a life spiraling out of control, is also impacted by feelings of marginalization and perceived discrimination. They feel separated from others based on ethnic or racial differences, cultural dissimilarities, social justice beliefs, or sexual orientations and gender identity. They become out of step with the greater society and often feel like an outsider (Bhui et al., 2012).

The discrimination and perception of social injustices lead to barriers to integration into mainstream society (Commission's Expert Group on European Violent Radicalisation [CEGEVR], 2008). They experience humiliation, deprivation, and stigmatization that may result in a high level of anger and frustration (Pressman, 2009; Schmid, 2013). Individuals experience real or perceived discrimination with little or no hope for a pathway to a better tomorrow (Sinai, 2005; 2012) and lack opportunities in their work and peer group to succeed (Schmid, 2013).

The experience of a tragic or overwhelming event often serves as a trigger or springboard for action or change. This could be a political event (McCauley and Moskalenko, 2008) or anger at political or foreign policy actions of their country (Pressman, 2009). It could be the loss of a family member, financial stress, the failure of a job, or a romantic loss (Drysdale et al., 2010). In these circumstances, the person feels trapped, has a lack of options, a low sense of self-esteem, and may be experiencing hopelessness, an existential crisis, or depression (ASIS, 2011; ATAP, 2006; Bhui et al., 2012; Meloy et al., 2014; O'Toole, 2002; Randazzo and Plummer, 2009; Turner and Gelles, 2003). The catalyst event or crisis enhances the grievances and may be mobilized through the group (Gill, 2007; Wiktorowicz, 2004).

Omar Mateen had lost his job as a prison guard after threatening to bring a gun to work and was unsuccessful gaining admission into the police academy before his 2013 attack at a Florida night club (Zimmerman, 2016). He tried to become a state trooper in 2011 and failed to gain admission into the police academy in 2015 (Swisher, 2016). There are reports he had a history of being mentally unstable, physically abusive, and was a long-time steroid user. He often used slurs and those who worked with him as security guards shared that he had a lot of hatred for people—black people, women, Jews, Hispanics, and gay or lesbian people (Times of Israel Staff, 2016).

So, does free fall occur and lead to a hardened point of view? Or does the hardened point of view occur and results in a free fall? It depends on the circumstances of the individual threat case. The interplay between these two factors, hardened point of view and a life in free fall, increases a concept referred to as a cognitive opening.

Cognitive Openings

A ***cognitive opening*** is a vulnerability in a person that allows others with an extremist point of view greater access to radicalize an individual toward violence. When a person experiences disenfranchisement and has

Table 6.1 Examples of Attacks with Free Fall

Date	*Attack*	*Details*
9/16/1991	The Luby's Shooting	Attacker had a history of stalking and was discharged from the Merchant Marines before his 1991 attack.
11/5/2009	Fort Hood Mass Shooting	The attacker killed 13 people in his Fort Hood attack after feeling marginalized and disenfranchised as a Muslim in the American Armed Forces.
2/18/2010	Austin Suicide Attack	The attacker was suicidal and was being audited by the IRS at the time of his attack.
4/7/2011	Rio de Janeiro Shooting	The attacker talked about a long history of bullying, depression, and a desire for suicide in a note before his 2011 attack in Rio de Janeiro.
2/23/2011	Attempt to Use Weapon of Mass Destruction	Attacker indicated that depression and isolation were contributing factors to his desire to build a weapon of mass destruction.
7/22/2011	Norway Attack	Attacker was socially isolated before his bombing and shooting attack in Norway.
8/2/2015	San Bernardino Shooting	Attacker increasingly socially disengaged from others at his work due to his religious perspective and had an altercation with his work before the shooting.

thoughts full of dissatisfaction and disillusionment, this increases their emotional vulnerability (Goli and Rezzei, 2010; Horgan, 2008). Thoughts of disconnection, isolation, and rejection of societal values further create a cognitive opening (Her Majesty's Government, 2011; Horgan, 2008; Pressman, 2009). Others common experiences include a disconnection from their social group, a rejection of societal values, and feelings of alienation and disengagement (CEGEVR, 2008; Taarnby, 2005).

This overall bleakness grows the cognitive opening, creating a space for a crisis to shake the individual's previously held beliefs (Bhui et al., 2012; Christmann, 2012; Wiktorowicz, 2004). One path to escalate violence in the individual is to exploit their dissatisfaction with protests as a method to create change (Horgan, 2008). This then leads to a willingness to seek new ways of bringing about change, including violence (Wiktorowicz, 2004). This influence could come from a group or a religious or political ideology that supports violent action as a clearer path (Pressman, 2009).

Dr. Adam Lankford offers an alternative to the idea that the violent actions of an attacker are based on a desire for change based on the religious, political, or social ideology. His research (Lankford, 2010; 2013) shows the issue of suicidality—manifested by a sense of hopelessness, depression, isolation, and failure—was a stronger motivator than the desire to achieve some larger societal message or culture shift. Other research has supported the theory of cognitive openings as associated with those vulnerable to radicalization (CEGEVR, 2008; Horgan, 2008; Pressman, 2009).

The desire to end chronic pain and commit suicide is a primary factor in most attacks. A suicidal person looks for a justification for their death in their attack plan, rather than sending a message to others through a violent attack. It is these thoughts of hopelessness, desperation, and a desire to take their own life that motivates the attack (ATAP, 2006; Dunkle et al., 2008; Lankford, 2010; 2013; Meloy et al., 2014; O'Toole, 2002; Randazzo and Plummer, 2009; Turner and Gelles, 2003; Vossekuil et al., 2002).

Another aspect that increases the cognitive openings is societal disengagement. They are separated from larger societal values and distrust those in the established order and may have experienced violence at the hands of an unjust authority in the past (CEGEVR, 2008; Pressman, 2009, Slootman and Tilley, 2006). Other concerns include long term isolation from others or an inability to create or maintain sexual or intimate relationships with others (Meloy and Moghaddam, 2005).

Affiliation with a Group

When an individual feels separated from others, they exhibit a strong desire to identify with a like-minded group, however they can find it (CEGEVR, 2008; McCauley and Moskalenko, 2008; Pressman, 2009). They desire any connection to community and solidarity that is offered (Her Majesty's Government, 2011). They desire to find connections to others in the community and share their viewpoint and strengthen their commitment to action. They are looking for those who would share their views and confirm existing beliefs and villainize a target (Meloy et al., 2014; Randazzo and Plummer, 2009; Van Brunt, 2012).

The group offers support for their extreme position (McCauley and Moskalenko, 2008) and helps legitimize their goals (Meloy and Moghaddam, 2005). Groups also may provide status or a title (Horgan, 2008) and a sense of approval and acceptance. (CEGEVR, 2008; Pressman, 2009). The group provides support for their political, religious, or ideological cause (Her Majesty's Government, 2011; Pressman, 2009) as well as providing opportunities for belonging and bonding (Pressman, 2009; Sageman, 2007).

Connection to Extremist Thoughts

To recap, an individual obtains a hardened point of view on a topic, and this often goes together with a sense of free fall, instability, and loss. This creates a cognitive opening and vulnerability for the individual that raises the risk of connecting to a group that shares their hardened viewpoints. Once the group affiliation occurs and they feel supported and part of the group, they often become exposed to increasingly extreme thoughts and

Table 6.2 Examples of Attacks with Groups Encouragement

Date	*Attack*	*Details*
9/20/2013	Russian Oil Rig	The attackers were involved in the attempted boarding and shutting down of the Russian oil rig Prirazlomnaya. Anzorovich "Jahar."
6/17/2015	Austin Suicide Attack	The attacker was connected to others on the internet who shared his beliefs related to triggering a race war.
10/1/2015	Umpqua Community College Shooting	The attacker admired and studied mass killings before his attack at Umpqua Community College.
10/15/2016	The Crusaders: Garden city Kansas	The attackers planned a bombing, all had links on their Facebook pages to conspiracy and anti-Muslim websites.

ideals. Given that they are often in an outsider position in society and struggle to feel connected to a community, they are more suspectable to the group pressure to continue to fit in and conform.

The group leadership may exert pressure that forces a crystallization of ideas from movement to action (McCauley and Moskalenko, 2008; Meloy and Moghaddam, 2005). The individual becomes increasingly exposed to radical ideas and shuts out ideas that don't align with the group's ideas (ASIS, 2011; ATAP, 2006; Glasl, 1999; Meloy et al., 2014; O'Toole, 2002; Randazzo and Plummer, 2009; Sokolow and Lewis, 2009; Sokolow et al., 2011; Turner and Gelles, 2003; Van Brunt, 2012).

They look to increase contact and connection with extreme subcultures within their local community (Sinai, 2005; 2012) or through friends, family, lovers, or a political event to learn more about the extremist movement (Gill, 2007; Her Majesty's Government, 2011; McCauley and Moskalenko, 2008; Schmid, 2013). They may also use the internet to seek more information about their viewpoint (Pressman, 2009; Weimann 2006). In some cases, this process may be escalated when the group has a charismatic leader or spiritual sanctioner of their beliefs (Horgan, 2008; Pressman, 2009; Sinai, 2005; 2012; Travis, 2008). The cognitive opening leads the individual to seek a religious or political ideology that echoes their concerns (Sinai, 2005; 2012). The leader then exploits this, taking advantage of the individual's vulnerability and weakness (Neumann and Rodgers, 2007). The leader seeks to shift the blame and focus to a target or enemy (Meloy and Moghaddam, 2005).

Justification for Violent Action

Before committing to violence, it is often necessary for the individual to achieve a sense of meaning and larger justification for their actions

(Meloy and Moghaddam, 2005). Similar to the military, there is period where moral disengagement and adherence to the mission objectives becomes a total focus (O'Toole, 2002; O'Toole and Bowman, 2011; Van Brunt, 2012; 2015). There includes a pervasive sense of anger and frustration toward the target and a desire for revenge (Pressman, 2009).

When a radicalized individual or group embraces violence as a justified pathway to achieve their political, religious, or social goals, this can transform to extremism and terrorism (Pressman, 2009). This justification includes a moral outrage, a desire for revenge and a willingness to die for a cause based on political, religious, or ideological goals (Bhui et al., 2012; Porta and LaFree, 2012; Pressman, 2009; Schmid, 2013). There is peer, family, and/or community support for violent action (Pressman, 2009) and they see violence as justified for their enemy (Horgan, 2008; Pressman, 2009).

Conclusion

We have discussed the process by which a hardened point of view leads to a cognitive opening, increasing the need for group affiliation. Once connected to the group, extremist thoughts and the pressure to commit violent action for a specific cause can increase the risk of violent action. While not all violent extremists follow this path, the combination of hardened thoughts, free fall, and personal loss do create a vulnerability in a person that can be exploited by groups looking to radicalize others toward extremist violence.

Moving Forward

Now that we understand the radicalization process as it ties to the individual, the next chapter provides a detailed literature review of dozens of cases where the radicalized individual moved forward to violence against specific groups targeted by white supremacists. It is these cases that will then support the development of an indoctrination rubric to better understand how far along an individual is on the path to radicalization and violence.

Keep The Conversation Going

- Think of a few recent terror attacks perpetrated by extremists. What were the attackers' grievances? What barriers do you think they encountered when trying to connect to others related to these grievances?
- Think of the risk factors associated with susceptibility to radicalization. How would parents or caregivers go about preventing their child from going down the pathway to violence? Think about ways to reduce access as well increasingly availability of positive social connections.

- What are some other ideas, connections, groups, or organizations that could be used to push against the connection an individual may have toward a more extremist group?
- Do you think in-person groups or online groups are a bigger threat to radicalization? Explain why. How does social media play into the increased risk for a person in pain looking for understanding and group connection?

References

ASIS International and the Society for Human Resource Management. (2011). *Workplace violence prevention and intervention: American National Standard.* Retrieved from http://ppcta.unl.edu/ctap/private/w/2014/Workplace%20Violence%20Prevention%20and%20Intervention%20Manual.pdf (Retrieved on 8/17/22)

Association of Threat Assessment Professionals (ATAP). (2006). *Risk Assessment Guideline Elements for Violence (RAGE-V): Considerations for Assessing the Risk of Future Violent Behavior.* (ATAP, Sacramento, CA).

Bhui, K.S., Hicks, M.H., Lashley, M., and Jones, E. (2012). A public health approach to understanding and preventing violent radicalization. *BMC Med.* 10, 16.

Christmann, K. (2012). Preventing religious radicalization and violent extremism: A systematic review of the research evidence. *Youth Justice Board for England and Wales.* Retrieved from https://assets.publishing.service.gov.uk/government/uploads/system/uploads/attachment_data/file/396030/preventing-violent-extremism-systematic-review.pdf (Retrieved on 8/17/22)

Commission's Expert Group on European Violent Radicalisation (CEGEVR). (2008). *Radicalisation processes leading to acts of terrorism.* Report Submitted to the European Commission. Retrieved from https://www.clingendael.org/sites/default/files/pdfs/20080500_cscp_report_vries.pdf (Retrieved on 8/17/22)

Drysdale, D., Modzeleski, W., and Simons, A. (2010). *Campus Attacks: Targeted Violence Affecting Institutions of Higher Education.* (United States Secret Service, United States Department of Education and Federal Bureau of Investigation, Washington, DC).

Dunkle, J.H., Silverstein, Z.B., and Warner, S.L. (2008). Managing violent and other troubling students: The role of threat assessment teams on campus. *J Coll Univ Law.* 34, 585–636.

Gill, P. (2007). A multi-dimensional approach to suicide *bombing. Int J Confl Violence.* 1, 142–159.

Glasl, F. (1999). *Confronting Conflict.* (Hawthorn Press, UK).

Goli, M. and Rezzei, S. (2010). *House of War: Islamic Radicalization in Denmark.* (Centre for Studies in Islamism and Radicalisation, Aarhus, Denmark).

Her Majesty's Government. (2011). *Extremism Risk Guidelines: ERG 22+ Structured Professional Guidelines for Assessing Risk of Extremist Offending.* (Ministry of Justice, UK).

Horgan, J. (2008). From profiles to pathways and roots to routes: Perspectives from psychology on radicalization into terrorism. *Ann Am Acad Poli Soc Sci.* 618, 80–94.

Lankford, A. (2010). *Human Killing Machines: Systematic Indoctrination in Iran, Nazi Germany, Al Qaeda, and Abu Ghraib.* (Lexington Press, Boston, MA).

Lankford, A. (2013). *The Myth of Martyrdom: What Really Drives Suicide Bombers, Rampage Shooters, and Other Self-Destructive Killers*. (St. Martin Press, New York).

McCauley, C. and Mosklenko, S. (2008).*Mechanisms of political radicalization: Pathways toward terrorism. Terror Political Violence*. 20, 415–433.

Meloy, J.R., Hoffmann, J., and Roshdi, K. (2014). Warning behaviors and their configurations across various domains of targeted violence. In *The International Handbook of Threat Assessment*.

Meloy, J.R. and Moghaddam F.M. (2005). The staircase to terrorism: A psychological exploration. *Am Psychol*. 60, 161–169.

Neumann, P. and Rodgers, B. (2007). *Recruitment and Mobilisation for the Islamist Militant Movement in Europe*. International Centre for the Study of Radicalisation and Political Violence. Retrieved from http://icsr.info/wpcontent/uploads/2012/10/1234516791ICSREUResearch Report_Proof1.pdf (accessed 9/6/17).

O'Toole, M.E. (2002). *The School Shooter: A Threat Assessment Perspective*. (FBI, Quantico, VA).

O'Toole, M.E. and Bowman, A. (2011). *Dangerous Instincts: How Gut Feelings Betray*., (Hudson Street Press, New York, NY).

Porta, D.D. and LaFree, G. (2012). *Guest editorial: Processes of radicalization and de-radicalization*. Int J Confl Violence. 6, 4–10.

Pressman, D.E. (2009). *Risk Assessment Decisions for Violent Political Extremism*. (Her Majesty the Queen in Right of Canada, Ottawa).

Randazzo, M. and Plummer, E. (2009). *Implementing Behavioral Threat Assessment on Campus: A Virginia Tech Demonstration Project*. (Virginia Polytechnic Institute and State University, Blacksburg, VA).

Sageman, M. (2007). *Radicalization of global Islamist terrorists*. United States Senate Committee on Homeland Security and Governmental Affairs. Retrieved from https://www.hsgac.senate.gov/download/062707sageman (Retrieved on 8/17/22)

Schmid, A.P. (2013). *Radicalisation, de-radicalisation, counter-radicalisation: A conceptual discussion and literature review*. The International Centre for Counter-Terrorism-The Hague 4, 2. Retrieved from http://www.icct.nl/app/uploads/download/file/ICCT-Schmid-Radicalisation-De-Radicalisation-Counter-Radica lisation-March-2013.pdf (Retrieved on 8/17/22)

Sinai, J. (2005). A conceptual framework for resolving terrorism's root causes. In The Root Causes of Terrorism: Myths, Reality and Ways Forward. T Bjorgo, ed.(Routledge, UK).

Sinai, J. (2012). *Radicalisation into extremism and terrorism*. Intelligencer J U.S. Intell Stud. 19, Summer/Fall.

Slootman, M. and Tillie, J. (2006). *Process of radicalization: Why some Amsterdam Muslims become radicals*. (Institute for Migrations and Ethnic Studies, University of Amsterdam, Netherlands).

Sokolow, B. and Lewis, S. (2009). *2nd Generation Behavioral Intervention Best Practices*. (The National Center for Higher Education Risk Management, Malvern, PA).

Sokolow, B., Lewis, S., Manzo, L., Schuster, S., Byrnes, J. and Van Brunt, B. (2011). *Book on BIT*. (National Behavioral Intervention Team Association, Malvern, PA).

Swisher, S. (2016). *Omar Mateen failed multiple times to start career in law enforcement*, state records show. Retrieved from www.sunsentinel. com/news/florida/fl-omar-mateen-fdle-records-20160616-story.html (accessed 1/13/17).

Taarnby, M. (2005). *Recruitment of Islamist terrorists in Europe: Trends and perspectives. Danish Ministry of Justice.* Retrieved from https://icsr.info/wp-content/uploads/2008/10/1234516791ICSREUResearchReport_Proof1.pdf (Retrieved on 8/17/22).

Times of Israel Staff. (2016). *Ex-coworker: Orlando shooter an 'unhinged racist misogynist'.* Retrieved from www.timesofisrael.com/ex-coworker-orlando-shooter-an-unhinged-racist-misogynist (Retrieved on 8/17/22).

Travis, A. (2008). *MI5 report challenges views on terrorism in Britain. Guardian.* 20, 558–579.

Turner, J. and Gelles, M. (2003). Threat Assessment: A Risk Management Approach. *United Nations Educational, Scientific and Cultural Organization (UNESCO). A Teachers Guide to the Prevention of Violent.* (Routledge, New York, NY).

Van Brunt, B. (2012). *Ending Campus Violence: New Approaches to Prevention.* (Routledge, New York, NY).

Van Brunt, B. (2015). *Harm to Others: The Assessment and Treatment of Dangerousness.*: (American Counseling Association, Alexandria, VA).

Vossekuil, B., Fein, R.A., and Reddy, M. (2002). *The Final Report and Findings of the Safe School Initiative.* (US Secret Service and Department of Education, Washington, DC).

Weimann, G. (2006). *Terror on the Internet: The New Arena, the New Challenges.* (United States Institute of Peace, Washington, DC).

Wiktorowicz, Q. (2004). Joining the Cause: Al-Muhajiroun and Radical Islam. *The Roots of Radical Islam.* (Department of International Studies, Rhodes College, Memphis, TN).

Zimmerman, M. (2016, June 15). *Orlando terrorist's chilling Facebookposts from inside club revealed.* Retrieved from https://www.foxnews.com/us/orlando-terrorists-chilling-facebook-posts-from-inside-club-revealed (Retrieved on 8/17/22)

7 Hatred in Action

A Review of Cases

Box 7.1 Key Take-aways

1. Of the 606 people killed and over 62,000 injured by white supremacists in the cases reviewed in recent history, this violence was primarily male generated against BIPOC, Jews, Muslims, U.S. government officials, LGBTQI+, Immigrants, women, and AAPI.
2. There are many other examples not included in this chapter. The cases chosen were a starting point to better understand the motivation of the attackers in order to develop improved violence risk assessment and management processes.

In this chapter, we will provide a list of violence or threat cases with white supremacist suspects and/or motives. Cases will be reviewed for common themes and escalations and will be used to help develop a White Supremacist Indoctrination Rubric (WSIR) to better understand the pathway to violence as it relates to white supremacy. They will also give the reader context into the three case studies introduced in Chapter 8 and referenced in the remainder of the book. This is not a complete list of such cases, but a sampling of higher profile or cases with more overt white supremacist or far-right motives from the last 30 years, mostly within the United States, as well as a handful of major attacks or events prior to that. A summary of the cases is included in Table 7.1

Box 7.2 Limitations

As with Chapter 3, we attempted to cast a wide, inclusive net on all of those affected by the hatred and pain that is grown and disseminated by the white supremacist movement. Without question, there are other pivotal cases that could be included in this chapter to bring our number from 100 into the 1,000s. It is our intent to provide a partial

DOI: 10.4324/9781003199656-7

reference to serve as exemplars for those violently impacted by the white supremacist movement. The authors acknowledge some cases are not included in this chapter, owing to space and time constraints.

Table 7.1 Summary of Key Case Factors

Descriptive element	*Data*	*Notes*
Total killed	606	When counts for those killed were estimated, we used the lowest estimate here. When the attacker was killed, that is included in these totals.
Total injured	62,479	When counts for those injured were estimated, we used the lowest estimate here. When the attacker was injured, that is included in these totals.
Male/female attackers	99/7	Only one case involved only female attackers, the Brooklyn attacks on Orthodox Jewish children (case 100). We included two large-scale events here, the Unite the Right rally (case 70) and the US Capitol Riots (case 94). The remaining cases involve a male/female pair acting together (cases 26, 45, 52, and 87).
Target/motive:		In some cases, the victims might not have been in the same category as the motive. In these cases, we are using the motive as the metric. For example, in case 5, the victims were white, but the motive was anti-Black, so that case is counting under the BIPOC section. Also, many of the cases had multiple motives/targets, so the total count here will be greater than 100.
BIPOC	35	Most of the violence in these cases was directed at Blacks/African Americans, and some were meant to include any non-white people. Two cases were directed specifically at Latino/Hispanic people, cases 83 and 85.
AAPI	3	While hate crimes against AAPI populations are on the rise, our focus was on attacks by white supremacists. This small number does not reflect the growing concerns of this population.
Immigrants	7	This is likely a low estimate, as many white supremacists consider almost all minorities to be immigrants or at least to not belong in the US. We only counted here those that clearly focused on immigrant populations.
Women	6	While misogyny is rampant among white supremacist organizations and thought, we did not specifically study domestic and partner violence and looked mainly toward violence directed at other minorities.

Descriptive element	*Data*	*Notes*
LGBTQIA+	9	This is another group that might be under-represented, as our search parameters would have excluded cases that were primarily about homophobia.
Jews	29	Second only to BIPOC in cases, antisemitism is a core tenet of white supremacy and a growing threat.
Muslims	15	In at least two cases (cases 24 and 25), the target was Muslims, but the attackers mistook members of other religious minorities for Muslim. These cases are included here.
Other religious minorities	1	This case involves an attack on a Sikh temple (case 48).
Government	10	These attacks were focused on anti-government and ani-police sentiments, often stemming from the belief that the government was too liberal.
Liberals	3	The anti-liberal sentiment that guided attacks on the government also led to these attacks.
Personal revenge	6	Personal revenge was a factor in these cases, which also included white supremacist motives or targets.
Mixed targets/ motives	3	These cases involved many suspects and we cannot determine motives for all participants. Included here are the eugenics programs (case 1), the Unite the Right rally (case 70), and the US Capitol riots (case 94).
Unknown	6	In these cases, the suspects had clear white supremacist beliefs and/or affiliations, but we cannot determine the exact motive or target in the attack.

1.	*Forced Sterilization*
Location:	United States
Date:	1907 – today
Weapons:	-
Deaths:	Unknown
Injured:	60,000+
Suspects:	US government
Target:	Mixed
Summary:	By 1913 most states had or would soon have eugenic sterilization laws, the first such law having passed in Indiana in 1907. Initially targeted toward white men, over time they increasingly targeted women and people of color, with Black women sterilized at more than three times the rate of white women and more than 12 times the rate of white men during the 1950s and 1960s. Forced sterilizations continued until 2010 in California prisons. In 2020, there were forced sterilizations performed in an ICE detention left in Georgia.

2.	*Tulsa Race Massacre*
Location:	Tulsa, OK
Date:	May 31, 1921 – June 1, 1921
Weapons:	Guns, explosives, arson
Deaths:	75–300 estimated
Injured:	800+
Suspects:	White mob
Target:	BIPOC
Summary:	Mobs of white residents attacked Black residents and their homes and businesses in the Greenwood District of Tulsa, also known as Black Wall Street, one of the wealthiest Black communities in the US. It began when a Black shoe shiner was accused of assaulting a white elevator operator. A group of 75 Black men went to the jail where he was being held to prevent him being lynched and ended up in an exchange of gunfire, which spurred the white mob into action.
3.	*Murder of Emmett Till*
Location:	Money, MS
Date:	August 28, 1955
Weapons:	Lynching
Deaths:	1
Injured:	-
Suspects:	Roy Bryant and J.W. Milam
Target:	BIPOC, personal revenge
Summary:	Till, a 14-year-old African American, was brutally murdered after being accused of offending a white 21-year-old woman in her family's grocery store. The woman's husband and his half-brother abducted him, beat and mutilated him, shot him in the head, and sunk his body in a river. They were acquitted by an all-white jury.
4.	*16th Street Baptist Church Bombing*
Location:	Birmingham, AL
Date:	September 15, 1963
Weapons:	Dynamite
Deaths:	4
Injured:	14–22
Suspects:	Thomas Blanton, Robert Chambliss, Bobby Cherry and Herman Cash
Target:	BIPOC
Summary:	Four member of a local Ku Klux Klan (KKK) chapter detonated 19 sticks of dynamite beneath the church steps. Four young girls were killed. The perpetrators were not convicted until 1977, 2001, and 2002.

5.	*Freedom Summer Murders*
Location:	Neshoba County, MS
Date:	June 21, 1964
Deaths:	3
Injured:	-
Suspects:	18 individuals
Target:	BIPOC
Summary:	The three victims were activists working with the Freedom Summer campaign registering African Americans in Mississippi to vote. They were arrested following a traffic stop and when they left the jail, they were followed and abducted. The lynch mob, including members of the KKK and local law enforcement, shot the activists at close range and buried their bodies in an earthen dam, where they were not discovered for two months.

6.	*Murder of Harvey Milk*
Location:	San Francisco, CA
Date:	November 27, 1978
Weapons:	Firearm
Deaths:	2
Injured:	-
Suspects:	Dan White
Target:	LGBTQ+, personal revenge
Summary:	Harvey Milk was the first openly gay man to elected to office in California. A disgruntled former employee on the Board of Supervisors, who had lost his job and was having problems at home, first shot the man who appointed someone else to his position, who was also a supporter of gay rights, then found and shot Milk. They had not got along at work, and although he denied it, White was known to be anti-gay. White suffered from depression and later committed suicide.

7.	*Greensboro Massacre*
Location:	Greensboro, NC
Date:	November 3, 1979
Weapons:	Firearms
Deaths:	5
Injured:	12+
Suspects:	American Nazi Party (ANP) and KKK members
Target:	BIPOC, personal revenge
Summary:	The "Death to the Klan" march had been organized by the Communist Workers Party. Members of the ANP and KKK arrived, and the marchers beat their cars with picket sticks and threw rocks at them. They responded by firing on the crowd of marchers with rifles and shotguns.

8.	*Murder of Alan Berg*
Location:	Denver, CO
Date:	June 18, 1984
Weapons:	Semi-automatic Ingram MAC-10
Deaths:	1
Injured:	-
Suspects:	Members of The Order
Target:	BIPOC, Jews, liberals
Summary:	Berg was an atheistic and liberal talk radio host. He was killed by members of The Order, who believed in killing all Jews and sending all Black people to Africa.

9.	*Murder of Mulugeta Seraw*
Location:	Portland, OR
Date:	November 13, 1988
Weapons:	Baseball bat
Deaths:	1
Injured:	-
Suspects:	Members of the East Side White Pride and White Aryan Resistance
Target:	BIPOC
Summary:	Three members of the white supremacist groups confronted two Black men, including Mulugeta, an Ethiopian student in the US to attend college, in front of his apartment. They beat him to death with a baseball bat and left him on the street. They admitted to killing him because of his race.

10.	*Luigi's Restaurant Shooting*
Location:	Fayetteville, NC
Date:	August 6, 1993
Weapons:	12-gauge pump action shotgun, 12-gauge shotgun,.22-caliber rifle
Deaths:	4
Injured:	8
Suspect:	Kenneth Junior French
Target:	LGBTQ+
Summary:	The 22-year-old Fort Bragg soldier opened fire in a restaurant in Fayetteville. During the attack, he yelled about politics and homosexuality, particularly in opposition to President Bill Clinton lifting the ban on gays in the military. French had been drinking heavily and watching violent movies prior to the attack and claims to have blacked out during it.

11.	*Brooklyn Bridge Shooting*
Location:	New York, NY
Date:	March 1, 1994

Weapons:	.380-caliber pistol, 9mm pistol, shotgun, stun gun
Deaths:	1
Injured:	3
Suspect:	Rashid Baz
Target:	Jews
Summary:	The Lebanese-born attacker shot at a van of 15 Chabad-Lubavitch Orthodox Jewish students. He was in possession of anti-Jewish literature, and the attack was at least in part a reaction to the attack at a Mosque in Hebron one week earlier.

12.	*Eugene Synagogue Attack*
Location:	Eugene, OR
Date:	March 20, 1994
Weapons:	High powered rifle
Deaths:	-
Injured:	-
Suspects:	Christopher Lord and George Dennis Smith, Jr.
Target:	Jews
Summary:	Two racist skinhead gang members fired a high-powered rifle with armor-piercing bullets at an unoccupied synagogue.

13.	*Oklahoma City Bombing*
Location:	Oklahoma City, OK
Date:	April 19, 1995
Weapons:	Fertilizer truck bomb
Deaths:	168
Injured:	680+
Suspects:	Timothy McVeigh and Terry Nichols
Target:	Government
Summary:	The two men destroyed more than one-third of the Alfred P. Murrah Federal Building with a truck bomb. Both held white supremacist and anti-government beliefs. McVeigh was the mastermind in the attack and was spurred on by the federal raids in Waco and Ruby Ridge. He had been bullied in school and came to believe the government was the ultimate bully.

14.	*Macedonia Baptist Church Arson*
Location:	Clarendon County, SC
Date:	June 21, 1995
Weapons:	Arson
Deaths:	-
Injured:	-
Suspects:	Timothy Adron Welch and Gary Christopher Cox

Target:	BIPOC
Summary:	In 1994 the Christian Knights of the KKK set up headquarters near the church. The next year, two members poured gasoline on the floor of the church and set it on fire, destroying the centuries-old building.

15.	*Murder of James Byrd, Jr.*
Location:	Jasper, TX
Date:	June 7, 1998
Weapons:	Truck
Deaths:	1
Injured:	-
Suspects:	Shawn Berry, Lawrence Brewer and John King
Target:	BIPOC
Summary:	Byrd accepted a ride from the three men, who then beat him and dragged him behind the pickup truck for three miles. He died about halfway through the ordeal. King had several racist tattoos and was affiliated with the Confederate Knights of America. He took pride in his crime and boasted about having made history.

16.	*Murder of Matthew Shepard*
Location:	Laramie, WY
Date:	October 6, 1998
Weapons:	
Deaths:	1
Injured:	-
Suspects:	Aaron McKinney and Russell Henderson
Target:	LGBTQ+
Summary:	The two men beat, tortured, and left Shepard to die tied to a barbed-wire fence. He was found 18 hours after the attack and died several days later from his injuries. Their intent was to rob him of money and drugs, and they attacked him after he put his hand on one of their knees.

17.	*London Nail Bombings*
Location:	London, England
Date:	April 17, 1999 – April 30, 1999
Weapons:	Nail bombs
Deaths:	3
Injured:	140
Suspect:	David Copeland
Target:	BIPOC, LGBTQ+

Summary: Over three weekends, nail bombs were detonated around London. The 22-year-old bomber was a neo-Nazi militant and member of the National Socialist Movement who was attempting to start a race war in England. He had a history of mental illness and drug use and police found Nazi memorabilia and a collage of bomb blasts in his home.

---

18. *Sacramento Synagogue Firebombings*

Location: Sacramento, CA

Date: June 18, 1999

Weapons: Firebombs

Deaths: -

Injured: -

Suspects: Benjamin Matthew and James Tyler Williams

Target: Jews

Summary: The pair of white supremacist brothers set fire to three Sacramento-area synagogues. No one was hurt in the fires, but they caused nearly $3 million in damages. The brothers were charged after an unrelated arrest for the murder of a gay couple (case 19). Benjamin was a member of the Christian Identity movement and studied white supremacy and antisemitism online.

---

19. *Murders of Gary Matson and Winfield Mowder*

Location: Redding, CA

Date: July 1, 1999

Weapons: .22-caliber gun

Deaths: 2

Injured: -

Suspects: Benjamin Matthew Williams and James Tyler Williams

Target: LGBTQ+

Summary: The white supremacist and antisemitic brothers shot and killed the couple in their bed. They confessed to killing the couple because they were gay and insisted their actions were justified because the Bible holds that homosexuality is a sin that must be punished by death. After their arrest for the murders, they were tied to the Sacramento synagogue firebombs (case 18).

---

20. *Midwest Drive-by Shootings*

Location: Illinois and Indiana

Date: July 2, 1999 – July 4, 1999

Weapons: .380-caliber pistol and.22-caliber pistol

Deaths: 3

Injured: 10

Suspect: Benjamin Nathaniel Smith

Target: BIPOC, AAPI, Jews

Summary:	Over the course of the 4th of July weekend, the 21-year-old targeted members of racial and ethnic minorities in a series of random drive-by shootings before killing himself. He was a white supremacist affiliated with the World Church of the Creator, whose leader had recently been denied his law license, and wanted to be a soldier of the Racial Holy War movement.

21.	*Los Angeles Jewish Community left Shooting*
Location:	Los Angeles, CA
Date:	August 10,1999
Weapons:	Uzi-type submachine gun, Glock 26 semi-automatic pistol
Deaths:	1
Injured:	5
Suspect:	Buford O. Furrow, Jr.
Target:	Jews
Summary:	The 37-year-old member of the Aryan Nations opened fire in the lobby of the Jewish Community left. His stated purpose was "killing Jews." Furrow had a history of mental illness and alcohol abuse.

22.	*Pittsburgh Killing Spree*
Location:	Pittsburgh, PA
Date:	April 28, 2000
Weapons:	.357 revolver
Deaths:	5
Injured:	1
Suspect:	Richard Baumhammers
Target:	BIPOC, AAPI, immigrants, Jews
eSummary:	The 34-year-old started his spree by shooting his 63-year-old Jewish neighbor and setting her house on fire. He then drove to a local synagogue, fired into its windows and spray-painted swastikas on the building. He proceeded to the India Grocer and shot two Indian Americans. From there, he shot at another synagogue and entered a Chinese restaurant and killed the Chinese manager and a Vietnamese American cook. He ended his killing spree at a Karate school, where he killed an African American man. The attacks were spread over two hours and 15 miles. Police found a white supremacist manifesto at his home. Baumhammers had a long history of mental illness and had talked in the past about suicide.

23.	*Conservative Synagogue Adath Israel of Riverdale Attack*
Location:	Bronx, NY
Date:	October 8, 2000
Weapons:	Molotov cocktails
Deaths:	-
Injured:	-

Suspects:	Mohammed Alfaqih and Mazin Assi
Target:	Jews
Summary:	The two men, aged 20 and 23, were charged with attempted arson as a hate crime for throwing a Molotov cocktail into the synagogue. The bomb failed to ignite. One of the attackers said he threw the bomb at "the rich Jews in Riverdale" because he believed they send money to Israel for "killing people."

24.	*Murder of Balbir Singh Sodhi*
Location:	Mesa, AZ
Date:	September 15, 2001
Weapons:	Firearm
Deaths:	1
Injured:	-
Suspect:	Frank Silva Roque
Target:	Muslims
Summary:	In the wake of the September 11 attacks, the 42-year-old attacker reportedly told friends he was "going to go out and shoot some towel-heads" and ranted about immigrants. He drove by Sodhi, who had a beard and wore a turban in accordance with his Sikh faith. The shooter mistook him for an Arab and shot and killed him. He proceeded to shot at a Lebanese American clerk at a gas station and outside the home of an Afghan family.

25.	*September 11 Revenge Killings*
Location:	Dallas, TX
Date:	September 16, 2001, September 21, 2001 and October 4, 2001
Weapons:	Firearms
Deaths:	2
Injured:	1
Suspect:	Mark Anthony Stroman
Target:	Muslims
Summary:	The day after a similar attack in Mesa, AZ (case 24), the 31-year-old began his killing spree by killing a Muslim Pakistani immigrant at a convenience store. Five days later, he shot a Bangladeshi immigrant at a gas station. Finally, on October 4th he killed a Hindu Indian immigrant at another gas station. The shooter identified as a white supremacist and was a member of the Aryan Brotherhood of Texas who sought revenge for the 9/11 attacks.

26.	*White Supremacist Terror Plot*
Location:	Boston, MA
Date:	April 19, 2002
Weapons:	-
Deaths:	-
Injured:	-

Suspects:	Leo Felton and Erica Chase
Target:	BIPOC, Jews
Summary:	The pair planned to blow up a series of African American and American Jewish institutions. They had begun acquiring bomb making materials and were arrested after attempting to use a counterfeit $20 bill at a coffee shop. Felton wanted to rid the United States of "mud people" – Asians, Blacks, Latinos, and Jews. Felton was half=Black and had been teased and ostracized as a kid. After being recruited by a white supremacist gang in an earlier prison stint, he began to identify as white and studied white supremacy and race theory.

27.	*Los Angeles International Airport Shooting*
Location:	Los Angeles, CA
Date:	July 4, 2002
Weapons:	.45-caliber handgun, 9mm handgun, knife
Deaths:	3
Injured:	5
Suspect:	Hesham Mohamed Hadayet
Target:	Jews
Summary:	A 41-year-old Egyptian national opened fire at the ticket counter of El Al, Israel's national airline. He had ties to an Islamist group that aimed to "understand truly and apply Islamic law in the 20th century under any circumstances."

28.	*Puzzles Lounge Attack*
Location:	New Bedford, MA
Date:	February 2, 2006
Weapons:	Hatchet, handgun
Deaths:	3
Injured:	4
Suspect:	Jacob D. Robida
Target:	LGBTQ+
Summary:	After confirming with the bartender that Puzzles Lounge was a gar bar, the 18-year-old swung a hatchet at a patron's head. He was tackled by other patrons but pulled out a handgun and began shooting. He fled the scene, picking up a woman in West Virginia and driving as far as Arkansas, where he murdered the woman and a police officer before killing himself. Police found weapons, Nazi regalia, and antisemitic writings at his home.

29.	*Seattle Jewish Federation Shooting*
Location:	Seattle, WA
Date:	July 28, 2006
Weapons:	.45-caliber handgun,.40-caliber handgun, knife
Deaths:	1
Injured:	6

Suspect:	Naveed Afzal Haq
Target:	Jews
Summary:	The shooter forced his way into the Jewish Federation, shooting into offices and holding the 14-year-old daughter of an employee as a hostage. The shooter was an American of Pakistani descent with few friends and a history of mental illness.

30.	*Murder of Sean Kennedy*
Location:	Greenville, SC
Date:	May 16, 2007
Weapons:	-
Deaths:	1
Injured:	-
Suspect:	Stephen Andrew Moller
Target:	LGBTQ+
Summary:	Kennedy was exiting a gay bar when he was punched so hard that it shattered his facial bones and separated his brain from his brain stem. The attack drew attention to the lack of a hate crime law in South Carolina and contributed to the passage of the federal Hate Crime Prevention Act of 2009.

31.	*Unitarian Universalist Church Shooting*
Location:	Knoxville, TN
Date:	July 27, 2008
Weapons:	12-gauge shotgun
Deaths:	2
Injured:	7
Suspect:	Jim David Adkisson
Target:	BIPOC, LGBTQ+, liberals
Summary:	Targeting the church because of its liberal teachings, the 58-year-old opened fire during a youth performance of *Annie Jr* until he was restrained by church members. He admitted to being motivated by hatred of Democrats, liberals, African Americans, and gays. He wrote a manifesto detailing these views and citing his inability to find work and that his food stamps were being cut. He had intended to keep shooting until police killed him.

32.	*Joliet Arson Case*
Location:	Joliet, IL
Date:	June 17, 2007
Weapons:	Arson
Deaths:	-
Injured:	-
Suspect:	Brian James Moudry
Target:	BIPOC

Summary:	The 36-year-old white supremacist set fire to the home of his African American neighbors. Nine people were home at the time, although none was injured. He had splashed gasoline on the home before setting it on fire. His goal was to upset the family and intimidate the owner from renting to African Americans in the future. The heavily tattooed arsonist had been in and out of psychiatric care for schizophrenia and had a history of suicide attempts.

33.	*Barack Obama Assassination Plot*
Location:	Tennessee
Date:	October 22, 2008
Weapons:	-
Deaths:	-
Injured:	-
Suspect:	Paul Schlesselman and Daniel Cowart
Target:	BIPOC
Summary:	Both men were neo-Nazi white power skinheads (one belonged to the Supreme White Alliance) who planned a killing spree of African Americans, including then-candidate Obama and students at a predominantly Black school. They were arrested on weapons charges after painting their car with swastikas and other neo-Nazi symbols and shooting at a church window.

34.	*Shooting of Pittsburgh Police Officers*
Location:	Pittsburgh, PA
Date:	April 4, 2009
Weapons:	Semi-automatic rifle, pump-action shotgun,.357 magnum revolver
Deaths:	3
Injured:	3
Suspect:	Richard Poplawski
Target:	Government
Summary:	After an argument, the shooter's mother called 9–1-1; he opened fire on the officers who responded. A member of Stormfront, his posts on a white supremacist website showed him to believe that Jews controlled society and there is a "Zionist occupation." Tattooed with racist symbols, Poplawsi hoped to write a book about the incident.

35.	*Bronx Terrorism Plot*
Location:	New York, NY
Date:	May 20, 2009
Weapons:	-
Deaths:	-
Injured:	-
Suspect:	Four Muslim men

Target:	Jews
Summary:	Four men were arrested in connection with a fake plot designed by an FBI informant. The plot involved shooting down military planes and blowing up two synagogues in the Bronx. None of the men had the money, knowledge, or skills to complete the plot.

36.	*United States Holocaust Memorial Museum Shooting*
Location:	Washington, DC
Date:	June 10, 2009
Weapons:	.22-caliber rifle
Deaths:	1
Injured:	2
Suspect:	James Wenneker von Brunn
Target:	Jews
Summary:	The 88-year-old entered the museum and fatally shot Museum Special Police Officer Stephen Tyrone Johns. Von Brunn self-published an antisemitic book and his website contained racist and antisemitic postings, including slur-filled rants against Black and Jewish court authorities that convicted him on other charges in the 80s. The attack took place shortly after Obama's visit to Buchenwald Concentration Camp.

37.	**Fort Hood Shooting**
Location:	Fort Hood, TX
Date:	November 5, 2009
Weapons:	Pistol,.357 Magnum revolver
Deaths:	14
Injured:	33
Suspect:	Nidal Hasan
Target:	Government
Summary:	The 39-year-old army psychiatrist opened fire in the Soldier Readiness Processing left, specifically targeting soldiers who were in uniform. He continued shooting outside, until he was eventually shot by responders. The attacker is a practicing Muslim who had visited radical Islamic websites and felt anguish over serving in a military that fought against Muslims and had justified suicide bombings. At his trial, he said his motive was wanting to save the lives of Taliban leadership in Afghanistan.

38.	*Jacksonville Mosque Bombing*
Location:	Jacksonville, FL
Date:	May 10, 2010
Weapons:	Pipe-bomb
Deaths:	-
Injured:	-

Suspect:	Sandlin Smith
Target:	Muslims
Summary:	The 46-year-old attacked the Islamic Centre of Northeast Florida with a pipe bomb. There were at least 60 people in the left at the time, although none weas injured or killed. He hated Muslims because of "our men going overseas, fighting and dying."

39.	*Tucson Shooting*
Location:	Tucson, AZ
Date:	January 8, 2011
Weapons:	Glock 19 semi-automatic pistol
Deaths:	6
Injured:	15
Suspect:	Jared Lee Loughner
Target:	Women, government
Summary:	US Representative Gabby Giffords and 18 others were shot at a constituent meeting in a supermarket parking lot. The 22-year-old attacker was fixated on Giffords and had posted online about the government brainwashing the citizens. He believed that women should not hold positions of power. Most of his online writings were conservative and anti-government. Loughner had lost his girlfriend, job, and school standing, turning to alcohol and other drugs.

40.	*Hardy Firebombing*
Location:	Hardy, AR
Date:	January 14, 2011
Weapons:	Molotov cocktails
Deaths:	-
Injured:	-
Suspects:	Gary Dodson, Jason Barnwell, Dustin Hammond, and Jake Murphy
Target:	BIPOC
Summary:	The men threw three Molotov cocktails into the couple's home because the victims were "a Black man living with a white woman."

41.	*Spokane Bombing Attempt*
Location:	Spokane, WA
Date:	January 17, 2011
Weapons:	Pipe bomb
Deaths:	-
Injured:	-
Suspect:	Kevin William Harpham

Target: BIPOC

Summary: A radio-controlled pipe bomb was found and defused along the Martin Luther King Jr. memorial march route. The 36-year-old white supremacist acted alone to place the shrapnel loaded bomb. He was a member of the racist National Alliance and posted more than a thousand racist and antisemitic articles online.

---

42. *Manhattan Terrorism Plot*

Location: Manhattan, NY

Date: May 11, 2011

Weapons: -

Deaths: -

Injured: -

Suspects: Ahmed Ferhani and Mohamed Mandouh

Target: Jews

Summary: The two men, aged 26 and 20, had planned to bomb various targets in Manhattan, including synagogues and churches. They were arrested trying to purchase weapons, including pistols and hand grenades. According to the NYPD, they "weren't driven by religion. It's really more politics and antisemitism."

---

43. *Murder of James Craig Anderson*

Location: Jackson, MS

Date: June 26, 2011

Weapons: Truck

Deaths: 1

Injured: -

Suspects Deryl Dedmon

Target: BIPOC

Summary: A group of white teenagers robbed and beat Anderson before one of them ran him over, killing him. The group had been drinking prior to the attack and went on a beer run, with Dedmon urging, "Let's go f-ck with some ni**ers."

---

44. *Norway Shooting*

Location: Oslo and Utøya, Norway

Date: July 22, 2011

Weapons: ANFO car bomb, Ruger min-14, Glock 34 pistol

Deaths: 77

Injured: 319+

Suspect: Anders Behring Breivik

Target: Muslims, government

Summary:	The attack started with a car bomb in Oslo within the executive government quarter, near the office of the prime minister. Less than two hours later, the 32-year-old right-wing extremist, dressed in a homemade police uniform, opened fire at a summer camp on Utøya island. About 90 minutes before the bombing, the attacker released a 1,518-page manifesto entitled *2083: A European Declaration of Independence*, in which he considers himself a knight dedicated to stemming the tide of Muslim immigration into Europe. Breivik had a history of mental illness and resented his liberal upbringing. He planned the attacks for nine years, acquiring materials and using video games for weapons practice.

45.	*Northwest Killing Spree*
Location:	Oregon and California
Date:	September 26, 2011 – October 3, 2011
Weapons:	Firearms
Deaths:	4
Injured:	-
Suspects:	Holly Grigsby and David Pedersen
Target:	BIPOC, Jews
Summary:	The pair's killing spree began when Pedersen killed his father and stepmother in Everett, OR. They then drove south, where they shot a teenager, thinking he was Jewish based on his name, and stole his car. The final victim was a 53-year-old Black man in northern California. Both suspects were white supremacists (Pedersen was the founder of a white-supremacist prison gang) who wanted to start a revolution by targeting Jewish leaders.

46.	*Murder of Trayvon Martin*
Location:	Sandford, FL
Date:	February 26, 2012
Weapons:	Firearm
Deaths:	1
Injured:	-
Suspect:	George Zimmerman
Target:	BIPOC
Summary:	Martin was walking back to his father's fiancée's house from a nearby convenience store when spotted by the 28-year-old Hispanic American resident. Zimmerman reported him to the police as suspicious then killed him a few minutes later in an altercation. Initially police did not arrest him because he claimed self-defense and used Florida's "stand your ground" law. He was eventually charged, but a jury acquitted him. Zimmerman has since posted racist and anti-Muslim message and images on social media, as well as apparent revenge porn.

47.	*Gilbert Arizona Killings*
Location:	Gilbert, AZ
Date:	May 12, 2012
Weapons:	Firearm
Deaths:	5
Injured:	-
Suspect:	J.T. Ready
Target:	Immigrants, personal revenge
Summary:	The 39-year-old was the founder and leader of a militia group and a member of the neo-Nazi National Socialist Movement. He was twice caught forcibly detaining immigrants on the Arizona-Mexico border and was under investigation related to immigrants found shot to death in the desert. On May 12, 2012, after an argument, he fatally shot his girlfriend, her daughter, and her daughter's boyfriend and infant daughter before killing himself.

48.	*Wisconsin Sikh Temple Shooting*
Location:	Oak Creek, WI
Date:	August 5, 2012
Weapons:	9mm semi-automatic pistol
Deaths:	8
Injured:	3
Suspect:	Wade Michael Page
Target:	Other religious minorities
Summary:	A mass shooting took place at the Sikh Temple of Wisconsin, where the 40-year-old white supremacist opened fire, killing seven people before turning the gun on himself. An army veteran, the heavily tattooed shooter had ties to white supremacist and neo-Nazi groups and was reportedly a member of the Hammerskins.

49.	*Missouri Mosque Fire*
Location:	Joplin, MO
Date:	August 6, 2012
Weapons:	Arson
Deaths:	-
Injured:	-
Suspect:	Jedediah Stout
Target:	Women, Muslims
Summary:	The 32-year-old was convicted of setting fire to the Islamic Society of Joplin and twice attempting to set fire to a Planned Parenthood clinic. He admitted to his anti-Muslim views and to targeting Planned Parenthood because of their reproductive health services.

50.	*Thwarted Death Ray Attack*
Location:	Albany, NY
Date:	June 2013
Weapons:	-
Deaths:	-
Injured:	-
Suspects:	Glendon Scott Crawford and Eric Feight
Target:	BIPOC, Muslims
Summary:	The men planned to build a radiation dispersal device, or dirty bomb, to target Muslims and then-president Obama with a lethal dose of radiation. Crawford, a member of the KKK, extensively researched potential targets, including local mosques. The two men designed and acquired parts for the device and built and tested a dispersal unit.

51.	*Overland Park Jewish Community left Shooting*
Location:	Overland Park, KS
Date:	April 13, 2014
Weapons:	Remington 870 shotgun, handgun
Deaths:	3
Injured:	1
Suspect:	Frazier Glenn Miller, Jr.
Target:	Jews
Summary:	Shootings occurred at the Jewish Community left of Greater Kansas City and Village Shalom, a Jewish retirement community. The 73-year-old shooter was the former KKK leader and neo-Nazi who had an accomplice buy the shotgun for him.

52.	*Las Vegas Walmart Shootings*
Location:	Las Vegas, NV
Date:	June 8, 2014
Weapons:	9mm pistols,.38 revolver, shotgun, knives
Deaths:	5
Injured:	-
Suspects:	Jerad and Amanda Miller
Target:	Government
Summary:	The couple killed two police officers at a restaurant declaring it "the beginning of the revolution." From there, they fled to a nearby Walmart where they killed an armed civilian who confronted them. Jerad was killed by police, while Amanda committed suicide. Detailed plans to "take over the courthouse and execute public officials" were found in their apartment. He believed in conspiracy theories and espoused hatred in the federal government and then-President Obama. Both posted images of themselves dressed as supervillains and expressed hatred for law enforcement. They also displayed white supremacist beliefs, supported the Patriot movement, and idolized the Columbine killers.

53.	*Thwarted Pittsburgh Bombing*
Location:	Pittsburgh, PA
Date:	July 27, 2014
Weapons:	IEDs and other bombmaking materials
Deaths:	-
Injured:	-
Suspect:	Eric Charles Smith
Target:	Unknown
Summary:	After a domestic violence incident, police searched the suspect's home and found approximately 20 IEDs, explosive materials and recipes, bombmaking literature, detonating devices, and white supremacist and Nazi paraphernalia. Smith, who has a history of mental illness, hosted gatherings of the "White Church Supremacists."

54.	*Charleston Church Shooting*
Location:	Charleston, South Carolina
Date:	June 17, 2015
Weapons:	Glock 41
Deaths:	9
Injured:	1
Suspect:	Dylann Roof
Target:	BIPOC
Summary:	The 21-year-old white supremacist opened fire during a Bible study at the Emanuel African Methodist Episcopal Church, one of the oldest Black churches in the United States, with the goal of starting a race war. On a website he owned, he posted a manifesto containing his opinions about several minority groups, including "Blacks," "Jews," "Hispanics," and "East Asians." At the time of the attack, Roof did not have a permanent home or job and was regularly using drugs and alcohol.

55.	*Lafayette Shooting*
Location:	Lafayette, LA
Date:	July 23, 2015
Weapons:	.40-caliber handgun
Deaths:	3
Injured:	9
Suspect:	John Russell Houser
Target:	Women, Jews

Summary: The 59-year-old opened fire at the Grand 13 movie theater during the film *Trainwreck*, killing two women and injuring nine other people before killing himself. He chose the movie based on its feminist themes and the lead actress's Jewish background. He had a history of anti-government and far-right views, and his online history shows that he was a supporter of David Duke, the Westboro Baptist Church, Adolf Hitler, the Oklahoma City bombers (case 13), and the Charleston shooter (case 54). He also had a history of mental illness, was estranged from his family, and was legally drunk as the time of the attack.

56.	*Thwarted "Hit Squad"*
Location:	Whitehall, NY
Date:	August 5, 2015
Weapons:	-
Deaths:	-
Injured:	-
Suspect:	Shane Robert Smith
Target:	Unknown
Summary:	The 24-year-old was convicted in 2016 after attempting to obtain fully automatic weapons. He advocated online for violence against racial and religious minority groups, attempting to form a "hit squad." He told an undercover officer, "I love violence." Two years after his release on those charges, he was arrested again when authorities found weapons and white supremacist materials in his home.

57.	*Umpqua Community College Shooting*
Location:	Roseburg, Oregon
Date:	October 1, 2015
Weapons:	Smith and Wesson M99, Taurus PT24/7, Hi-Point CF-380, Glock 19, S&W M642–2
Deaths:	10
Injured:	8
Suspect:	Christopher Harper-Mercer
Target:	Personal revenge
Summary:	A 26-year-old student at Umpqua Community College killed an assistant professor and eight students and injured eight others before killing himself. During the attack, he spared one student, giving them a package for the police that contained his writings, which referenced past mass killers and detailed his motivations, stating that he had "no friends, no job, no girlfriend." Witnesses state that he asked victims about their religion during the attack. He had a history of mental illness and had recently been placed on academic probation.

58.	*Minneapolis Protest Attack*
Location:	Minneapolis, MN
Date:	November 23, 2015

Weapons:	Firearms
Deaths:	-
Injured:	5
Suspects:	Nathan Gustavsson, Allen Scarsella, Daniel Macey, and Joseph Backman
Target:	BIPOC
Summary:	The men, aged 21–27, hoped to disrupt and record the protest of the recent police killing of 24-year-old Jamar Clark. Scarsella brought a weapon and shot at protestors, wounding five Black men. Police found weapons and white supremacist paraphernalia in their residences.

59.	*Chesterfield Church Attack Plot*
Location:	Chesterfield County, VA
Date:	January 2016
Weapons:	-
Deaths:	-
Injured:	-
Suspects:	Charles Halderman, Ronald Beasley Chaney III, and Robert Doyle
Target:	BIPOC, Jews
Summary:	The three men plotted an attack on Black churches and Jewish synagogues in Virginia, with the goal of starting a race war. They planned to rob a local jeweler to fund the attacks. Halderman was associated with the Aryan Brotherhood.

60.	*Ohio Restaurant Machete Attack*
Location:	Columbus, OH
Date:	February 11,2016
Weapons:	Machete, filet knife, automobile
Deaths:	1
Injured:	4
Suspect:	Mohamed Barry
Target:	Unknown
Summary:	The 30-year-old attacker entered the Nazareth Restaurant and attacked customers with a machete. He fled the scene and collided his car into another vehicle. He was killed by police when we lunged at them with the knife. He was known to the FBI for making radical comments.

61.	*Murder of Jo Cox*
Location:	Birstall, West Yorkshire, England
Date:	June 16, 2016
Weapons:	Knife,.22 hunting rifle
Deaths:	1
Injured:	1

Suspect:	Thomas Alexander Mair
Target:	Government
Summary:	Cox was a member of the British parliament and a member of the Labour Party. She was shot and stabbed multiple times by the 53-year-old, who wanted to advance white supremacism and nationalism. He targeted Cox because she was "one of the collaborators" and a "traitor" to white people. Mair was linked to the neo-Nazi group National Alliance.

62.	*Minneapolis Shooting*
Location:	Minneapolis, MN
Date:	June 29, 2016
Weapons:	.38 handgun
Deaths:	-
Injured:	2
Suspect:	Anthony John Sawina
Target:	Muslims
Summary:	After leaving a bar with friends, the 26-year-old encountered a group of five Somali men wearing traditional *qamis*. He and his friends shouted anti-Muslim insults and when the men objected, he drew a gun and began shooting at the Somalis.

63.	*Munich Shootings*
Location:	Munich, Germany
Date:	July 22, 2016
Weapons:	Glock 17 semi-automatic pistol
Deaths:	10
Injured:	36
Suspect:	David Ali Sonboly
Target:	Unknown
Summary:	The 18-year-old opened fire at a McDonald's and shot others in the street outside and a nearby shopping mall, before killing himself. He supported the far-right and was proud to share the same birthday as Adolf Hitler. He had researched mass shootings and committed this attack on the fifth anniversary of the Norway attacks (case 44). He had a history of mental illness and was isolated from and bullied by his peers in school.

64.	*Garden City Thwarted Attack*
Location:	Garden City, KS
Date:	October 14, 2016
Weapons:	Firearms, explosives
Deaths:	-
Injured:	-
Suspects:	Patrick Eugene Stein, Curtis Allen and Gavin Wright
Target:	Immigrants, Muslims

Summary:	The three members of a Kansas militia group plotted to bomb an apartment complex populated mostly by Somali Muslim immigrants, spurred to action by the Pulse nightclub shooting. With the help an FBI informant, police found weapons and bomb making materials in their residences.

65.	*Myrtle Beach Thwarted Attack*
Location:	Myrtle Beach, SC
Date:	December 2016
Weapons:	-
Deaths:	-
Injured:	-
Suspect:	Benjamin McDowell
Target:	Jews, Muslims
Summary:	An undercover agent formed a relationship with the 31-year-old, who made friends with white supremacist groups and got racist tattoos while in prison on another charge and had a history of mental illness. He told the FBI agent that he was panning an attack in the name of white power and praised the Charleston Church attacker (case 54). He talked about wanting to commit violence against Jewish and Muslim people. Because of that earlier conviction, he could not legally own a gun and was arrested when he bought one from the undercover agent.

66.	*Quebec City Mosque Shooting*
Location:	Quebec City, Canada
Date:	January 29, 2017
Weapons:	Glock 17, semi-automatic rifle
Deaths:	6
Injured:	19
Suspect:	Alexandre Bissonnette
Target:	Muslims
Summary:	Six worshippers were killed, and five others were injured, when the 27-year-old opened fire after evening prayers at the Islamic Cultural Centre of Quebec City. The shooter regularly visited Islamophobic websites and researched mass shooters. He espoused far-right, white nationalist, and anti-Muslim views.

67.	*Murder of Timothy Caughman*
Location:	New York, NY
Date:	March 20, 2017
Weapons:	Sword
Deaths:	1
Injured:	-
Suspect:	James Harris Jackson
Target:	BIPOC

Summary:	The 28-year-old white supremacist stabbed Caughman multiple times while he was collecting recycling. He turned himself into police and admitted that he traveled from Maryland to New York with the intention of killing Black men to prevent them having interracial relationships with white women. His YouTube channel contained alt-right, neo-Nazi, Holocaust denial, incel, pro-Trump, and white nationalist content.

68.	*Portland Train Attack*
Location:	Portland, Oregon
Date:	May 26,2017
Weapons:	Knife
Deaths:	2
Injured:	1
Suspect:	Jeremy Joseph Christian
Target:	BIPOC, Muslims
Summary:	The self-described white nationalist shouted racist and anti-Muslim slurs at two Black teenagers on a train and attacked three men who confronted him. Christian, who had no permanent address, posted about his extremist views online, praised the Oklahoma City bombers (case 13), and had participated in alt-right rallies.

69.	*Finsbury Park Attack*
Location:	London, England
Date:	June 19, 2017
Weapons:	Lufton box van with tail lift
Deaths:	1
Injured:	10
Suspect:	Darren Osborne
Target:	Muslims
Summary:	The 47-year-old drove a van into pedestrians at a London park, near the Muslim Welfare House and the Finsbury Park Mosque. The attacker had turned against Muslims after the London Bridge attack on June 3, 2017, when Islamic terrorists drove a van into pedestrians. His intended target was the Al-Quds day march and he hoped to kill march attendees Labour Party leader Jeremy Corbyn and London mayor Sadiq Khan. He had recently attempted suicide and had a history of mental illness and drug and alcohol abuse. He rented the van several days before the attack and had been sleeping in it.

70.	*Unite the Right Rally*
Location:	Charlottesville, VA
Date:	August 11–12, 2017
Weapons:	Automobile
Deaths:	3

Injured:	49+
Suspect:	James Alex Fields, Jr., alt-right proteste
Target:	Mixed
Summary:	The Unite the Right rally brought together far-right groups including the alt-right, neo-Confederates, neo-fascists, white nationalists, neo-Nazis, Klansmen, and right-wing militias. They met in Charlottesville to protest the removal of the statue of Robert E. Lee from what had been known as Lee Park. Protestors clashed with counter-protestors and a white supremacist protestor rammed his car into a crowd of counter protestors. One counter-protestor, Heather Heyer, was killed and 35 others were injured in that attack. At least 14 others were injured in other clashes during the rally, including DeAndre Harris, who was beaten by a group of six men in a parking garage after an altercation with a group of white supremacists.

71.	*White Supremacist Domestic Violence*
Location:	Harris County, TX
Date:	October 2017
Weapons:	-
Deaths:	-
Injured:	1
Suspect:	William Fears IV
Target:	Women
Summary:	The 30-year-old white supremacist was arrested for choking his girlfriend and in regards to his plea deal, he talked about hating women and blamed her for his conviction. Fears had attended the Unite the Right rally as a member of Vanguard America. He had recently been involved in an altercation at a venue where a well-known white supremacist was speaking in which he praised Hitler and urged another man to shoot at protestors.

72.	*Aztec High School Shooting*
Location:	Aztec, NM
Date:	December 7, 2017
Weapons:	9mm Glock
Deaths:	3
Injured:	-
Suspect:	William Atchison
Target:	Unknown
Summary:	A former student at the school, the 21-year-old white supremacist killed two students in a hallway, fired several rounds into a classroom, and then killed himself as police approached him. He had posted on pro-Hitler forums and websites and joked about school shootings. His online writings were racist, antisemitic, and anti-LGBT and he had drawn neo-Nazi symbols on his body prior to the attack. He referred to other mass shooters and was in contact with the 2016 Munich attacker (case 63).

73.	*Murder of Blaze Bernstein*
Location:	Orange County, CA
Date:	January 10, 2018
Weapons:	Knife
Deaths:	1
Injured:	-
Suspect:	Samuel Woodward
Target:	LGBTQ+, Jews
Summary:	Bernstein was killed by a former classmate who was a member of the Atomwaffen Division, entrusted with vetting new members. Bernstein was Jewish and openly gay.

74.	*Unite the Right Domestic Violence*
Location:	Paoli, IN
Date:	March 13, 2018
Weapons:	-
Deaths:	-
Injured:	1
Suspect:	Matthew Heimbach
Target:	Women
Summary:	The prominent neo-Nazi, who was a major promoter of the Unite the Right rally (case 70), was arrested after attacking his wife and the husband of his mistress (who co-founded the Traditionalist Worker party with Heimback). He has engaged in gender- and race-based violence on many occasions.

75.	*United States Mail Bombing Attempts*
Location:	United States
Date:	October 22, 2018 – November 1, 2018
Weapons:	Pipe bombs
Deaths:	-
Injured:	-
Suspect:	Cesar Sayoc, Jr.
Target:	Government, liberals
Summary:	Sixteen packages containing pipe bombs were mailed to several Democratic politicians and other critics of Trump. The 56-year-old perpetrator was staunchly pro-Trump and anti-liberal, and a believer in right-wing conspiracy theories. Sayoc has a history of steroid abuse, financial trouble, and anxiety and was living in his van at the time of the incidents.

76.	*Kentucky Kroger Shooting*
Location:	Jeffersontown, KY
Date:	October 24, 2018
Weapons:	Firearm

Deaths:	2
Injured:	0
Suspect:	Gregory A. Bush
Target:	BIPOC
Summary:	On the afternoon of October 24, the 51-year-old had tried to enter a predominantly Black church, but found the doors locked. Shortly after this, he entered the Kroger and fatally shot Maurice Stallard then went outside and killed Vicki Lee Jones. Both victims were African American. He had a history of mental illness and had become increasingly polarized during the 2016 presidential campaign and posted frequently on Twitter about Black-on-Black crime and making racial insults.

77.	*Tree of Life Shooting*
Location:	Pittsburgh, PA
Date:	October 27, 2018
Weapons:	AR-15 semi-automatic rifle, 3 Glock.357 semi-automatic pistols
Deaths:	11
Injured:	7
Suspect:	Robert Gregory Bowers
Target:	Jews
Summary:	During Shabbat morning services, the 46-year-old entered the Tree of Life, or L'Simcha Congregation, and opened fire. The shooter was a white nationalist who posted antisemitic conspiracy theories online and had cut ties with his friends and family in the years leading up to the attack.

78.	*Christchurch Mosque Shootings*
Location:	Christchurch, New Zealand
Date:	March 15, 2019
Weapons:	Two AR Style riddles, 12-gauge Mossberg 930, 12 gauge Rander 870 shotgun,.357 Magnum level-action rifle,.223-caliber Mossberg Predator bolt-action rifle
Deaths:	51
Injured:	40
Suspect:	Brenton Harrison Tarrant
Target:	Immigrants, Muslims
Summary:	During Friday prayers, over the course of about 15 minutes, the 28-year-old entered two mosques, opening fire at each. He livestreamed the first attack on Facebook and prior to the attack published an online manifesto titled *The Great Replacement*. It contains anti-immigrant sentiments and neo-Nazi symbolism. He planned the attack for two years, after becoming obsessed with Islamic extremist terror attacks.

79.	*Escondido Mosque Fire*
Location:	Escondido, CA
Date:	March 24, 2019
Weapons:	Arson
Deaths:	-
Injured:	-
Suspect:	John Timothy Earnest
Target:	Muslims
Summary:	The Islamic left of Escondido was set on fire and the driveway was graffitied with references to the Christchurch shootings (case 78). No suspect was found until police were able to link the Poway Synagogue shooter (case 81) to the fire.

80.	*Louisiana Black Church Fires*
Location:	Port Barre, LA and Opelousas, LA
Date:	March 26, 2019 – April 4, 2019
Weapons:	Arson
Deaths:	-
Injured:	-
Suspect:	Holden Matthews
Target:	BIPOC
Summary:	Three historic black churches were set on fire by the 21-year-old over the course of ten days. The arsonist was influenced by Norwegian black metal musicians who committed similar attacks in the 1990s.

81.	*Poway Synagogue Shooting*
Location:	Poway, CA
Date:	April 27, 2019
Weapons:	Smith and Wesson M&P15 rifle
Deaths:	1
Injured:	3
Suspect:	John Timothy Earnest
Target:	Jews
Summary:	The 19-year-old opened fire in the Chabad of Poway synagogue on the last day of Passover. He attempted to livestream the attack on Facebook and had posted an antisemitic and racist letter on 8chan before the shooting. After this attack, authorities were able to link the attacker to the fire at the Islamic left of Escondido (case 79).

82.	*Dallas Courthouse Shooting*
Location:	Dallas, TX
Date:	June 17, 2019
Weapons:	AR-15 style rifle

Deaths:	1
Injured:	1
Suspect:	Brian Isaack Clyde
Target:	Unknown
Summary:	The 22-year-old opened fire near the courthouse before entering the building and continuing to fire. One person was injured before police killed the shooter. He was an army veteran who self-radicalized online, posting extreme far-right views including Nazism, misogyny, incel philosophies, and transphobia. In 2016 his brother had contacted the FBI about Clyde's fascination with guns and suicidality.

83.	*Garlic Festival Shooting*
Location:	Gilroy, CA
Date:	July 28, 2019
Weapons:	AK-47 style automatic rifle
Deaths:	4
Injured:	17
Suspect:	Santino William Legan
Target:	BIPOC, immigrants
Summary:	The 19-year-old gunman opened fire near an inflatable slide at the festival. Earlier that day, the shooter, who was described as a loner, used Instagram to encourage people to read the book *Might is Right*, a proto-fascist manifesto, and to complain about overcrowding and "hordes" of Latinos.

84.	*North Miami Beach Synagogue Shooting*
Location:	North Miami Beach, FL
Date:	July 28, 2019
Weapons:	Firearm
Deaths:	-
Injured:	1
Suspect:	Carlints St. Louis
Target:	Jews
Summary:	A gunman pulled up outside the Young Israel of Greater Miami Temple, got out of the car, and shot a 68-year-old man who was waiting outside. He then got back in the car a drove away.

85.	*El Paso Shooting*
Location:	El Paso, Texas
Date:	August 3, 2019
Weapons:	WASR-10 (AK-47 style automatic rifle)
Deaths:	23
Injured:	23

Suspect:	Patrick Wood Crusius
Target:	BIPOC, immigrants
Summary:	The 21-year-old attacker open fire at a Walmart. He targeted Latinos and wrote extensively about being inspired by the New Zealand shooter (case 44) and the far-right conspiracy theory called the *Great Replacement*. He wrote a manifesto entitle *An Inconvenient Truth* and argued for white supremacy and a national call to action to stop the growing migrant invasion of the country. Crusius has a history of mental illness and was described as a loner and standoffish who had been teased in school.

86.	*Bomb Possession*
Location:	Birmingham, AL
Date:	October 2019
Weapons:	IEDs
Deaths:	-
Injured:	-
Suspect:	James David Kircus
Target:	BIPOC, personal revenge
Summary:	The 54-year-old as found to have made IEDs at an auto salvage company where he was working while living at a half-way house for federal prisoners. He had detonated several airbags "for fun." He was a self-described white supremacist who planned to kill two women who he believed turned him in on another charge and to blow up the half-way house in order to kill the Black people there.

87.	*Jersey City Shooting*
Location:	Jersey City, NJ
Date:	December 10, 2019
Weapons:	AR-15 rifle, 12-guage shotgun, 2 9mm handguns
Deaths:	6
Injured:	3
Suspects:	David Anderson and Francine Graham
Target:	Jews, government
Summary:	The attackers shot and killed a police officer who approached them while they were in a stolen vehicle. They then entered the JC Kosher Supermarket and opened fire before being killed by police. The shooters were suspects in at least two other murders, including that of a Jewish man. Anderson (47) had made anti-police and antisemitic posts on social media. Both he and Graham (50) were African American and were linked to the Black Hebrew Israelite movement, which vilifies white and Jewish people.

88.	*Monsey Hanukkah Stabbing*
Location:	Monsey, NY
Date:	December 28, 2019
Weapons:	Large knife or machete
Deaths:	1
Injured:	4
Suspect:	Grafton E. Thomas
Target:	Jews
Summary:	On the seventh night of Hanukkah, a masked man invaded the home of a Hasidic rabbi and began stabbing guests. The suspect, 37, is an African American with several previous arrests and a history of mental illness and drug use who had maintained journals expressing antisemitic views. He was suspected in the previous stabbing of an Orthodox Jewish man and had shown support of the Black Hebrew Israelite movement.

89.	*Gun Rally Plot*
Location:	Richmond, VA
Date:	January 16, 2020
Weapons:	Assault rifle
Deaths:	-
Injured:	-
Suspects:	Patrik Mathews and Brian Lemley
Target:	BIPOC
Summary:	The men, who are members of the white supremacist group The Base, had plans to carry out an attack at a pro-gun rights rally in Richmond, with the goal of starting a racial civil war. The two had attended military-style camps with other members of The Base and had built an assault rifle they had tested at a gun range.

90.	*Hanau shootings*
Location:	Hanau, Hesse, Germany
Date:	February 19, 2020
Weapons:	Glock 17, CZ 75 Shadow, Sig Sauer P226, Walther PPQ M2 (.22)
Deaths:	11
Injured:	5
Suspect:	Tobias Rathjen
Target:	Immigrants
Summary:	The 43-year-old attacker targeted two shisha bars in Hanau's central square, killing nine people there before killing his mother and himself. He published a racist manifesto on his website that discussed eugenics, paranoia, and misogyny. He wrote about his struggles with mental illness and identified as an incel. He expressed hatred for people from the Middle East, Asia, and North America and for German citizens who allowed immigrants into their country.

91.	*Murder of Ahmaud Arbery*
Location:	Glynn County, GA
Date:	February23, 2020
Weapons:	Shotgun
Deaths:	1
Injured:	-
Suspects:	Travis McMichael, Gregory McMichael and William Bryan
Target:	BIPOC
Summary:	The three men chased Arbery with their truck while he was out jogging before fatally shooting him. They claim to have suspected him of committing burglary in the neighborhood. One of the men recorded the event on his cell phone. No arrests were made until public outcry after the video was released by one of the attackers.

92.	*Murder of George Floyd*
Location:	Minneapolis, MN
Date:	May 25, 2020
Weapons:	-
Deaths:	1
Injured:	-
Suspect:	Derek Chauvin
Target:	BIPOC
Summary:	As Floyd was being arrested on suspicion of using a counterfeit $20 bill, the 44-year-old white police officer knelt on Floyd's neck for over nine minutes while he was handcuffed and lying face-down in the street. Two other officers assisted in the arrest and a third prevented bystanders from intervening. Videos made by witnesses became public and spurred worldwide protests against police brutality and police racism.

93.	*Boogaloo Killings*
Location:	Oakland, CA and Ben Lomond, CA
Date:	May 29, 2020 and June 6, 2020
Weapons:	Rifle, improvised explosive devices (IEDs)
Deaths:	2
Injured:	4
Suspects:	Steven Carrillo and Robert Justus
Target:	Government
Summary:	On May 29, there was a drive-by shooting in front of the federal courthouse in Oakland that killed a security officer. Over a week later, Santa Cruz County sheriff's deputies were shot at and attacked with IEDs. The suspects were associated with the boogaloo movement, a far-right anti-government extremist movement. Carrillo was also spurred by his wife's suicide two year's prior and the stress of the pandemic.

94.	*United States Capitol Attack*
Location:	Washington, DC
Date:	January 6, 2021
Weapons:	Various
Deaths:	5
Injured:	Unknown number of protestors (at least five hospitalized); at least 138 police officers (at least 15 hospitalized)
Suspects:	Trump supporters
Target:	Mixed
Summary:	After Trump and others claimed fraud in the election, a rally turned violent as his supporters breached the US Capitol. Rioters chanted "Hang Mike Pence," vandalized and looted offices, and occupied the Senate chamber. Pipe bombs were discovered near the Republican National Committee offices and many of the rioters were violent against law enforcement. Many of the rioters displayed racist and antisemitic imagery and included far-right militants and white supremacist group members.

95.	*Shul of Bal Harbour Attempted Break-in*
Location:	Surfside, FL
Date:	February 7, 2021
Weapons:	-
Deaths:	-
Injured:	-
Suspect:	Unidentified man
Target:	Jews
Summary:	A man was arrested for attempting to forcibly enter the Shul, one of the largest synagogues in South Florida. The Shul's security members approached his parked car, where he was overheard speaking Arabic and appeared to be under the influence. He began running toward the building and was stopped by security.

96.	*Atlanta Massage Parlor Shootings*
Location:	Atlanta, GA
Date:	March 16, 2021
Weapons:	9mm semi-automatic pistol
Deaths:	8
Injured:	1
Suspect:	Robert Aaron Long
Target:	AAPI, women
Summary:	The 21-year-old attacked three massage parlors in the Atlanta area. He told police that his sex addiction conflicted with his Christianity. He saw the massage parlors as sources of sexual temptation. He had recently lost his girlfriend over his frequent visits to massage parlors and his parents threw him out of the house the night of the attacks.

97.	*Los Angeles Restaurant Attack*
Location:	Los Angeles, CA
Date:	May 18, 2021
Weapons:	-
Deaths:	-
Injured:	2
Suspects:	Xavier Pabon and Samer Jayylusi
Target:	Jews
Summary:	The two assailants were part of a pro-Palestinian caravan when they exited their vehicles and asked if any diners were Jewish. They attacked two men who identified as such while yelling racial slurs.

98.	*London, Ontario Truck Attack*
Location:	London, ON, Canada
Date:	June 6, 2021
Weapons:	Pickup truck
Deaths:	4
Injured:	1
Suspect:	Nathaniel Veltman
Target:	Muslims
Summary:	The attacker mounted the curb and rammed a pickup truck into a family of Muslim Pakistani Canadian pedestrians at an intersection. Police believe he planned the attack in advance.

99.	*Denver Yeshiva Killing*
Location:	Denver, CO
Date:	August 18, 2021
Weapons:	Firearm
Deaths:	1
Injured:	1
Suspects:	Seth James Larhode, Isaiah James Freeman, Aden Sides, Noah Loepp-Hall and Samuel Fussell
Target:	Jews
Summary:	Five young men, ages 18–21, killed Shmuel Silverberg in a drive-by shooting outside Yeshiva Toras Chaim. The suspects claim they were not targeting the Jewish school specifically, but this was part of a larger crime spree that included multiple carjackings at gunpoint and the shooting of a robbery victim.

100.	*Brooklyn Attacks*
Location:	Brooklyn, NY
Date:	November 26–28, 2021
Weapons:	-

Deaths:	-
Injured:	3
Suspects:	Three unidentified women
Target:	Jews
Summary:	Three women attacked at least three Jewish ultra-Orthodox children who were wearing traditional Jewish attire. The youngest child was a three-year-old boy who they slapped across the face. Two days later, they approached an 18-year-old girl and pulled her to the ground. Later they slapped a nine-year-old boy on top of his head several times.

8 Introduction to Three Case Studies

Box 8.1 Key Take-aways

1. Three cases are provided as examples to be used to describe the White Supremacist Indoctrination Rubric reviewed in Chapter 11 as well as offer case examples for assessment and treatment approaches in Chapters 14, 15, and 16.
2. Hank is a high school junior who, along with some friends, has begun to openly discuss white supremacist ideology in their school and use racists slurs against other students.
3. Jesse is a college student who engages in debate and arguments with social justice groups and in the classroom, defending the principles of the white supremacist movement.
4. Dawson is a community college student who is deeply connected to the white supremacist movement and is openly talking and recruiting others to his cause.

The first half of this book provided a foundation of understanding related to the rise of the white supremacist movement. The harm caused by this growing threat spreads across the Black, Jewish, and Muslim communities, as well as women, LGBTQI+, and those of Asian background. Now that the white supremacist issue is well understood and conceptualized, it is the time to address it.

Perhaps one of our first reactions to hearing someone sharing white supremacist rhetoric, seeing someone proudly wearing a symbol outlined in chapter four, or witnessing someone targeting someone they believe is inferior is to become angry or enraged. The question that often plagues us is, does this reaction take them further down the pathway to violence or does it begin to dissuade them and offer alternative explanations? This is complicated as some acts such as physical assault, terrorist threats or yelling hate slurs at a marginalized individual cannot be met with dialogue and an expression of empathy. There is, however, an opportunity to

DOI: 10.4324/9781003199656-8

work with those who are asked to complete therapy as part of a mandated assessment or treatment or by concerned parents, and this opens the possibility of working with the individual within a therapeutic setting.

The three cases below are hypothetical, based on actual case data outlined in Chapter 7 and the authors' experiences. The basic fact patterns are established in this chapter and discussion questions on each case are included to provide the reader opportunities to consider the contextual elements of each case. Moving forward, we will address the assessment of risk as well as offer treatment suggestions for each case across various therapeutic modalities.

Hank

Hank is a junior high school student in a small, rural school district. There are two hundred students in the high school and most students also attended one of two local elementary schools and the same middle school. The school district is set within a conversative political community where gun ownership rates are high, and hunting is a common pastime. Hank's father and older brother, David, are avid hunters and Hank joins them regularly. Hank's mother works as an administrator at their church and his father is a manager at a factory about an hour from their home. Hank has two younger sisters, one in elementary school and the other in middle school. David works part time at the local hardware store.

Hank and David never got along well. Hank is more introverted and socially shy, while David played football in high school, had lots of friends, and dated several popular cheerleaders. Hank has always felt less than David, as he is not athletic and has never dated despite asking a few girls out. Hank feels down and sad most of the time and is unsure things will ever get better. He doesn't feel invested in any of his academics, doesn't have many friends and is frustrated women aren't interested in him. He does talk to two childhood friends, Chris and Austin, about how his brother calls him gay because he has never had a girlfriend and about his frustrations with girls at their school. Hank says, "They keep dating these freaking Chads who treat them like shit. I swear, these bitches get what they deserve. Nice guys always finish last."

Austin's father has been involved in the Proud Boys movement, becoming more involved in recent months as news of a local factory being relocated to China has come out. Austin talks to Chris and Hank about immigrants taking hard-working Americans' jobs and disparages the Black Lives Matter movement, claiming it was funded by Jewish interests to destabilize the country. Austin shares, "All the immigrants and blacks think about is how bad it is for them and how everything is about slavery. It's the same with the Jews...freaking Anudda Shoah and everything is about the Holocaust. Like we don't have it hard."

Hank joins a few online chat groups to learn more about what the "real problem" is in the country. He posts on Twitter a quote from the Charleston shooter's manifesto, "I see all this stuff going on, and I don't see anyone doing anything about it." Austin pressures both Hank and Chris to "man up" and do something about the overtaking of our country. The three of them talk about girls at school and how they are attracted to either money, like the Jews, or the athletic, dumb blacks. Hank says to them, "I can see how all this works. Everything is set up against us. Something needs to change. They're taking over."

Hank continues to become more involved in online chat groups and gets into an argument with his brother about fake media and how girls at the high school chase the wrong guys. David snaps back at Hank and says, "Ha, I never had any problem with the girls – maybe it's because you are a beta-cuck, little fag-bitch. Probably need to stop sucking meat with your two wanking Nazi friends." Hank's father throws a dinner roll across the table that strikes David in the head. He then says, "I'm not gonna tolerate that kind of language at my dinner table. Particularly when you can't even get a full-time job, Mr. Football." The two continue to argue and Hank retreats to his room in tears. He turns on the computer and signs into a chat room to find solace.

Hank continues to isolate himself over the next few weeks and misses several days at school. The school guidance counselor calls Hank's mother out of concern for his missed classes, increased signs of depression, wearing a cap with an 88 on it and a shirt with RAHOWA, bullying from other students, and a conflict in the cafeteria with a female student he called a Jewish slur. They strongly recommend that Hank meets with a counselor.

Questions to Consider:

a Discuss the issues of intersectionality that occur in this case (previously outlined in Chapter 3).
b What are some of the challenges in addressing Hank's growing white supremacist beliefs given the influence from his friends?
c How does Hank's difficulty at school, in his family relationships, and with dating increase the risk of radicalization?
d If you were Hank's friend and concerned with the escalation you are seeing, what might you do or say to influence him in a different direction?
e If you were Hank's therapist, where would you start on the assessment of risk? What kind of goals would you have for his treatment?

Jesse

Jesse is a first semester freshman at a small liberal arts college. In his Introduction to Political Thought class, Jesse expresses very intellectualized thoughts regarding politics and nationalism. He argues that America was stronger prior to more lax immigration policies and that the U.S. should adopt a more nationalistic policy. He argues for states' rights to create separate but equal schooling for white and non-white citizens and supports the idea that citizens should need a passport or driver's license to vote. When speaking, he uses terms like "those people," "illegals," and "aliens."

In class, other students argue strongly against Jesse's points, and the arguments become increasingly heated. At one point, a classmate calls him a neo-Nazi, bigoted racist, and Proud Boy. Jesse argues back that he believes in none of those concepts, but rather "I argue for individuals to take pride in their own heritage and cultural experiences. Whites should not be made to feel guilty for things their ancestors did, nor be ashamed or taught critical race theory, which lacks scientific rigor."

Students around campus continue to escalate against Jesse, calling him a Nazi, racist, and ignorant. He argues back to them while remaining calm and offers some rather disturbing political statements. He challenges a social justice group that has a Black Lives Matter table with the idea that All Lives Matter, explains his support for Kyle Rittenhouse, and argues the Jews are no longer a marginalized group, but own the majority of the wealth in the United States.

During a talk on campus related to free speech, Jesse wears a Swastika on his clothes and an empty holster on his belt as part of an "empty holster protest." Other students confront him about the Swastika and he says, "It's actually a Hindu symbol of peace that was co-opted by the German Nazi Party." Another student punches him and is taken into custody by campus police. Jesse ends up in counseling the next day, frustrated and upset by the lack tolerance to different opinions on the campus. He tells his therapist on intake, "I came to this school because it claimed to be a place to engage in critical thinking and explore ideas. What I get instead is violence and hatred. I really don't understand this at all."

Questions to Consider:

a From your campus perspective, what are the limits of free speech vs. hate speech? How would the Swastika incident be handled on your campus? How would the empty holster protest be handled on your campus?
b What role do faculty have in finding a way to engage students in debate and discussion in class and what limits do they have to set on the boundaries of these conversations?
c Do you feel as if Jesse is escalating as a dangerous individual? Does his behavior seem to be trolling or something different?
d What are some of the challenges for mental health treatment providers who find Jesse's viewpoint offensive? Is there a place for referral or denying Jesse care based on these beliefs?

Dawson

Dawson is a community college student working on a technical degree in automotive welding. He often comes to class in a blue denim jacket with the letters 88 written on one sleeve along with a pit bull, a shield with the radiation symbol, and patches with the words "I have nothing to say" and the phrase "RAHOWA." Dawson is very outspoken in his membership in several white supremacist groups and brags to classmates about attending protests aimed at keeping our nation pure. He keeps his head shaved bald and has several visible tattoos that include the number 88 and a pit bull. He has few friends at school and works at a local bar while pursuing training to become certified in automotive welding and crash repair. He has been in an on again, off again relationship that often escalates into shouting, yelling, and threatening each other. On one occasion, Dawson choked his girlfriend because she needed to "know her place because men are superior and make the rules."

Dawson tells one classmate that he has several weapons at home including shotguns, an AR-15 platform, and enough ammunition to "give those ovens in WW II a run for their money." He frequently talks about the three percenters and the need for a racial holy war. Other students in the class laugh Dawson off as a good-natured, harmless guy who got wrapped up in some extreme Nazi stuff. People in class tend to ignore him when he goes on his white supremacist rants, but one day last week he was so angry about a local progressive rally he said "I swear if anyone pushes me on this today, we are gonna have a day of the rope f-*king tomorrow. I'll pull some James Byrd and Matthew Shepard shit."

Dawson is finally confronted by the instructor when another student told him, "Dawson is basically telling everyone he is going to start hanging black people and Jewish people. You really need to do something. It's beyond creepy. It's starting to scare me." The instructor talks to Dawson after class and asks him to stop the racist talk. Dawson does not take this well and says, "I can't do anything in this country. It's just like Spencer says, we can't limit immigration, because Hitler. We can't be proud of ourselves as Europeans, because Holocaust. White people can be Christian, but not too Christian, because Auschwitz...what we need is for the 3% to rise up and fix this mess we call a country."

The instructor isn't sure what to do and makes a report to the campus Behavioral Intervention and Threat Team. He shares his concerns that Dawson has been disrupting other students and escalating his rhetoric about race, immigration, and religion. The instructor says, "Look, he seems like a nice kid. But someone must do something. I can't teach like this."

Questions to Consider:

a What concerns do you see with a student like Dawson?
b Where does Dawson's right to free speech end? Does any of his behavior violate the student code of conduct at your school?
c If you were the instructor, would you feel comfortable intervening with Dawson and asking questions like these to better understand the context?
d How might a campus BIT address this behavior through its process?

Moving Forward

In the upcoming chapters, we will discuss the importance of using a structured system of risk assessment when determining the dangerousness of threats or escalating behaviors. This will involve identifying both the risk and protective factors in each scenario, applying a specific rubric regarding white supremacist indoctrination, and conducting a violence risk assessment. Once the level of risk is assessed initially, the next step in each of these cases will be to examine the best practice approaches to treatment and management of the potential risk.

9 Identifying the Risk Factors

Box 9.1 Key Take-aways

1 For those new to the work of violence risk assessments and risk factors, there is a review of Dr. Van Brunt's writing in this area.
2 **Affective violence** is often immediate, unplanned, and emotional. **Predatory or targeted violence** is premediated, mission-oriented, and the type of violence behind mass shootings and larger attacks. **Lethality** refers to the overall risk of death. **Transient threats** have little lethality risk while **substantive threats** have a much higher lethality risk.
3 **Fixation and focus** refer to the narrowing down on a target of a threat from a larger group to a more narrowly defined target. **Action and time imperative** refer to the date, time, and place an attack might occur.
4 13 risk factors for targeted violence are reviewed along with five environmental risk factors. Case examples from the previous chapter are included for context.

There is some utility in separating out those white supremacists who are escalating on the pathway to violence when compared to those who are not escalating to violence. This is a delicate issue; any white supremacist ideology is problematic and a cause for concern, but some are so deeply invested in the belief system that they feel justified and sometimes even called to act violently in support of their beliefs and fears.

When assessing the risk of violence, it is essential to examine not just the risk factors but the protective factors that serve to off-set the escalation toward violence. Stabilizing factors can be seen as the off-ramp for an individual accelerating on the pathway to violence. These protective or anchor factors will be reviewed in the following chapter. We mention these here because as you explore the risk factors, consider the question, for this risk factor, what supports or counteractions could be in place in

DOI: 10.4324/9781003199656-9

the person's life to work to tamp down, mitigate or remove this risk factor from the equation?

Dr. Brian Van Brunt, an author of this book, has written several other books and articles that are worth mentioning here. While this chapter is unique and related directly to the specific issue of white supremacy, it can be seen as an evolution of previous work. For those interested in this evolution, please refer to Table 9.1. Full references for each of these works are included at the end of the chapter.

Table 9.1 Review of Van Brunt's Work on Risk Factors

Book or Article	*Year*	*Summary*
Ending Campus Violence: New Approaches to Prevention	2012	Published by Taylor and Francis, this book explored targeted violence in the college campus setting. The Structured Interview for Violence Risk Assessment (SIVRA-35) was created during this time and remains one of the most common violence risk assessment processes used at colleges and universities.[1]
Harm to Others: The Assessment and Treatment of Dangerousness	2015	This book, published by the American Counseling Association. outlines an evidence-based approach to violence risk assessment and treatment for the K-12 and college/university populations. The SIVRA-35[1] is demonstrated here through two detailed case studies.
"Violence Risk Assessment of the Written Word (VRAW^2)"	2015	Published in NABITA's *Journal of Behavioral Intervention Teams (J-BIT)*, this article outlines an approach to assessing social media and written threat through the VRAW[1] assessment tool.
"Assessing Threat in Written Communications, Social Media, and Creative Writing"	2016	Published in the *Journal of Violence and Gender*, this article further outlines the process in assessing threat in online and written formats.
"An exploration of the risk, protective, and mobilization factors related to violent extremism in college populations."	2017	This article was the foundation for the Extremist Risk Intervention Scale (ERIS). This violence risk assessment process examines the interplay between risk and protective elements and mobilization factors.[1]
An Educator's Guide to Assessing Threats in Student Writing	2020	This book, published by Taylor and Francis, advances the research on written and social media threat and outlines a more streamlined system called Looking Glass.[1]
Understanding and Treating Incels	2020	Published by Taylor and Francis, this book looks at a specific subset of predatory violent attackers, those who follow the involuntary celibate ideology. This text created the basis for the Incel Indoctrination Rubric

When addressing the assessment of risk, it is useful to ask the question, risk for what? Are we looking at assessing the risk for suicide? For getting into an argument at a bar and punching a bouncer? For showing up at a protest with an AR-15 to help "keep the peace?" In this chapter, we are looking to address the risk of a certain type of violence known as ***predatory or targeted violence.*** This type of violence requires forethought, planning and is focused on completing a mission or objective. The violence involves the development of strategies, tactics, and logistics (Meloy, 2000; 2006; Meloy et al., 2011; O'Toole, 2014; Meloy et al., 2014; Van Brunt, 2015a). The attacker here is driven by a desire to inflict pain on someone or a group that has wronged them or caused, either directly or perceived, their unfortunate life events. They adopt a distant stance, take countermeasures to avoid being detected by others and often proceed with a military precision in their planning.

Affective violence, by contrast, is poorly planned and reactive to a situation that occurs. This violence is escalated by biological changes such as a rapid heartbeat, blood pooling in the center torso and the release of adrenaline. This violence can be seen when a person raises their voice, threatens others around them, pumping themselves up and down to escalate (Grossman, 1996; Grossman and Siddle, 2000; Howard, 1999; Hart et al., 2011; Hart and Logan, 2011; Meloy, 2000; 2006).

Escalation in the targeted violence we are focused on involves a narrowing down onto a specific targeted group or system the attacker is wishing to harm. This is the violence progression we see in school shootings and mass causality attacks. O'Toole describes this mission-oriented violence this way:

> Mission-oriented shootings are hardly impulsive crimes. They are well-planned and can involve days, weeks, months, even years of preparing and fantasizing about the crime. The planning is strategic, complex, detailed, and sufficiently secretive to minimize the risk of being detected and maximize the chances for success. The planning does not occur in a vacuum—during this phase, mission-oriented shooters make many decisions, including the types of weapons and ammunition they will use and where to obtain it, the clothes they will wear, the location of the assault, who the victims will be, what they will do at the location, and the date and time of the shooting"
>
> (p. 9)

Those who engage in this kind of mission-oriented violence often share their plans with others through "leakage" on social media or through verbal or written means (O'Toole, 2014). Most attackers share statements about their intent prior to their attacks (Horgan et al., 2016; Lankford, 2013; Meloy and O'Toole, 2011; Meloy et al., 2014; Pollack et al., 2008; Van Brunt, 2012; Vossekuil et al., 2002). Attackers often leave small clues, hints, or comments to telegraph their future actions. These provide opportunities to detect an attack plan prior to implementation. O'Neill et al. write, "Writings, drawings, and other forms of individual expression reflecting violent fantasy and causing a faculty member to be fearful or concerned about safety should be evaluated contextually for any potential threat" (2008, pp. 32–33).

Risk Factors

Risk factors identify the personality traits, behavioral indicators, social and peer interactions, environmental stressors, threats, acquisition of or access to lethal means, and other contextual clues that have been noted in those who move forward with a targeted attack plan. These factors are based on the research of dozens of researchers, professional organizations, and government agencies including Meloy (2000; 2006), Hart and Logan, (2011), Fein et al. (1995), O'Toole (2000; 2002), Turner and Gelles (2003), Lankford (2016; 2018), Calhoun and Weston (2009), Van Brunt (2012; 2015; 2016; 2020), de Becker (1997), the National Behavioral Intervention Team Association (NABITA) (Sokolow et al., 2019), the Association of Threat Assessment Professionals (2006), the Department of Justice and the Federal Bureau of Investigation (2017), the National Threat Assessment Center (NTAC) (2018; 2019), and the United States Postal Service (2007).

As mentioned earlier, when assessing overall risk, it is critical to balance these risk factors with the protective, stabilizing, and anchor factors. When conducting a violence risk assessment (VRA), one should avoid

Table 9.2 Summary of Targeted and Predatory Violence Risk Factors

Direct threat	*Indirect threat*	*Lack mental support*	*End of a relationship*
Access to weapons	Lack peer support	Explosive reactions	Inability to date
Hardened thoughts	Lack family support	Intimidates others	Hopelessness
Social isolation	Loss of job	Lacks empathy	Last act behavior
Victim of bullying	Decline in academics	Polarized thoughts	Legacy token
Substance abuse	Acquiring weapons	Glorified violence	Feeling persecuted
Authority Conflict	Suicide attempt	Lacking remorse	Leaking attack plan
Fixation on target	Focus on target	Action plan for attack	Time frame for attack
Fantasy rehearsal	Rejection	Financial loss	Catalyst event
Feeling trapped	Poor anger outlets	Fame seeking	Objectification

emphasizing any single risk factor, such as weapons access or mental illness, without regard to the context of other risk factors. While someone who is experiencing manic, bi-polar symptoms, is off their medication, and has access to firearms poses a considerable increase in the risk of violence, simply evaluating the presence of mental illness and firearms access is not a sufficient VRA process.

Our goal is to better establish the risk of those with white supremacist ideologies escalating to targeted or predatory violence. This can be done by employing a three-stage process:

a Determining the presence of risk factors (this chapter) and protective factors (Chapter 10);
b Assessing how deeply they have been indoctrinated into the white supremacist ideology (Chapter 11); and
c Estimating their movement toward action (Chapter 12).

Quality of Threat

Threats come in different shapes and sizes. All threats are not considered equal and simply making a threat does not mean the threatener will carry it out. As a threat is reported, there should be a careful determination if the threat is substantive leakage connected to an actionable attack or if it is more transient in nature, expressing frustration, feelings of powerlessness, or a desire to intimidate or troll others for a reaction. As this determination is being made, it should be noted that any direct threat should initially be considered serious and necessitates an appropriate response. Any threats must be balanced against the data to determine the likelihood of an attack (Scalora et al., 2010; Turner and Gelles, 2003). Scalora et al. (2010) write:

> Unlike disruptive and other forms of aggressive behavior, violent or directly communicated threat always requires immediate investigation and evaluation. While most communicated direct threats do not end in violence, this can only be determined after directly questioning and assessing the student in question.
>
> (p. 5)

Threats can be either substantive or transient (Cornell, 2010), hunting or howling (Calhoun and Weston, 2009). Transient threats, or howling, are typically made in reaction to an intense, emotional, and passionate conflict. They are often made to protect reputation or "save face" and rarely have lethality or a high likelihood of follow up or action. Cornell (2010) cites in his research these types of threats make up approximately 70% of threats made in primary and secondary schools. Hunting behavior, in contrast, often conceals a more substantive intent to harm others in a predatory, mission-oriented attack. Substantive threats are more lasting and intentional, reaching beyond the current incident. In comparison to transient threats, substantive threats are 36 times more likely to be carried out (Burnette et al., 2018). Table 9.3 outlines several different types of threat examples.

Threat ***lethality*** represents the extent to which a particular threat has a high likelihood of resulting in death. For example, the possession of a firearm and ammunition combined with a threat to shoot up a LGBTQ+ rally on campus has a high likelihood of lethality whereas a transient threat to "make them shut up" by a student without access to a firearm would likely have a lower lethality. Assessments of lethality might be easy to determine based on a threat or could require deeper exploration into social media, past behavior, and determination of weapons access.

Table 9.3 Examples of Various Types of Threats

Type of Threat	*Example*
Direct	"We need to kill all of the Jews or they will just keep taking everything we have from us."
Indirect/Vague	"Men are to lie with women, and not to lie with other men. There will be a reckoning coming soon for the Sodomites"
Direct with Action/ Time Imperative	"You thought January 6th was bad? Wait until you see what happens on the next January 6th. We will reclaim our country from the illegals, the Jews and the deviants. Tune in!"
Conditional Ultimatum	"If the Blacks don't stay out of our neighborhood at night, they are going to learn about what lynching really feels like, up close and personal."
Transient	"The Jews control everything. If you don't believe that, you are asleep. The only way we will Make American Great Again is to take it back from their greedy hands."
Substantive	"If those bitches don't shut their mouths in front of the student union at the Dyke Table of Awareness, I'm going to come by to show every single one of them how a real man handles a woman— with my f-cking fist."
Howling	"Wake up, White America. All lives matter and if you don't speak up, your voice will be covered in hot, black tar."
Hunting	"Today is the day that I take action. The next SJW who approaches me is getting a face full of something special I made in chemistry class."
Vague, but Direct	"Dean Roberts needs to be taken out. Her words need to be silenced and her voice drowned out."
Direct, but Vague	"Maybe anyone with a BLM sign outside should be given a real lesson on why all lives matter. They are outside until 3pm today with their little protest."

For those new to the VRA process, Turner and Gelles (2003) provide a particularly accessible book on the topic that outlines several key terms useful to understand related to threats. ***Action and time imperative*** refer to the time and location of an attack. If the threat contains a high degree of detail, this should be considered a heightened risk of the attack being carried out. If someone posts online, "The day of the rope will be this Friday at 9 p.m." this is a higher concern than, "One of these days, there will be a reckoning for the Jews and Blacks." The terms ***fixation and focus*** relate to a narrowing down on a specific target when assessing a particular threat. ***Fixations*** are hardened points of view, bordering on obsession, concerning a certain group being at fault and deserving of punishment. A ***focus*** builds off a fixation and further narrows onto a smaller group or a single person. For example, "I'm going to make those Asians pay for the COVID disease they brought to our country" would be a fixation on Asian-Americans and Pacific Islanders. The threat, "I'm going to fire-bomb the corner store and rid our neighborhood of those rice eaters for eating those bats and killing American Patriots" would include both a fixation and focus.

Risk Factors for Targeted, Predatory, Mission-Oriented Violence[2]

1. ***Actionability*** is the term used to describe if an individual has access to means and materials to carry out an attack. For example, someone might threaten to kill Black students at a school who are perceived as getting special treatment, but the threat is lowered in actionability if they have no weapon access, knowledge, or ability to acquire a weapon. If a threatener has access to guns or possesses firearm experience (e.g., they have taken a combat handgun course) or can obtain a weapon from a peer, this escalates the risk. Most school shooters gained access to firearms in the home or from the home of a relative, both secured and unsecured (National Threat Assessment Center, 2019). While firearms present a high level of concern, the VRA should determine if a potential attacker has access to any weapons, not just firearms.

Most of the cases we reviewed in Chapter 7 were completed attacks, where action was taken. One case where violence may have been prevented if the risk had been properly assessed was the shooting of the Pittsburgh police officers (case 34). In her 9–1-1 call, the shooter's mother told the operator that her son was armed, but this information was not relayed to the police officers heading to the scene.

CASES: 1–25, 27–32, 34, 36–41, 43–49, 51–55, 57, 58, 60–64, 66–94, 96–100

2.A ***hardened point of view*** is a locked and fixed way of seeing the world that is resistant to other counterpoints. The individual holds a strong investment tied to these beliefs and they are often unwilling or unable to shift from these ideas (O'Toole, 2002; Sokolow et al., 2014; Van Brunt, 2012; 2015a). Sokolow et al. (2014), write, "The individual begins to selectively attend to his or her environment, filtering out material or information that doesn't line up with his or her beliefs. Stances begin to harden and crystalize" (p. 7). They hold a strong passion about their beliefs and filter out any other information that does not support these ideas. Most commonly, these beliefs center on religion, politics, academic expectations, social justice, or relationships (National Threat Assessment Center, 2019; Van Brunt, 2016; Van Brunt et al., 2017). What differentiates these strong beliefs from simple opinions is the passion and emotion behind these ideologies, a rejection of any other viewpoints, and the reinforcement of these beliefs through other personal experiences and networks (Sageman, 2007).

We saw this hardened point of view in most of the cases we reviewed, given that the motivation for almost all the attacks was white supremacy or other prejudices. In Joliet, IL, a man was so steeped in white supremacist beliefs that he set the home of Black family on fire with nine people inside, eight of whom were children (case 32). In the fall of 2018, sixteen Democratic politicians and other critics of President Trump were sent pipe bombs in the mail from a man who felt justified by his pro-Trump, anti-liberal beliefs.

CASES: 2–5, 7–41, 43–45, 47–55, 57, 58, 60–83, 85–90, 93, 94, 96–98

3. ***Drivenness and a justification for violent action*** describe an attacker who is dedicated to committing violence in the name of a particular cause (Association of Threat Assessment Professionals, 2006; Deisinger et al., 2014; Meloy et al., 2011; Turner and Gelles, 2003; United States Postal Service, 2007). Prior to the implementation of violence, they attribute their actions to the advancement and greater good of their cause (Moghaddam, 2005). As they escalate on the pathway to violence, they morally disengage from any external ethical or moral standards, objectify their target, and focus on mission completion. (O'Toole, 2002; O'Toole and Bowman, 2011; Van Brunt, 2012; 2015a). There is often an intense sense of rage and blame placed toward the target and completion of the mission provides a secondary achievement to obtain revenge (Pressman, 2009). The attacker sees violence as a natural consequence directed at the source (Horgan, 2008; Pressman, 2009).

This is another factor in most of the cases reviewed, where white supremacy provided the justification for violence. The men who murdered a gay couple in Redding, CA (case 19) felt justified by their religious beliefs and their interpretation of the Bible's condemnation of homosexuality. A man in Hardy, AR, was able to use his white supremacy to justify firebombing an interracial couple's home (case 40). Ahmaud Arbery's killers felt so justified they released the video of the event, which eventually led to their conviction (case 91).

CASES: 4, 5, 8, 10, 12–14, 17–19, 21, 23–27, 29–33, 35–39, 41, 44, 45, 49, 50, 52, 54–56, 59, 61, 64–68, 70, 75, 77–81, 85, 87, 89, 90, 93, 94, 96

4. ***Grievance or dangerous injustice collection*** is a trait many of us have experienced. The difference here is the grievance and injustice collecting takes on a dangerous characteristic where the grievance or injustice becomes a justification for violence. In their 2017 study, Gill et al. (2017) found just over half (56%) held a grievance against a particular person or entity. These grievances are most often held against those in positions of power. The attacker holds them responsible for real or imagined unfairness and difficulties. O'Toole described the injustice collector as "a person who feels 'wronged,' 'persecuted' and 'destroyed,' blowing injustices way out of proportion, never forgiving the person they felt has wronged them" (O'Toole & Bowman, 2011, p. 186). An individual can have a grievance about almost anything, though they are most commonly held against high stakes issues related to retaining a job, academic success, or a relationship.

While white supremacist thought is riddled with supposed grievances and injustices made against white people, the cases listed here include more specific grievances held by the suspects. For instance, in 1955, Emmett Till was killed by a white woman's family after he spoke with her in a grocery store (case 3). In their minds, this supposed offense was enough to justify his murder. More recently, the rioters at the US Capitol were convinced that the 2020 election was being stolen and held the vice president and democratic politicians responsible.

CASES: 3, 6, 13, 23, 36, 41, 44, 52, 54, 57, 61, 69–71, 75, 78, 85, 86, 90, 94

5. Most attackers are ***suicidal*** (Association of Threat Assessment Professionals, 2006; Dunkle et al., 2008; Lankford, 2010; 2013; 2018; Meloy et al., 2014; National Threat Assessment Center, 2019; O'Toole, 2002; Randazzo and Plummer, 2009; Turner and Gelles, 2003; United States Postal Service, 2007; Vossekuil et al., 2002). The NTAC (2019) found half of the attackers had shared or demonstrated behavior related to suicide or self-harm. Lankford (2018) conducted a meta-analysis of targeted violence from 1974 until 2008 and found 70–90% of the attackers experienced suicidal thoughts or behaviors prior to their attack. They would express indifference toward life, hopelessness, and a lack of confidence about the future. They were disempowered, misunderstood, and lost. This does not excuse their violence or seek to explain away their hatred, but rather provides insight into what motivates them to attack.

Several of the attackers we reviewed committed suicide during the attack or had discussed suicidal thoughts in the past. When police entered the movie theater in Lafayette, they found the shooter's body along with his victims (case 55). The shooter at the Dallas Courthouse (case 82) had a history of suicidal ideation and his family is convinced the attack was designed as a suicide by police.

CASES: 6, 20, 22, 28, 31, 32, 37, 47, 48, 52, 55, 57, 63, 69, 72, 82, 83, 90

6. ***Mental illness*** can be an aggravating factor when conducted at VRA, particularly when related to thought disorders, depression, and bi-polar disorder (Van Brunt and Pescara-Kovach, 2019). Most of those who carry out attacks experience psychological, behavioral, or developmental symptoms (National Threat Assessment Center, 2019). With more than half of attackers receiving one or more mental health treatments prior to their attack, mental illness awareness remains a factor of concern. However, it is not a substitute for a collaborative, multidisciplinary threat assessment (National Threat Assessment Center, 2019). In their study of 115 attackers from 1990 until 2014, Gill et al. (2017) found that 44% of the sample had a history of substance abuse and 41% had a diagnosed mental health disorder.

This factor was present in several of the cases reviewed, and may have been present in more, given that it is not always diagnosed. In one notable case, nine months before attacking a Jewish Community Center (case 21), the attacker showed up drunk and suicidal at a psychiatric hospital. He threatened workers with a switchblade and was taken to jail. Over the course of those nine months, his mental health was evaluated several times.

CASES: 6, 17, 21, 22, 24, 26, 29, 32, 39, 44, 45, 53, 55, 57, 63, 65, 69, 75, 76, 80, 85, 88, 90

The ***use of substances,*** particularly stimulants, impacts decision making, increases isolation, fosters disengagement, and reduces impulse control. Alcohol lowers inhibition and provides a catalyst to turn thoughts into violence. A history of drug or substance use, particularly methamphetamines or amphetamines, cocaine, or alcohol, has been connected to both affective and targeted violence. (Association of Threat Assessment Professionals, 2006; O'Toole and Bowman, 2011; Turner and Gelles, 2003; United States Postal Service, 2007). In Chapter 12, the concept of disinhibitors will be introduced and substance use is often cited as a disinhibitor for violence.

We know substances were directly involved in several of the attacks reviewed. The shooter at Luigi's restaurant (case 10) had been drinking all day prior to the attack and may have blacked out during the attack. James Anderson's killers had also been drinking prior to the attack and were on a beer run when they decided to attack (case 43).

CASES: 10, 16, 17, 21, 30, 31, 38, 39, 43, 45, 54, 55, 62, 69, 75, 80, 88, 90

7. Many who engage in targeted violence experience an inability to understand different perspectives. This ***lack of empathy and remorse for actions*** is an aggravating factor in a violence risk threat assessment. In a 2019 study, the NTAC found most attackers were victims of bullying. Victims of bullying do not have anyone focusing on their safety, pain, and feelings, which increases the risk of them disregarding the feelings, pain, and safety of others. They often seek to intimidate, act superior to others and/or have an intolerance to individual differences (Association

of Threat Assessment Professionals, 2006; O'Toole, 2002; Turner and Gelles, 2003; Van Brunt, 2012).

This factor was present in many of the cases, and one of the defining traits of white supremacy is lacking empathy for those who don't fit the cis, white, and straight ideal. While the white supremacist who attacked his girlfriend pled guilty (case 71), in a video uploaded to social media, he denied his guilt and said he signed the plea agreement "because of a statement a woman made against me. And this is why I hate women."

CASES: 1, 2, 3, 4, 5, 7, 8, 9, 10, 11, 13, 15, 17, 18, 19, 20, 21, 22, 24, 25, 26, 28, 31, 32, 34, 35, 36, 37, 38, 39, 40, 41, 42, 43, 44, 46, 49, 51, 52, 54, 56, 57, 64, 67, 68, 70, 71, 73, 74, 75, 76, 77, 78, 79, 80, 81, 86, 88, 89, 90, 91, 93, 94, 96, 99

8. When potential attackers experience frustrations, pain or feel overwhelmed, they engage in ***fantasy rehearsals*** to reduce their anxiety. These fantasies involve them confronting, punishing and/or destroying the target of their perceived injustices. These fantasies might emerge through writing, drawing, or creating content on social media. The subject perseverates on the wrongs they perceived having been done to them and enact elaborate revenge or punishment plots. O'Neill et al. (2008) stress the importance of exploring these communications: "Writings, drawings, and other forms of individual expression reflecting violent fantasy and causing a faculty member to be fearful or concerned about safety, should be evaluated contextually for any potential threat" (pp. 32–33). O'Toole (2014) writes, "Mission-oriented shootings are hardly impulsive crimes. They are well-planned and can involve days, weeks, months, even years of making preparations and fantasizing about the crime" (p. 9).

Many of the cases reviewed had clear evidence of fantasy rehearsal. The shooter in Norway (case 44) planned his attack for almost a decade, acquiring supplies, practicing for the attack using video games, and writing a lengthy manifesto. Several other attackers wrote manifestos, including the Umpqua Community College shooter (case 57) and the Charleston church attacker (case 54).

CASES: 10, 13, 14, 17, 19, 22, 25, 26, 33, 41, 44, 50, 51, 54, 56, 71, 74, 81, 85–89

9. ***Feelings of isolation and hopelessness*** are common among those who plan targeted violence. Many attackers have experienced discrimination based on a marginalized status and expressed despair and hopelessness about a better tomorrow (Sinai, 2005; 2012). They might also experience a lack of social or advancement opportunities at home, school, or work (Schmid, 2013). Most experience chronic isolation and/or an inability to create or maintain sexual or intimate relationships with others (O'Toole, 2002; Van Brunt et al., 2017). The NTAC (2019) found nearly two-thirds of the attackers they studied either spoke about their sadness, depression, or loneliness, or these appeared through their behaviors. It is common for many attackers to share these thoughts and feelings with others or

write about them online or in school assignments. As with suicidal behavior, the identification of isolation and hopelessness as a risk factor is not to provide an excuse for the violence, but rather to point out an important area for intervention.

We did not see this as often in these cases as we do in mass shooting violence, especially in school shootings. This is largely because so many of the attackers we reviewed found support and connection in white supremacist groups, both in person and online. However, we did see this isolation in such cases like the Fort Hood shooter (case 37) who felt separate from his colleagues in the military as he sought revenge for the killing of Muslims around the world and the shooter in Hanau, Germany (case 63) who identified as an incel and had lost hope of ever having a successful romantic relationship.

CASES: 37, 38, 57, 63, 75, 82, 90, 93, 96

Box 9.2 Why Should I Care How They Feel?

We often received this question when exploring the risk factors related to marginalization and feelings of isolation or hopelessness. These risk factors are highlighted to draw attention to the known factors that move someone down the path toward violence, rather than as any apology or explanation for their hateful perspective. If this book is to reach its stated goal, identifying the foundational thinking of the white supremacist and moving them away from these beliefs and any potential violence, then the key to unlocking this door to is shift their behavior. We wanted to share with the reader that a difficult part of this work is putting aside the desire to hate those who hate, instead of trying to understand what drives their hatred and carefully and methodically move them off this path away from violence.

10. ***Marginalization*** is also experienced by those who express white supremacist ideologies. In fact, prior to recent political shifts in the United States, Nazis and white supremacists were a common target for most Americans. Even today, someone expressing sympathy or supporting the white supremacist ideology are not viewed kindly by most of the population. These resulting feelings of marginalization by those affiliated with this viewpoint might be based on social factors, ethnic or racial differences, cultural dissimilarities, or diverse gender expression (Langman, 2009; Lankford, 2013; Sue, 2010). This results in a perceived threat to those they identify with, causing a sense of moral outrage (Bhui et al., 2012; Sageman, 2007). While unlikely to be admitted in a public setting, there certainly are intense feelings of frustration, despair and anger experienced by the white supremacist as they experience judgement, unfair treatment, discrimination, and violence.

While many white supremacists feel marginalized in their whiteness (this corresponds to the idea of the Great Replacement, where immigrants and minorities are taking the place of white culture), it's hard to know how many of the attackers studied held to that belief. We did clearly see feelings of marginalization in some cases. The man who was arrested as part of a plot to blow up a series of African American and American Jewish institutions (case 26) was interesting in that his father was African American, but after his parents split, he felt separate and marginalized when staying with his father and embraced his white side and denied his Black side, becoming a white supremacist.

CASES: 26, 37, 57, 63, 68, 87, 88, 94

11. ***Fascination with violence*** (Mohandie, 2014; National Threat Assessment Center, 2019; O'Toole, 2002) is a risk factor that at least half of those experience while planning their attacks. When engaged in a VRA, there should be a careful exploration of the subject's investment, obsession, or fixation on violence. This could include studying past attacks, watching media that shows firing squads, torture, or sensationalized violence against particular groups, drawing pictures or writing essays with similar themes.

When these are discovered in written narratives, they should be explored through a structured process (Meloy et al., 2011; National Threat Assessment Center, 2019; Van Brunt, 2012; 2015a). A specific example of this would be the system developed by Van Brunt in his book an *Educator's Guide to Assessing Threats in Student Writing* (Van Brunt, Lewis, and Solomon, 2020).

This was present in many of the cases, as many of the attackers were members of violent groups, such as the Ku Klux Klan, and/or wrote online about their violent belief system. The London nail bomber (case 17) had a collage of bomb blasts in his home. The man convicted on weapons charges in Whitehall, NY (case56) had written online advocating violence against racial and religious minorities and told an undercover officer, "I love violence." The El Paso shooter (case 85) wrote extensively about finding inspiration in the New Zealand attacks (case 78).

CASES: 8, 11, 17, 26, 44, 47, 48, 52, 53, 55–57, 63, 65, 66–68, 71, 72, 78–82, 85, 86, 89

12. The ***desire for fame*** is present as a motivating factor for this kind of targeted violence. Lankford (2016) describes 24 offenders who directly shared their desired attention and fame and/or directly contacted media organizations to obtain this attention. Those who feel marginalized, bullied, teased, or isolated expressed a desire for attention and seek retribution for this perceived injustice (Bhui et al., 2012; Sageman, 2007). There is a connection here to those suicidal attackers who plan terrorist actions and "produce martyrdom videos, murals, calendars, key chains, posters, postcards, and pennants with the names and photos of past suicide terrorists, they show potential participants that committing a suicide attack is a path to fame and glory" (Lankford, 2018, p. 6).

Most of the attackers we reviewed were interested in furthering their cause but didn't express much interest in fame for themselves. We did see this desire for fame in some cases though, as when James Byrd's killer (case 15) boasted that he had made history and when the Christchurch attacker livestreamed his attack on Facebook (case 78).

CASES: 13, 15, 17, 20, 31, 34, 36, 37, 52, 78, 81, 91

13. As part of the escalation on the pathway, attackers often engage in ***objectification and depersonalization*** toward their target (Van Brunt, 2012; 2015a). Grossman (1996) writes about this related to military training in his book *On Killing*. He described how many soldiers are loathe to kill, but this aversion is overridden by training soldiers to depersonalize enemy combatants. An example occurs in writing and social media posts, where the potential attacker shares a dehumanized view of their target. They might use hostile language, insulting, images or diminishing/misogynistic objectification focused on separating themselves from their target (Van Brunt, 2016; 2020).

This factor was present in many of the cases reviewed, as white supremacism by its nature depersonalizes those outside the ideals they hold. The government's forced sterilization of women and people of color (case 1) is one clear example. The shooter at the Kroger in Jeffersontown, KY (case 76) targeted African Americans and clearly thought them less than white, telling a white man he encountered during his attack, "Whites don't shoot whites."

CASES: 1–5, 8, 9, 12, 14, 15, 17–22, 25, 30, 31, 35, 36, 40–42, 48–52, 54, 57, 63, 64, 67, 70–74, 76–78, 81, 85–87, 89, 90, 93, 99

Environmental Factors

1. ***Catalyst events*** occur when there is a significant loss that occurs in a person's life that causes an escalation in attacker planning. This could be anything the person holds dear in their life such as failing a particularly important class, losing a romantic relationship, being fired from a job, being involved in domestic abuse, drug use, or criminal charges, or the death of a close friend or family member. Similar to the catalyst in a chemical reaction, these events create an intensification in the action and time imperative related to an attack. They might also increase feelings of hopelessness, despair and increase pressures to plan and take action. This is different than just having a bad day or reaction to a difficult time (National Threat Assessment Center, 2019), but rather leave the person escalated toward action or without the stabilizing and protective factors needed to keep them from putting an attack plan in motion.

Some of the catalyst events we saw were personal, as with the murder of Harvey Milk (case 6), whose killer had recently lost his job, or the Umpqua Community College shooter (case 57), who had recently been placed on academic suspension. Some catalyst events were more external, like the attack in Hebron spurring on the Brooklyn Bridge shooter (case 11).

CASES: 2, 3, 5–7, 10, 11, 16, 20, 24, 25, 34, 36, 47, 57, 58, 64, 68–70, 91, 92, 94

2. The ***experience of teasing and bullying*** are additional escalating factors for the attacker. (Van Brunt, 2012; 2015). Many students struggling with bullying and it remains a key factor in NTAC's 2019 research on targeted violence in schools. They define bullying as "unwanted, aggressive behavior among school-aged children with an intent to do physical, social, or emotional harm; which involves a real or perceived power imbalance; and is, or could be, repeated" (National Threat Assessment Center, 2019, p. 33). Bullying and teasing might be physical, social, property, or cyber. About one-third of attackers in their study engaged in bullying, often as part of a persistent pattern of behavior which lasted for weeks, months, or years.

Bullying was not explored in many of the resources available on these cases, as it often is when looking at younger perpetrators of school violence, so we don't know the true extent to which it was a factor, but we did see it in some cases. The shooter in Munich, Germany (case 63) was bullied by his peers in school, and this is thought to have been a driving force in his attack. Similarly, the El Paso shooter (case 85) was teased in school and isolated from his peers.

CASES: 17, 26, 37, 63, 85

3. ***Free fall*** describes a wide range of problems an attacker might experience in their community, school, work, primary support group, and/or social circle. These problems could include, illness, financial pressures, death of a close friend, unemployment, chronic depression or worry, isolation, difficulty adjusting to a new life circumstance (e.g., new school), failing an academic program or internship, being terminated from work, or blocked upward mobility based on their personal characteristics such as race, ethnicity, religious beliefs, or appearance (Bhui et al., 2012; Schmid, 2013; Travis, 2008). For those in a free fall, there is little hope for improvement and this often leads to further isolation, suicidality and feelings of despair. As problems spiral (conflicts in the home, academic, legal or disciplinary actions, or other personal issues), there is little preventing them from looking for an escape.

In his manifesto, the shooter at the Unitarian Universalist church in Knoxville (case 31) wrote not only about his political views, but about his inability to find a job and that his food stamps were being cut. He had issues with drugs and alcohol and had been divorced five times. He was suicidal and had intended to keep shooting until he was killed by police.

CASES: 6, 31, 34, 38, 39, 45, 57, 75, 93, 96

4. When there is a rapid or intense ***decrease in academic or work progress***, this can be a catalyst event and lead to further escalation. In many attack cases, the loss of academic or workplace connection becomes the final straw that overwhelms the individual and moves them closer to an attack. Failure to progress in work and school can directly contribute to other areas of life beginning to become unstable. Gill et al. (2017) write:

> 63% experienced long-term stress. Examples of this include academic frustration stemming from learning disorders; difficulty maintaining employment and failure in business ventures; disabling injuries from automobile and work accidents; long-term financial debts; a range of mental health issues including depression, bipolar disorder, and post-traumatic stress disorder; being a victim of sexual/physical abuse in childhood; an inability to establish appropriate social relationships; and long-lasting discord in marriages and romantic relationships (p. 711).

We saw this in several cases, including the attack on US Representative Gabby Giffords (case 39). The shooter had lost both his job and his standing at school.

CASES: 6, 31, 39, 57, 96

5. The ***social isolation*** that occurs when the person has vastly different beliefs from the majority and/or when they see increases in teasing and bullying, is another cause for escalation (O'Toole, 2002; Sokolow et al., 2019; Van Brunt, 2012; 2015a; 2015b). In their study, Gill et al. (2017) found that 75% of attackers spoke about their sadness, depression, or loneliness, or appeared through their observable behaviors to be experiencing these feelings. This isolation makes the potential attacker feel alone in their thinking and that violence as the only way to be seen. This isolation is often observed by those around the attacker as they isolate themselves, withdrawing from others, appearing sad, or crying.

Several of the attackers we reviewed isolated themselves from friends and family prior to their attacks, including the Tree of Life shooter (case 77), who had cut ties in the years leading up to the attack. The El Paso shooter (case 85) was described as a loner and standoffish.

CASES: 17, 22, 29, 37, 39, 48, 57, 63, 77, 78, 83, 85, 90

A word of caution. Simply experiencing difficulties in life does not turn one into a mass shooter. Rather, of those who have moved forward with an attack, these are the experiences that have bene studied and noted upon examination. Conducting a VRA requires the assessor to gather information about their current stressors and a contextual exploration to determine if there are additional stressors that are still impacting them. Next, these stressors are balanced with an assessment of their protective and stabilizing influences in their life. Stress is manageable when the individual has the supports and scaffolding needed while returning to balance (National Threat Assessment Center, 2018).

Moving Forward

This chapter has offered a detailed exploration of common risk factors and threat assessment terms. The next chapter outlines the protective and stabilizing factors that must be considered alongside the risk factors to create a balanced calculation of the overall risk. Chapter 11 then brings a more detailed lens of how ideology of white supremacy contributes to the overall assessment of risk. For those unfamiliar with a VRA, Chapter 12 outlines several contemporary, research-based approaches to estimate the risk of predatory violence in each presented scenario.

Discussion Questions

- What do you think would be the most critical risk factors for targeted or predatory violence that are mentioned in this chapter?
- How would you manage the balance between understanding risk factors alongside the reality that most of us (who are not planning a violent attack) have experienced each of these risk factors at one time or another?
- This predatory violence appears to be a problem amongst males much more than females. What are some reasons that would explain this difference between genders?
- If you had to list three additional factors that you believe would cause someone to move closer to an escalation of violence, what would these factors be?

Notes

1 For more information or training on the SIVRA-35, VRAW2, ERIS or Looking Glass please contact www.nabita.org
2 The cases referenced are detailed in Chapter 7. Our research was conducted using public records, so cases might not be included in every category that might apply if the information was not available.

References

Association of Threat Assessment Professionals. (2006). *Risk Assessment Guideline Elements for Violence (RAGE-V): Considerations for Assessing the Risk of Future Violent Behavior*. Sacramento, CA.

Bhui, K., Hicks M., Lashley, M., and Jones, E. (2012). A public health approach to understanding and preventing violent radicalization. *BMC Med., 10*(16).

Burnette, Datta, and Cornell, D. (2018). The Distinction Between Transient and Substantive Threats. *National Institutes of Justice Report.*

Calhoun, F. and Weston, S. (2009). *Threat Assessment and Management Strategies: Identifying the Howlers and Hunters*. Boca Raton, FL: CRC Press.

Cornell, D. (2010). Threat Assessment in the College Setting. *Change Magazine* (January/February), pp. 9–15. www.changemag.org,

de Becker, G. (1997). *The gift of fear and other survival signals that protect us from violence*. New York, NY: Dell.

Deisinger E., Randazzo M., and Nolan J. (2014). Threat assessment and management in higher education: Enhancing the standard of care in the academy. In

The International Handbook of Threat Assessment, J.R. Meloy and J. Hoffmann, eds. New York, NY: Oxford University Press, pp. 107–125.

Dunkle, J.H., Silverstein, Z.B., and Warner S.L. (2008). Managing Violent and Other Troubling Students: The Role of Threat Assessment Teams on Campus. *Journal of College and University Law, 34*(3): 585–636.

Fein, R., Vossekuil, B., and Holden, G. (1995). *Threat assessment: An approach to targeted violence: National Institute of Justice in Action*. Washington, DC: National Institute of Justice.

Gill, P., Silver, J., Horgan, J., and Corner, E. (2017). Shooting Alone: The Pre-Attack Experiences and Behaviors of U.S. Solo Mass Murderers. *J Forensic Sci*, 62(3), pp. 710–714.

Grossman, D. (1996). *On killing: The psychological cost of learning to kill in war and society*. Lebanon, IN: Little, Brown and Company Back Bay Books.

Grossman, D. and Siddle, B. (2000). Psychological effects of combat, in *Encyclopedia of Violence, Peace and Conflict*. UK: Academic Press.

Hart, S. and Logan, C. (2011). Formulation of violence risk using evidence-based assessment: The structured professional judgment approach. In *Forensic Case Formulation*, P. Sturmey, M. McMurran, eds. Chichester: Wiley-Blackwell, pp. 83–106.

Hart, S., Sturmey, P., Logan, C., and McMuran, M. (2011). Forensic case formulation. *International Journal of Forensic Mental Health*, 10, 118–126.

Horgan, J. (2008). From profiles to pathways and roots to routes: Perspectives from psychology on radicalization into terrorism. *Ann Am Acad Poli Soc Sci.*, 618, 80–94.

Horgan, J., Shorland, N., Abbasciano, S., and Walsh, S. (2016). Actions speak louder than words: A behavioral analysis of 183 individuals convicted for terrorist offenses in the United States from 1995 to 2012. *J Forensic Sci*, 61, 1228–1237.

Howard, P. (1999). *The Owner's Manual for the Brain: Everyday applications from Mind-Brain Research* (2nd Ed.). Austin, TX: Bard Press.

Langman, P. (2009). Rampage School Shooters: A typology. *Aggression Violent Behav.*, 14, 79–86.

Lankford, A. (2010). *Human Killing Machines: Systematic Indoctrination in Iran, Nazi Germany, Al Qaeda, and Abu Ghraib*. Boston, MA: Lexington Press.

Lankford, A. (2013). *The myth of martyrdom: What really drives suicide bombers, rampage shooters, and other self-destructive killers*. New York, NY: Palgrave Macmillan.

Lankford, A. (2016). Fame-seeking rampage shooters: Initial findings and empirical predictions. *Aggression and Violent Behavior*, 27, 122–129.

Lankford, A. (2018). Identifying Potential Mass Shooters and Suicide Terrorists with Warning Signs of Suicide, Perceived Victimization, and Desires for Attention or Fame. *J Pers Assess.*, 5, 1–12.

Meloy J. (2000). *Violence Risk and Threat Assessment: A Practical Guide for Mental Health and Criminal Justice Professionals*. San Diego, CA: Specialized Training Services.

Meloy, J.R. (2006). The empirical basis and forensic application of affective and predatory violence. *Australian and New Zealand Journal of Psychiatry*, 40, 539–547.

Meloy, J., Hoffmann, J., Guldimann, A., and James, D. (2011). The role of warning behaviors in threat assessment: An exploration and suggested typology. *Behav Sci Law*, 30, 256–279.

Meloy, J.R., Hoffmann J., Roshdi K, et al. (2014). Warning behaviors and their configurations across various domains of targeted violence. In *The International*

Handbook of Threat Assessment. J.R. Meloy and J. Hoffmann, eds. New York, NY: Oxford University Press, pp. 39–53.

Meloy, J.R. and O'Toole, M. (2011). The concept of leakage in threat assessment. *Behavioral Sciences and the Law*. Advance online publication.

Moghaddam, F. (2005). The staircase to terrorism: A psychological exploration. *Am Psychol.*, 60, 161–169.

Mohandie, K. (2014). Threat assessment in schools. In J.R. Meloy and J. Hoffman (eds), *The International Handbook of Threat Assessment* (pp. 126–147). New York, NY: Oxford University Press.

National Institute of Mental Health. (2017). Suicide prevention. Retrieved from www.nimh.nih.gov/health/topics/suicide-prevention/index.shtml.

National Threat Assessment Center. (2018). Enhancing school safety using a threat assessment model: An operational guide for preventing targeted school violence. US Secret Service, Department of Homeland Security.

National Threat Assessment Center. (2019). Protecting America's Schools: A United States Secret Service Analysis of Targeted School Violence. United States Secret Service, Department of Homeland Security.

O'Neill, D., Fox, J., Depue, R., and Englander, E. (2008). *Campus Violence Prevention and Response: Best practices for Massachusetts higher education*. Applied Risk Management, LLC.

O'Toole, M.E. (2000). *The school shooter: A threat assessment perspective*. Quantico, VA: National Center for the Analysis of Violent Crime, Federal Bureau of Investigation.

O'Toole, M.E. (2002). *The School Shooter: A Threat Assessment Perspective*. Quantico, VA: FBI.

O'Toole, M.E. (2014). The Mission-Oriented Shooter: A New Type of Mass Killer. *Journal of Violence and Gender*, 1(1), 9–10.

O'Toole, M.E. and Bowman, A. (2011). *Dangerous Instincts: How Gut Feelings Betray*. , New York, NY: Hudson Street Press.

Pollack, W., Modzeleski, W., and Rooney, G. (2008). Prior knowledge of potential school-based violence: Information students learn may prevent a targeted attack. Washington, DC: United States Secret Service and United States Department of Education.

Pressman, D. (2009). *Risk Assessment Decisions for Violent Political Extremism*. (Her Majesty the Queen in Right of Canada, Ottawa.)

Randazzo, M. and Plummer, E. (2009). *Implementing Behavioral Threat Assessment on Campus: A Virginia Tech Demonstration Project*. Blacksburg, VA: Virginia Polytechnic Institute and State University.

Sageman, M. (2007). Radicalization of global Islamist terrorists. United States Senate Committee on Homeland Security and Governmental Affairs. Retrieved on December 7, 2019 from www.hsgac.senate.gov/download/062707sageman.

Scalora, M., Simons, A., and Vansly, S. (2010, February). Campus Safety: Assessing and Managing Threats. *FBI Law Enforcement Bulletin*. Washington, DC: Federal Bureau of Investigation.

Schmid, A.P. (2013). Radicalisation, de-radicalisation, counter-radicalisation: A conceptual discussion and literature review. The International Centre for Counter-Terrorism-The Hague, 4(2). Retrieved on March 26, 2020 from https://icct.nl/publication/radicalisation-de-radicalisation-counterradicalisation-a-conceptual-discussion-and-literature-review.

Sinai, J. (2005). A conceptual framework for resolving terrorism's root causes. In *The Root Causes of Terrorism: Myths, Reality and Ways Forward*, T. Bjorgo, ed. London: Routledge.

Sinai J. (2012). Radicalisation into extremism and terrorism. *Intelligencer J U.S. Intell Stud.*, 19, Summer/Fall.

Sokolow, B.A., Lewis, W.S., Van Brunt, B., Schuster, S., and Swinton, D. (2014). *The Book on BIT* (2 ed.), Berwyn, P.A.The National Behavioral Intervention Team Association.

Sokolow, B., Van Brunt, B., Lewis, W., Schiemann, M., Murphy, A., and Molnar, J. (2019). *The NaBITA Risk Rubric*. King of Prussia, P.A. The National Behavioral Intervention Team Association.

Sue, D. (2010). *Microaggressions in everyday life: Race, gender, and sexual orientation*. Hoboken, NJ: John Wiley & Sons.

Travis, A. (2008). MI5 report challenges views on terrorism in Britain. *The Guardian*, August 20.

Turner, J. and Gelles, M. (2003). *Threat Assessment: A Risk Management Approach*. New York, NY: Routledge.

United States Postal Service. (2007). Threat Assessment Team Guide, Retrieved on November 30, 2019 from www.nalc.org/workplace-issues/resources/manuals/pub108.pdf.

Van Brunt, B. (2012). *Ending Campus Violence: New Approaches to Prevention*. New York, NY: Routledge.

Van Brunt, B. (2015a). *Harm to Others: The Assessment and Treatment of Dangerousness*. Alexander, VA: American Counseling Association.

Van Brunt, B. (2015b). Violence Risk Assessment of the Written Word (VRAW2). *Journal of Behavioral Intervention Teams (JBIT)*, 3, pp. 12–25.

Van Brunt, B. (2016). Assessing Threat in Written Communications, Social Media, and Creative Writing. *The Journal of Violence and Gender*, 3(2), pp. 78–88.

Van Brunt, B., Lewis, W., and Solomon, J. (2020). *Educator's Guide to Assessing Threats in Student Writing*. New York, NY: Routledge.

Van Brunt, B., Murphy, A., and Zedginidze, A. (2017). An Exploration of the Risk, Protective, and Mobilization Factors Related to Violent Extremism in College Populations. *The Journal of Violence and Gender*, 4(3), pp. 81–101.

Van Brunt, B. and Pescara-Kovach, P. (2019). Debunking the Myths: Mental Illness and Mass Shootings. *Journal of Violence and Gender*, 6(1), pp. 53–63.

Van Brunt, B. and Taylor, C. (2021). *Understanding and treating incels: Case studies, guidance, and treatment of violence risk in the involuntary celibate community*. London: Routledge.

Vossekuil, B., Fein, R., Reddy, M., Borum, R., and Modzeleski, W. (2002). *The final report and findings of the safe school initiative: Implications for the prevention of school attacks in the United States*. Washington, DC: United States Secret Service and United States Department of Education.

10 Identifying the Protective Factors

Box 10.1 Key Take-aways

1. Protective and stabilizing factors offer a counterbalance to risk factors for white supremacist violence.
2. Questions related to each protective factor are provided to incorporate into violence risk assessments to consider the presence of attitudes, behaviors, and skills that can promote non-violence.
3. Elements of the five protective factors can be used in education and training settings in addition to therapy design to help individuals and groups develop attributes helpful in the prevention of violent action and other extremist activities.

Dr. Amy Murphy is an assistant professor at Angelo State University and program coordinator for the graduate program in student development and leadership in higher education. We often write and present together on violence prevention. She contributed to this book by sharing her perspectives in this chapter on protective factors, the elements that can counterbalance risk factors for white supremacist violence.

Imagine the weight that must drag an individual down toward extremist violence. The previous chapter examined risk factors that can push and pull an individual toward extreme ideas, activities, and ultimately escalating to violence. The weight of trauma, transition, perceived failure, and distress becomes too heavy, and individuals seek out others to blame and remedies for the pain, anger, and lack of control. This chapter considers how to counterbalance the weight of the risk factors by describing **protective and stabilizing factors**.

Centers for Disease Control and Prevention define protective factors as:

> "individual or environmental characteristics, conditions, or behaviors that reduce the effects of stressful life events. These factors also increase an individual's ability to avoid risks or hazards and promote

DOI: 10.4324/9781003199656-10

> social and emotional competence to thrive in all aspects of life, now and in the future."
>
> (2018, para. 2)

In contrast to risk factors, protective factors add stability and support to an individual's experience and create a defense against elements that could incite or motivate violence. Protective factors can serve as a counterbalance to risk factors for white supremacist violence.

Protective factors can be used by practitioners to inform their work in two ways:

1 Protective factors support threat assessment work by outlining attitudes, behaviors, characteristics, or conditions that support non-violent actions.
2 Protective factors inform our efforts to prevent radicalization and can be used in educational programs and therapy design.

As each protective factor is described, we will include examples of threat assessment questions connected to the factor to use when considering the presence of the factor in individuals.

Scope of Protective Factors

The social-ecological model provides a framework for understanding the scope of protective factors important to consider in violence prevention (Centers for Disease Control and Prevention, 2021). Table 10.1 lists some of the protective factors across the range of the social-ecological model. While it is important to consider individual characteristics, it is also critical to consider the context and environment around the individual and their impact on their need and desire for white supremacist involvement and their exposure to alternative ways of being and thinking.

As we move through the chapter, we will define and describe some of the most critical protective factors related to counterbalancing risk factors for white supremacist violence. As with risk factors, no one individual protective factor is predictive of non-violence. These factors should be considered in combination and as part of an overall assessment of risk and threat. The protective factors identified as important to threat assessment, treatment, and prevention of white supremacist engagement and violence are:

- Environmental and emotional stability
- Social health and connection
- Access and satisfaction with non-violent outlets
- Empathy
- Cognitive clarity and pluralistic awareness

Table 10.1 Overview of Protective Factors

Individual Protective Factors Individual attitudes, beliefs, and behaviors	• Sense of purpose, mattering • Demonstrates resilience • Prosocial behaviors (empathy, kindness, compassion, consequence awareness) • Positive future orientation • Impulse control, self-control
Relationship Protective Factors *Social groups, peers, and family behaviors and influences*	• Social health and connection, sense of belonging • Positive and trusting relationships • Open and healthy communications in families • Engaged with prosocial organizations • Actively disengaging from white supremacist organizations
Community Protective Factors *Characteristics and conditions of physical and social environment*	• Participation in multicultural and social justice education • Cybersafety and information literacy in online communities • Trauma-informed schools and organizations • Access to resources to support transitions out of military and law enforcement organizations. • Stimulated and rewarded in non-violent arenas
Societal *Social and cultural norms*	• Prioritize and support antiracism and diversity initiatives • Restorative justice and nonjudicial interventions

Environmental and Emotional Stability

Many violent actors find that the world around them is filled with disruption, difficulty and erratic changes. When considering the counterbalancing protective factors, we want to consider the presence of both environmental and emotional stability. Environmental and emotional stability are when an individual's life experiences have consistency and constancy, and their reactions to change or crisis represent a similar calm and resilience.

Environmental stability involves a stable personal, professional, and/or academic life. When transitions occur, the individual has access to and participates in resources to assist them. When difficulty occurs, it is moderate in nature and not made more complex by multiple occurrences happening all in one time period or layering upon one another. An individual can often manage one life transition, but it becomes more complex when confronted with changes and challenges in other areas of life as well. Those with high environmental stability have resources to help them cope with disruptive life events or difficulties.

Emotional stability examines the individual's psychological steadiness, impulse control, and frustration tolerance, which guides their reaction to crisis and concerns. Frustrations and resentment related to circumstances are short-term, and the individual is able to identify ways to make things better and find solace in opportunities for a better tomorrow. This protective factor explores the individual's resilience, their positive future orientation, and their emotional response to upheaval and difficulty. Positive future orientation is sometimes seen as "the capacity to imagine a positive future for the self, the community, and the world" (Miconi et al., 2020, p. 344). The corresponding risk factors are lacking emotional control, becoming increasingly frustrated and resentful, blaming others for their circumstances, and perceiving themselves as a victim with few options. The ability to manage emotions and build emotional stability can be taught by focusing on conflict management skills, increasing recognition of triggers for anger and frustration, and identifying ways to resolve anger and frustration without violence.

Environmental and emotional stability can also consider the ongoing impact of family circumstances, trauma history, poverty, incarceration, and exposure to crime, but here it is more about their ongoing response to it and access to resources to assist them in managing histories of concerns. Resilience is positively correlated with positive life outcomes and buffers against histories of negative experiences (Powell et al., 2020). There are a variety of strategies linked to promoting resilience and positive future orientation. We can learn a great deal from the social and emotional learning efforts in schools. Dr. Kevin Powell has explored interventions for at-risk youth focusing on positive psychology and building resilience. His "Resilience Protective Factors Checklist" can offer a good supplement when assessing or treating an individual (Powell, 2020). An individual with high environmental and emotional stability has a sense of resilience and feels a level of significance in their lives in the face of challenging or negative life experiences.

Remember, recruitment efforts by extremist organizations often target those that are victims or feel like victims of their circumstance. Significance felt by the individual has been found to prevent the need for extremist engagement and violence in their search for more meaning and worth (Jasko et al., 2016). Fathali Moghaddam, when discussing Islamic fundamentalists driven toward terrorism, reminds us that individuals who see themselves and/or their collective social groups as facing extinction because of the various threats to their way of life seek stability and significance (2009). Increasing this protective factor involves looking for the presence of or ways to add steadiness and strength to a person's situation so they do not feel threatened or fearful for their way of being. This includes finding opportunities for social mobility to improve their situation when concerns are present.

Related Threat Assessment Questions:

1 Is the individual engaged and rewarded by a job, career, or academic pursuit?
2 Does the individual experience consistency and steadiness personally?
3 When challenges occur, does the individual respond with relative calm and/or is anger and frustration short-lived?
4 Does the individual have access to resources and support related to histories of trauma and difficulty?
5 Does the individual see opportunities to improve or better their situation?

Social Health and Connection

More often than not, those acting on white supremacist ideologies are involved online or in person with groups or organizations sympathetic to or encouraging of similar ideals. Thus, this second group of protective factors becomes even more critical. The initial lure of these organizations is often more about belonging and purpose than the specific ideology of white supremacy. Individuals who feel disillusioned with existing social relationships and connections are more susceptible to the sense of community provided. White supremacist violence is mostly perpetrated by men. Several research studies exploring men and masculinity highlight this "gendered" concern and how frustration, shame, and emasculation influence the search for new connections and the correlation between gender-based violence and terrorism (Kimmel, 2018; Van Brunt and Taylor, 2021; Windisch, 2021).

> "These young men feel entitled to a sense of belonging and community, of holding unchallenged moral authority over women and children, and of feeling that they count in the world and that their lives matter. Experiencing threats to the lives they feel they deserve leads these young men to feel ashamed and humiliated. And it is this aggrieved entitlement–entitlement thwarted and frustrated–that leads some men to search for a way to redeem themselves as men, to restore and retrieve that sense of manhood that has been lost."
>
> (Kimmel, 2018, p. 10)

Those without social supports and social safety are more vulnerable to extremist groups and ideas.

The negative impact of actual or perceived marginalization and discrimination based on an individual's identity is a key risk factor. Kimmel supports this idea, "it is this sense of victimhood—that they are the new victims of the politically correct, multicultural society—that lends a degree of righteousness to their political activities" (Kimmel, 2018, p. 20). This is counterbalanced if the individual has social connections and supportive relationships that promote a sense of belonging and purpose outside of those extremist groups. These same relationships and connections also support disengaging with a white supremacist organization, especially when positive relationships and experiences shift how the individual views what is occurring in the organization or their relationship with the group. Becoming a parent, a new romantic relationship, or the influence of family are catalysts for self-reflection and disillusionment with the white supremacist group (2018).

Those with high social health and connections experience positive and trusting relationships with family, friends, and significant others. More importantly, they feel a sense of belonging and safety in those relationships. Sense of belonging is often seen as a basic human need that motivates and stimulates our behaviors (Strayhorn, 2012). It is particularly important during times of transition and entry into groups and for those that are or perceive themselves to be marginalized. A sense of belonging relates to three elements: do I belong, how do I feel, and what will I do. Thus, for our purposes, sense of belonging in non-violent social groups is important in terms of how a person feels and their future behaviors. Sense of belonging is also connected to mattering, which "reflects a person's need to feel significant in the eyes of other people," including being noticed by others, cared about by others, relied upon by others, valued by others, and others being concerned about what happens to them and their success (Flett, 2018). When others ask what they want and think, express belief in them and their capabilities, let them know they need them and rely on them, invest time and energy in them, and celebrate their accomplishments and efforts, people feel that they matter.

Related Threat Assessment Questions:

1. Does the individual have positive connections to family, friends or organizations that are not affiliated with white supremacist activities?
2. Does the individual feel a sense of belonging and mattering in existing relationships?
3. Is there a healthy awareness of masculinity, a positive view of the feminist perspective, and a positive self-worth?
4. Is someone reaching out and connecting with the individual to give them positive social support?

Access To and Satisfaction with Non-violent Outlets

We consider access to non-violent outlets a protective factor. There is a need for individuals to improve their life situation, gain status and belonging, and in some cases to advance an ideology or cause. We know from a variety of perspectives and research that radical and extremist thought does not necessarily equate to violent action. It has been proposed that radicalization and violent action exist on a spectrum and that interventions should be tailored accordingly (Abay Gasbar et al., 2020). This becomes important when we consider outlets on the spectrum that do not include violent activity. This protective factor highlights the need for non-violent outlets that can satisfy some of the needs discussed earlier.

Those drawn to white supremacist violence often experience psychological stimulation from fighting and confrontation. The group affiliation as we discussed in the previous protective factor offers a feeling of victory or reward that they are unable to attain otherwise (Windisch et al., 2018). Unfortunately, the need for affiliation and respect from the group often results in the individual needing to "perform" for the group, further increasing involvement in aggressive and violent activities. This protective factor considers if the individual has access to alternative, non-violent outlets to provide a source of stimulation, engagement, reward, and fun, like participation in sports activities, school or work experiences, or other organizations. For those with grievances against the government or others, this involvement in non-violent outlets can mean opportunities to contribute to a cause, voice opinions, or advocate for points of view without the need for violence. Even the opportunity to voice opinions without judgement can offer protection against the need to use violence to feel seen and heard. The need for non-violent outlets can be redirected into seeking out positive social and individual action, such as former white supremacist attempting restorative activities to repair harm previously caused or to help others disengage from communities of extremism and violence.

There is a cautionary note here especially as we see more non-violent but active supporters of white supremacist ideology. Knight and Keatley call these individuals "idealogues, fundraisers and 'keyboard warriors'" (2020). Extremist thought, anger, frustration, and resistance can remain nonviolent for individuals. Social justice education has often explored the role of non-violence and mobilization of communities (Butler, 2020). Violence and nonviolence are closely connected and when assessing risk and threat it is critical to consider the full array of risk and protective factors and not to rely on one characteristic or behavior as a determinate of future violence.

Related Threat Assessment Questions:

1 Is the individual involved with organizations or activities unrelated to white supremacist groups that are stimulating, rewarding, engaging, and/or fun?
2 Does the individual have non-violent opportunities to discuss, advocate for, and take action related to points of view, areas of concern, and grievances?
3 Is the individual beginning to actively disengage with extremist groups?
4 Is the individual committed to positive social or individual action?

Empathy

Empathy is the ability to see into another person's world and their perspective. It has been shown in research to exist in different amounts in people (Lanzoni, 2018). The presence of empathy is often connected to a pathway of nonviolence (Chialant et al., 2016; Van Brunt, 2015). In fact, in some research on peace psychology and nonviolent conflict resolution among nations, realistic empathy has been explored as not only "perceiving another person's experience of life through that person's eyes and appreciating that person's emotional reactions," but also "seeing each other without distortion" (Schwebel, 2006). When an individual can see someone "without the add-ons of demonization, and to see...without the rose-colored glasses that manage to block out one's own role in precipitating conflict" (Schwebel, 2006, p. 196), they are better able to understand the perspectives of others and less likely to take harmful actions against them.

Empathy is an important protective factor especially when other elements of risk are at play. When an individual is in a freefall and surrounded by an unstable environment seeking those to blame without a supportive place to land, they might identify others to blame for why things are the way they are. It becomes more difficult to place that blame on others when we can realistically see others for their own circumstances, challenges, hopes, and beliefs. Dehumanization, objectification, and the projection of hostility onto others are attitudes and behaviors associated with a justification for violent action toward others. Empathy is about seeing the mental and emotional life of an individual and as such promotes nonviolence and conflict resolution. Empathy is also linked to other prosocial behaviors and characteristics, such as compassion, helping skills, and consideration of the welfare of others.

There can be an incentive for individuals to learn the skill and behavior of empathy since it is often connected to marketability and employability skills such as leadership. Individuals can become empathetic toward others and take on a realistic perspective of their lives if they have the opportunity and are willing to take on new experiences, participate in new activities, and observe different environments. Becoming more empathic involves putting aside judgments of those who are not like us and attempting to understand their behaviors and attitudes, especially those with different social and cultural backgrounds.

Related Threat Assessment Questions:

1. Can the individual consider the perspectives of others?
2. Can the individual recognize blind spots, difficulties, or biases in understanding the experiences of others?
3. Is the individual willing to listen to and learn about the experiences of others?

Cognitive Clarity and Pluralistic Awareness

Our final protective factor considers the individual's cognitive processes and how they think and reason. This relates to how they identify and receive information to inform their perspectives and how they consider differing perspectives and ideas. With the growth in extremist groups operating and broadly sharing information online, work related to preventing violent extremism involves the information and media literacy and other educational initiatives related to critical thinking and problem-solving skills (United Nations Educational, Scientific and Cultural Organization, 2018). When individuals are armed with critical thinking skills to evaluate sources of information, they are less likely to be misled or inspired by misinformation and conspiracy theories. The United Nations specifically discusses antisemitism as an area that is critically impacted by misinformation in addition to bias and prejudice. Unfortunately, some engaged in extremist activities might not have access to alternative sources of information. They operate in an echo chamber where their ideas and perspectives are not challenged. When assessing for the presence of this protective factor, we should consider access to alternative sources of information in addition to overall information literacy. When individuals have the ability to evaluate sources of information and content of messages and an understanding and awareness of their own bias and stereotypes, this creates a cognitive clarity that can act as protection against radicalization to extremist ideas.

Critical thinking and information literacy skill involves exploring information to better understand the history, culture, behaviors, experiences, and values of others. At the most basic level, when an individual can understand the impact of their actions on others and the moral engagement to minimally avoid negative consequences of their actions, this can help prevent a movement toward violent action. This protective factor is closely connected to empathy discussed earlier and the idea of global competence which includes the ability to investigate the world and recognize and weigh perspectives (Jackson, 2017). When individuals have a global competence and self-awareness, they can see the value in inclusive participation and diversity, and they can balance opposing viewpoints. Individuals might also have access to and take part in various diversity, equity, and inclusion activities or trainings in their workplace or educational settings that promote these ideals. It is important to note here that engaging in these types of activities means an acknowledging bias, prejudice, and white supremacist norms and behaviors, which can be very challenging. For some, this challenge can make them feel more under attack and marginalized. This brings us full circle to the importance of developing critical thought, pluralistic awareness, empathy, and global competence as protective factors.

Related Threat Assessment Questions:

1. Can the individual understand and evaluate sources of information and the content of messages?
2. Does the individual have access to alternative sources of information?
3. Is the individual open minded and able to consider differing perspectives?
4. Does the individual engage in diversity, equity, or inclusion activities or trainings?
5. Does the individual interact and engage with those different from them in positive ways, especially minority and other under-represented groups?

Moving Forward

This chapter has examined the stabilities and supports that counter-balance the risk of extremist violence. In addition to helping inform violence and risk assessments, the protective factors identified throughout the chapter can be used in educational and prevention activities. We must look beyond risk factors and consider the corresponding protective factors at the individual, relationship, community, and society levels. Violent extremism and white supremacist violence does not develop in a vacuum and cannot be prevented in one. Prevention requires collaborative and integrated interventions targeted at multiple aspects of individual and community experiences.

Discussion Questions:

1. How can we promote skill-building related to the various protective factors in educational settings and communities?
2. What other attitudes, behaviors, and skills have the potential to prevent violent extremism?
3. Consider the risk factors in the previous chapter and the protective factors in this chapter, together how do they help you to better understand the movement to extremist violence?

References

Abay Gaspar, H., Daase, C., Nicole, D., Julian, J., and Manjana, S. (2020). Radicalization and political violence: Challenges of conceptualizing and researching origins, processes and politics of illiberal beliefs. *International Journal for Conflict and Violence*, 14(2), 1–18. doi:10.4119/ijcv-3802.

Butler, J. (2020). *The force of nonviolence: An ethico-political bind*. Verso.

Centers for Disease Control and Prevention. (2018, August 7). Adolescent and school health. www.cdc.gov/healthyyouth/protective/index.htm.

Centers for Disease Control and Prevention. (2021, January 28). Violence Prevention. www.cdc.gov/violenceprevention/about/social-ecologicalmodel.html.

Chialant, D., Edersheim, J., and Price, B.H. (2016). The dialectic between empathy and violence: An opportunity for intervention? *The Journal of Neuropsychiatry and Clinical Neurosciences*, 28(4), 273–285.

Flett, G. (2018). *The psychology of mattering: Understanding the human need to be significant*. Elsevier.

Jackson A. (2017). The antidote to extremism. *Educ Leadership*, 74, 18–23.

Jasko, K., LaFree, G., and Kruglanski, A. (2016). Quest for significance and violence extremism: The case of domestic radicalization. *Political Psychology*, 1–17. doi:10/1111/pops.12376.

Kimmel, M.S. (2018). *Healing from hate: How young men get into—and out of—violent extremism*. University of California Press.

Knight, S. and Keatley, D. (2020). What do we know about radicalization? A commentary on key issues, findings and a framework for future research for the scientific and applied community. *International Journal of Conflict & Violence*, 14(2), 1–7.

Lanzoni, S. (2018). *Empathy: A History*. Yale University Press.

Miconi, D., Oulhote, Y., Hassan, G., and Rousseau, C. (2020). Sympathy for violent radicalization among college students in Quebec (Canada): The protective role of a positive future orientation. *American Psychological Association Psychology of Violence*, 10(3), 344–354. doi:10.1037/vio0000278.

Moghaddam, F.M. (2009). The new global American dilemma and terrorism. *Political Psychology*, 30(3), 373–380.

Powell, K. (2020). Resilience Protective Factors Checklist (RPFC-CLIN). www.kevinpowellphd.com/resources.

Powell, K., Rahm-Knigg, R., and Conner, B. (2020). Resilience protective factors checklist (RPFC): Buffering childhood adversity and promoting positive outcomes, *Psychological Reports*, 124(4), 1437–1461.

Schwebel, M. (2006). Realistic empathy and active nonviolence confront political reality. *Journal of Social Issues*, 62(1), 191–208.

Strayhorn, T.L. (2012). *College students' sense of belonging: A key to educational success for all students*. Routledge.

United Nations Educational, Scientific and Cultural Organization. (2018). Preventing violent extremism through education: Effective activities and impact. https://en.unesco.org/preventingviolentextremismthrougheducation.

Van Brunt, B. (2015). *Harm to Others: The Assessment and Treatment of Dangerousness*. Alexandria, VA: American Counseling Association.

Van Brunt, B. and Taylor, C. (2021). *Understanding and treating incels: Case studies, guidance, and treatment of violence risk in the involuntary celebate community*. Routledge.

Windisch, B. (2021). A downward spiral: The role of hegemonic masculinity in lone actor terrorism. *Studies in Conflict & Terrorism*. doi:10.1080/1057610X.2021.1928894.

Windisch, S., Simi, P., Blee, K., and DeMichele, M. (2018). Understanding the micro-situational dynamics of white supremacist violence in the United States. *Perspectives on Terrorism*, 12(6) 23–37.

11 Developing the White Supremacist Indoctrination Rubric

Imagine yourself, or someone you know, having a strong connection to a sports team. Think about how they talk about the team, how they are immersed in the statistics related to wins and losses, maybe even how they play interactive parallel games such as fantasy football. They spend time, money, and energy in following and rooting for their team. It is likely very difficult to talk them out of their point of view, and as passionate as they might be about their players, they are likely just as passionate (or more so) about those rivals who stand in the way of their team's victory. They might follow the team on social media, travel to games, wear the uniform and logo of the team, and feel strongly connected to the entire experience. The team and experience give them a sense of identity.

This is a useful thought exercise for the reader to keep in mind when reading this chapter. If our goal is to ultimately prevent an escalation to violence, then our approach should explore the risk and protective factors, have an assessment of how far into the white supremacist ideology they have invested, and apply a research-based violence risk assessment that blends these elements. In this chapter, we will move beyond the risk and protective factors outlined in the two previous chapters and focus on depth of exposure and buy-in the subject has in the white supremacist movement.

The White Supremacist Indoctrination Rubric

The authors have spent considerable time in their careers developing threat assessment rubrics and have learned the importance of not only creating a research-based, reliable approach, but one that is easy to teach and apply. Even if the approach is based on literature and does an excellent job of assessing risk, it must also be something that can be taught and used by the professional doing the assessment.

The White Supremacist Indoctrination Rubric (WSIR) adopted here is based on five words starting with the letter A: ***Appearance, Affiliation, Absorption, Acquisition, and Appointment.*** Each will be described briefly in this section and then described in more detail with reference to the cases

DOI: 10.4324/9781003199656-11

reviewed in Chapter 7. Finally, this rubric will be applied to the three case studies introduced in Chapter 8.

Box 11.1 Some Words of Caution

Each of these five concepts should be viewed in context. Risk factors for violence should always be taken in context and single items should be cautiously interpreted. Someone who has a particular love for pit bulls might be mistaken for being connected to the movement. Simply having firearm knowledge might not be a concern if they do not have other areas of concern such as anger toward a specific group, threats of violence, or history of using racists slurs. A person might have once acquired a tattoo connected to a hate group but has since abandoned their affiliation and actively work against the group. This concept of taking data in context is discussed further in the next chapter as we explore how to conduct a violence risk assessment (VRA).

Appearance: Appearance is the outward manifestation of the inward thoughts of the white supremacist. This can include tattoos, patches, uniforms, logos, insignia, and clothing frequently worn by those in the movement. Certain hair styles (such as the bowl cut and shaved head) have been adopted by white supremacist movements. While the swastika has many religious and cultural applications beyond the appropriation of the image by the German Nazi party, it has been used for decades as a symbol of hate and its use as a symbol of white supremacy is common.

There are several examples of cases where the appearance of the individual was a clear warning sign to their escalation toward action. At least one of James Byrd's killers (case 15) had tattoos of racist imagery, including the words "Aryan pride." The arsonist in Joliet, IL (case 32) was heavily tattooed including "W" and "P" on his temples and had carved an inverted cross on his forehead with a hot nail. The shooter at Aztec High (case 72) was not tattooed but had drawn neo-Nazi symbols on his body prior to the attack.

Cases:[1] 12, 15, 26, 32–34, 44, 65, 72, 94

Appearance will be rated on a 1–5 scale with one representing the lowest level of concern and five representing the highest level of concern. The scale is outlined in Table 11.1.

Affiliation: Affiliation refers to the groups and organizations the individual knows about, has considered joining, or is an active or previous member of. These groups exist both in-person and online, so any assessment should explore both possibilities. Obtaining tattoos or branding related to a white supremacist group demonstrates a potentially deeper commitment to the group's particular manifesto.

Table 11.1 Appearance Rating

Level	*Label*	*Description*
1	None	Here there are no indications of tattoos, clothing, hair styles or symbolism related to the white supremacist movement.
2	Passing Interest	They show interest in tattoos, symbols, clothing, or imagery associated with the movement. They might reference or wear tentatively some small affectation (e.g., drawing in marker on the skin or an esoteric music group associated with the movement, such as Horna or Behemoth).
3	Casual Collection	They have some items of clothes that include symbols from the white supremacist movement (see Chapter 4). They wear these occasionally at gatherings or other locations where others are wearing the symbols or clothing as well. They might have tattoos related to the movement, but they are small and in easily concealable locations.
4	Conscious Display	They have many items of clothing with white supremacist symbols, logos, or phrases. They might also have multiple tattoos that are visible and difficult to conceal. They might shift clothing or conceal tattoos to fit into a work setting or social setting, but often they can be found communicating a clear message through their clothes (e.g., Identity Evropa triangle, blood drop cross symbol).
5	Consistent Style	They are regularly found in clothing with white supremacist logos, phrasing or images and/or have visible tattoos, often on the neck or forearm, that are not easily concealed and convey their connection to the movement. They have adopted a hair style and other mannerisms connected to the white supremacist movement. They encourage others to wear and display white supremacist symbols.

There are several examples where the affiliation with a hate group offered a warning sign of their escalation toward action. Of the 100 cases reviewed, the suspects in at least 37 of them were directly affiliated with a group or organization that aligned with their beliefs. This includes cases from decades ago, like the Ku Klux Klan members who blew up the 16th Street Baptist Church in 1963 (case 4), and more recent cases, like the Atomwafffen Division member who murdered a Blaze Bernstein in 2018 (case 73) and the member of the boogaloo movement that killed security and law enforcement personnel in 2020 (case 93).

Cases: 4, 5, 7–9, 12, 14, 15, 17–21, 26, 27, 33, 34, 45, 47, 48, 50, 51, 53, 59, 61, 64, 65, 70, 71, 73, 74, 87–89, 93, 94, 97

Affiliation will be rated on a 1–5 scale with one representing the lowest level of concern and five representing the highest level of concern. The scale is outlined in Table 11.2.

Absorption (of Knowledge): Absorption of knowledge reflects the gathering of knowledge related to the history and philosophy of the white

Table 11.2 Affiliation Rating

Level	*Label*	*Description*
1	None	They have no affiliation (online or in-person) with any group that expresses extremist, white supremacist, or hate-based ideologies.
2	Passing Interest	They have looked at some groups online but have not requested more information or joined any newsletters or memberships. Their online exploration exists on mainstream sites. They maybe have considered attending a local meeting, protest, or convention, but have not done so in person.
3	Casual Exploration	They have downloaded some online materials and are actively learning about the movement. They might have a local connection, group, or organization they have begun talking to and have attended a meeting, protest, or convention to learn more about the movement.
4	Active Membership	They have connections to several online resources with white supremacist content, many on dark web sites and forums, and have attended meetings, protests, or other group activities. They might have multiple accounts to hide their identity and follow those who hold white supremacist beliefs and/or active hate content directed to targeted groups (e.g., Blacks, Jews, LGBTQI+).
5	Leadership/ Recruitment	They maintain active membership to groups both online, especially on dark web sites and forums, and in-person, where they have administrator, moderator, or other leadership status. They have acquired written materials, pamphlets, or flyers and share these with others. They have an active social media presence that expresses white supremacist beliefs and/or active hate content to targeted groups (e.g., Blacks, Jews, LGBTQI+). Their profile photo is a hate symbol or personal photo with their hate group.

supremacist movement. It refers to how much the individual has studied and learned about the group and how willing they are to follow these doctrines. This information could be acquired in person, online, or as part of an oral tradition within a group or organization. They might have categorized the information for easier reference and/or share information with others to spread the message of hate.

Similarly high numbers of cases as those that included an affiliation with groups or organization showed a clear and purposeful absorption of knowledge. Even in the early days of the internet, we see attackers such as the London nail bomber (case 17) with significant understanding of the movement and collections of memorabilia. As information has become more readily available, we see more and more attackers studying previous attacks, as the Las Vegas Walmart shooters (case 52) and the Umpqua

Community College shooter (case 57) did. Several attackers were so steeped in knowledge they were able to write lengthy manifestos, including the Charleston church shooter (case 54) and the shooter in Norway (case 44).

Cases: 17–20, 22, 26, 28, 36, 37, 44, 51, 53–55, 57, 58, 63, 66, 70–74, 77–79, 81–83, 85–90, 94

Absorption will be rated on a 1–5 scale with one representing the lowest level of concern and five representing the highest level of concern. The scale is outlined in Table 11.3.

Acquisition (of Weapons): Acquisition of weapons refers to learning about, collecting, storing, and training with various weapons. Weapons can include bomb-making materials, firearms, poisons, radioactive materials, knives, and swords. Understanding the progression from interest to intense training assists in estimating the level of lethality. As mentioned in the text insert, simply having a weapon should not be the only data point used in the estimation of targeted violence risk but is important contextual information.

Table 11.3 Absorption of Knowledge Rating

Level	*Label*	*Description*
1	None	They know very little about the white supremacist movement and might suggest that it was over with the German Nazi Party.
2	Passing Interest	They have reviewed some material, perhaps read a book or manifesto, related to the movement. This is done more out of passive curiosity than direct pursuit.
3	Casual Exploration	They have acquired some knowledge about the movement and are looking to learn more. This could be through conversations with local members in-person or through joining online chat groups or membership websites. They might have some materials, images or documents saved, but these are limited to just a handful.
4	Focused Learning	They have acquired a good amount of knowledge about the movement and have read several of the key texts, such as those written by Camus or Mason. They have information saved that includes dozens of images, documents, and manifestos regarding white supremacy and hate focused on groups such as Jews, LGBTQI+, Blacks or Asians to better defend their points. They share and talk with others about their study.
5	Historian/ Marketer	Their knowledge of the movement, ideologies and beliefs is detailed and well-researched. They make use of a catalog or classification system to store information and are always looking to acquire more. They have sophisticated counter-arguments to those they debate and adopt a creative and manipulative use of social media. They publish and/or sell materials, logos, patches, stickers, and insignias to others.

There are several examples where the collection and training with firearms provided a clear warning sign related to the lethality potential during an attack. While almost all the completed attacks we studied obtained weapons at some point (the exception used either physical violence or non-traditional weapons, such as motor vehicles), we see many cases where the weapons were acquired shortly before and specifically for the purpose of carrying out the attacks. The Oklahoma City bombers (case 13) stole or purchased the bomb making materials they needed during the year leading up to the attack and stored them in rented sheds. The attacker in Norway (case 44) went to great lengths to hide his preparations, using shell companies and traveling to other countries. The Aztec High shooter (case 72) legally purchased the weapon he used just a month before the attack.

Cases: 2–8, 10–14, 17–29, 31–34, 36–42, 44–58, 62–66, 69, 72, 75–87, 89–91, 93, 96, 98, 99

Acquisition will be rated on a 1–5 scale with one representing the lowest level of concern and five representing the highest level of concern. The scale is outlined in Table 11.4.

Appointment (to Mission): Appointment to mission refers to the commitment the individual has when moving from idea to action related to targeted violence. They are preparing or already feel ready to commit action against a particular group in the service of their group's mission.

There are several examples where the appointment to mission became a clear fixation and focus prior to an attack. While not every attacker studied was driven by commitment to a group or specific ideology, many provided clear examples of this appointment to mission. From the murder of Alan Berg by members of the Order in 1984 (case 8) to the Ku Klux Klan members who set fire to the Macedonia Baptist in 1995 (case 14) to the Ford Hood shooter in 2009 (case 37) who visited radical Islamic websites to the Black Hebrew Israelite followers who attacked a kosher market in 2019 (case 87), we saw this appointment to mission over and over throughout the cases we reviewed.

Cases: 3–6, 8–14, 17–21, 23–29, 31, 32, 36–39, 41, 44, 45, 48–51, 54, 55, 57, 61, 63, 64, 66, 69, 70, 75,77–79, 81, 85, 87–90, 93, 94

Appointment will be rated on a 1–5 scale with one representing the lowest level of concern and five representing the highest level of concern. The scale is outlined in Table 11.5.

The Application of the White Supremacist Indoctrination Rubric

Given the experience the authors have with training thousands on violence risk assessment rubrics, we wanted to provide you with potential tools to help with practical application. To that end, there is a visual scoring sheet included in Figure 11.1 that can be used to record scores.

Table 11.4 Acquisition of Weapons Rating

Level	*Label*	*Description*
1	None	They have no interest and little knowledge related to weapons or dangerous materials. They have not previously fired a gun.
2	Passing Interest	They own no they weapons but have used a firearm on occasion at a range or while hunting. They have a basic knowledge of weapons.
3	Casual Exploration	They own or have easy access to a handgun or rifle. They have acquired the firearm for personal protection or hunting, but do not talk about using it in an active or targeted way against a group. They have taken basic firearm safety courses or have the equivalent knowledge. They might show interest in other dangerous materials such as explosives, poisons or the like and read about these online or talk about them in person. They might have begun to acquire a few secondary items such tactical gear, bulletproof plating or rapid-fire/high-capacity magazines.
4	Soldier	They own multiple firearms or other weapons and have acquired them to be prepared for the coming conflicts (e.g., race war, insurrection). They have studied tactics and have taken combat firearm courses. They have multiple weapon systems (e.g., handgun, distance rifle with optics, rapid fire capacity, shotgun and/or explosives). They practice with others and stockpile ammunition and/or do their own reloading (making ammunition). They belong to a group or militia to support their training and work as a collective.
5	Specialist/ Officer	They have acquired deep knowledge of firearms and have stockpiled dozens of weapons. They might have a specific area of expertise such as firing from a distance or attacking a crowd or protest group. They belong to one or more groups and teach/support others in their acquisition of weapons skills. They train frequently to prepare for the coming conflict and have specific plans detailing how the firearms, explosives, tactical gear, optics or other weapons will be used against specific groups. They study previous attacks to learn how to be more effective in their killing.

Table 11.5 Appointment to Mission Rating

Level	*Label*	*Description*
1	None	There is no mission considered and no commitment to any type of action against any group.
2	Passing Interest	They have a partial understanding and perhaps even agree with some of the white supremacist group's ideology (e.g., standing against critical race theory, anti-BLM, supporting a nationalist/isolationist policy), but have not joined a group, attended a protest or are considering action.

3	Casual Exploration	They have researched various groups, protests, and rallies and have expressed interest in attending. They either have attended a single event or two or have plans to attend a convention or group meeting soon. They feel aligned with the group's goals and mission yet are hesitant to become fully immersed or committed to action.
4	Active Directive	They are connected to a group and looking for ways to assist the group's mission forward. They align with the group's ideology, and they might have engaged in protests, rallies, harassing behavior, or pseudo-militaristic tactics and training. They target other groups or protests to counter their messaging and look for ways to harm and disenfranchise those who they stand against. At this stage, there is no active plans for deadly violence, but harassment, threatening, and affective violence occur.
5	Pathway to Violence	They are connected to a group or sub-group committed to violent action against those they hate (e.g., Jews, Blacks, Asians, LGBTQI+). They have acquired the weapons needed and engaged in training and tactics to carry out a mission. The time, location and date might not be chosen yet, but they are certain it will occur in the future and depending on the group and planning, they are actively involved in the recruitment and/or training of others to engage in violence to bring their vision of how the world should be to fruition.

Figure 11.1 WSIR Scoring

In the next section, we will apply the WSIR to the three cases outlined in Chapter 8. We hope this will aid the reader in putting this theory into practice.

Hank

As you might recall from Chapter 8, Hank is a junior high school student in a small, rural school district. Hank is shy, has never dated, and is often teased by his older brother. His friend's father is involved in the Proud Boys movement and Hank begins to explore ideas online related to the "real problem" in this country. Family conflict continues with racist and

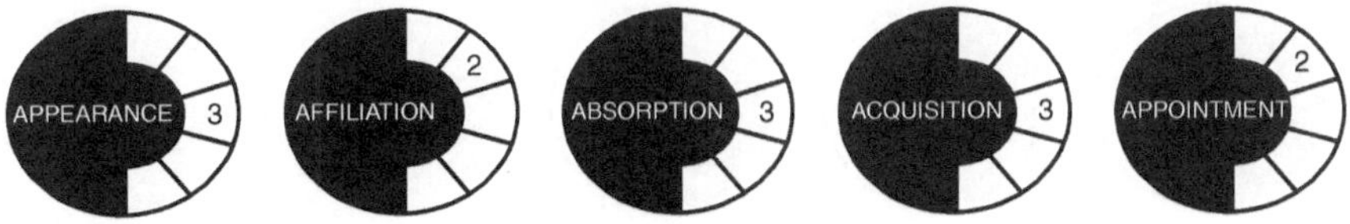

Figure 11.2 WSIR: Hank

homophobic slurs frequently used, along with violence and threats of violence. Hank becomes increasingly depressed around the conflicts, begins to miss school, and calls another student a racist slur.

Hank is confronted by the school for wearing an 88 cap and a shirt with "RAHOWA" on it, both concerning white supremacist symbols representing *Casual Collection* (3) on **Appearance**. He does not appear to be overly connected with any group beyond a *Passing Interest* (2) on **Affiliation**. Hank looks online for materials and would likely be at the *Casual Exploration* phase (3) on **Absorption**. Hank's father takes him hunting, so this would lead to *Casual Exploration* (3) on **Acquisition**. Hank seems to have a *Passing Interest* (2) in terms of **Appointment** to a mission.

A few points to clarify on a rationale for Hank's scoring:

- A few items are known through the case study details but should be explored to determine whether they are the "tip of the iceberg" or should be taken at face value. For example, does the 88 cap belong to Hank or someone else? The racial holy war shirt is more concerning, and the same question remains. Are these the extent of his collection or does he have more such items?
- Hank's online connection is mentioned but would need further exploration as well. Are there multiple usernames? Does he serve in an administrator or moderator capacity? Have these connections resulted in any in-person meet ups, conventions, or social engagements?
- Given Hank's family conflict, the bullying he faces, his difficulty dating and his depression, there might be more of an **Appointment** concern, since things are not going well in his life. This should also be an area of further focus and exploration.

Jesse

Jesse is a college student in a political science class who frequently gets into trolling and intellectual debates with other students around social justice issues. He claims to want to share his free speech with others and is called a Nazi and racist for his beliefs.

Jesse has worn a swastika on his clothes representing *Passing Interest* (2) on **Appearance**. He is knowledgeable about many different groups but does not appear be overly connected with any group beyond a *Passing*

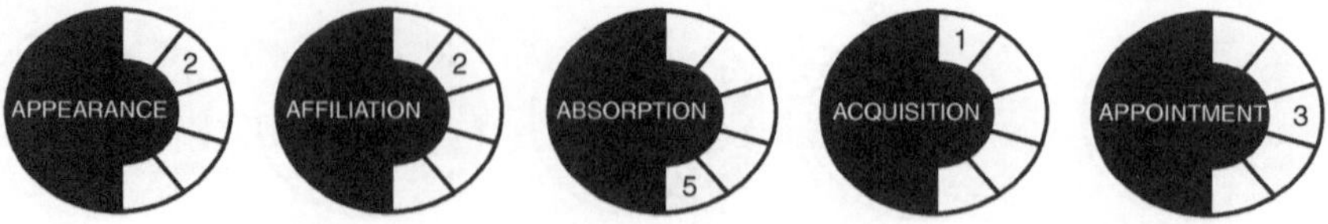

Figure 11.3 WSIR: Jessie

Interest (2) on **Affiliation.** Jesse has detailed and cataloged knowledge of white supremacist thought and would likely be at the *Historian/Marketer* phase (5) on **Absorption**. Jesse does not appear from the case study to have any knowledge or experience with weapons so this would lead to *None* (1) on **Acquisition**. Jesse seems to have an *Active Directive* (3) in terms of **Appointment** to a mission.

A few points to clarify on a rationale for Jesse's scoring:

- As with the previous case discussion with Hank, our knowledge of the case is limited to the case study and there are a few areas that would require further exploration. For example, is there only the one swastika or does he wear other symbols he has collected over time? Weapons are not mentioned but could very well be something he has studied as well. This would be an important area to explore.
- In terms of the **Appointment** being higher up at *Active Directive*, this is more for his commitment to spreading the ideas and challenging others who have a different opinion. Jessie does not appear to be engaged in any direct violence, more of an incitement to conflict and aggressive action.
- Similarly, the *Historian/Marketer* level on **Absorption** relates to his knowledge acquisition used for debate and public rhetoric. There does not appear to be any other motive than challenging and getting into debate with others; however, this should be explored in more detail.

Dawson

Dawson is a community college student with white supremacist ties who directly advocates for violence. He references previous attacks and is part of several different groups.

Dawson wears multiple symbols of concern including the pit bull, 88, RAHOWA, and the Atomwaffen symbol and has several visible racist

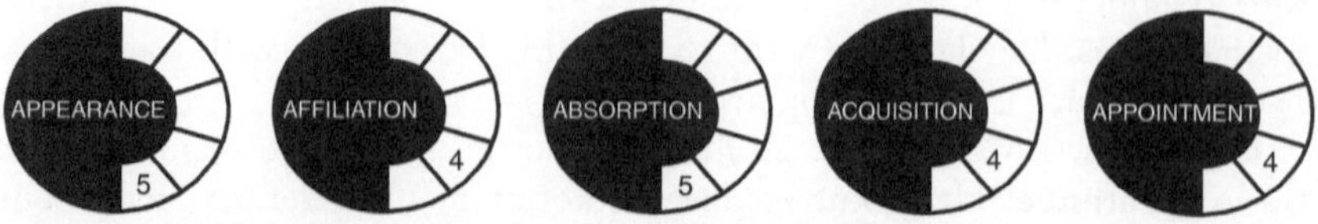

Figure 11.4 WSIR: Dawson

tattoos. This represents a *Consistent Style* (5) on **Appearance**. He is knowledgeable about many different groups and claims membership in several of them indicating *Active Membership* (4) on **Affiliation**. Dawson has detailed and cataloged knowledge in white supremacist thought and casually references previous attacks as justification for his anger. This would likely be at the *Historian/Marketer* phase (5) on **Absorption**. Dawson mentions owning multiple firearms and gives the impression he is preparing for violence, indicating a *Soldier* phase (4) on **Acquisition**. Dawson seems to have an *Active Directive* (4) in terms of **Appointment** to a mission.

A few points to clarify on a rationale for Dawson's scoring:

- Dawson offers numerous concerns details in his case study and provides a useful example of outlining a higher level of risk. The consistency of his style and presence of multiple white supremacist clothing, tattoos and markings moves him to the highest level on the **Appearance** scale.
- His knowledge of the movement and use of phrases raise the rating for him on the **Absorption** scale to the highest level as well. The desire to challenge and/or convert others to his thinking is a higher level of risk as well.
- While **Acquisition** is rated higher at level 4, there would need to be more detail about teaching these skills to others to move him higher on the acquisition stage.
- In terms of commitment to a mission, Dawson has a high level of **Appointment**, although there seems to be a lack of fixation and focus onto a particular target, rather Dawson seems more reactive to the possibility of causing problems with multiple targets.

Moving Forward

This chapter provides a useful outline of a rubric to gauge the level of white supremist indoctrination a person is engaged in. This level of indoctrination should then be used as part of a violence risk assessment process while added an analysis of risk and projective factors. The assessment then provides the direction for the treatment to reduce the risk for violence escalation. The next chapter outlines the process by while a violence risk assessment is crafted and allowing the assessment to better inform the treatment approaches outlined in Chapter 13. We then return to Hank, Jessie, and Dawson to look more specifically at their VRAs and treatment considerations.

Note

1 The cases referenced are detailed in Chapter 7. As in Chapter 9, our research was conducted using public records, so if the information was not available, cases might not be included in every category that might apply.

12 Conducting a Violence Risk Assessment

A Violence Risk Assessment (VRA) for an individual with a white supremacist ideology requires the careful balancing of the risk (Chapter 9) and protective (Chapter 10) factors with the White Supremacist Indoctrination Rubric (Chapter 11). The goal of the VRA is to better understand the degree of escalation and lethality of a potential attack, weighed against the possibility of simply believing in the dominance of whites, trolling for attention, or blustering immaturely. A VRA looks to estimate the likelihood of an attack plan having lethal intentionality through the exploration of substantive threats and planning.

For those new to the VRA process, it is essential to be aware these are not used to predict future violence or profile an individual based on a list of characteristics. Instead, VRAs should be seen as fluid processes used to understand the escalation toward lethal violence and identify intervention strategies to reduce the likelihood of the individual moving further down the pathway to violence. The assessment of this risk is determined by asking contextual questions concerning the nature of the threat and risk and applying expert systems, threat rubrics, and research-based interview techniques to better estimate the level of potential dangerousness. These assessments consider multiple perspectives and areas of subject matter expertise and make use of contextual information to better understand the escalation on the pathway to violence. O'Toole wrote in 2000, "In general, people do not switch instantly from nonviolence to violence. Nonviolent people do not 'snap' or decide on the spur of the moment to meet a problem by using violence. Instead, the path toward violence is an evolutionary one, with signposts along the way (p. 7)." A quality VRA accomplishes this through careful questioning and analysis of the risk and protective elements that occur contextually. The VRA process determines the presence of fixation and focus on a particular target and the presence of an action or time imperative which directs their personal action motivated by their frustration, anger, and dissatisfaction (Turner and Gelles, 2003).

While there are many approaches to the behavioral threat assessment process, the White Supremacist Indoctrination Rubric (WSIR) should be used as a component of the overall process, not as a substitution for the

DOI: 10.4324/9781003199656-12

VRA process. For further reading, the book *Harm to Others: The Treatment and Assessment of Dangerousness* (Van Brunt, 2015) offers a detailed approach to the threat assessment process using the SIVRA-35. Other approaches include the RAGE-V (Association of Threat Assessment Professionals, 2006), the HCR-20 (Hart and Logan, 2011), and MOSIAC (de Becker, 1997).

The VRA process should also consider the dangers of conflating mental illness and targeted violence. It is often assumed that violence occurring in these targeted attacks is directly connected to mental illness, an assumption that lacks supporting evidence (Knoll and Annas, 2016; Van Brunt and Pescara-Kovach, 2019). Mass shootings and violence like that which occurred during the US Capitol attacks on January 6th, 2021 is the result of a dozen of multi-faceted elements (National Threat Assessment Center, 2018; 2019; Jarvis and Scherer, 2015). The Federal Bureau of Investigation, Secret Service, and the Department of Homeland Security have shared research that consistently makes the point that there is no singular profile for a mass casualty attacker, but rather these attacks arise from a series of risk factors escalating an individual toward an attack while they are simultaneously experiencing evaporating stabilizing influences. This is also true of white supremacists. Even those that score on the very highest levels of the WSIR, should not be immediately assumed to be someone who will carry out an attack. It is the combination of the white supremacist ideology along with an analysis of the risk and protective factors that provides an understanding of the current risk.

A mental health diagnosis is never the sole cause of targeted violence, although this message often becomes lost in a sea of media coverage and public opinion that portrays mental illness as causal to the escalation of mass shootings. Mass shootings by people with serious mental illness represent one percent (1%) of all gun homicides each year (Knoll and Annas, 2016). The fear exists, however, and the public demands answers to prevent these kinds of attacks from happening again. The term "probability neglect," coined by Sunstein in 2003, describes the tendency to probability and overrate small risks, especially ones that might be easier to mitigate or cause a more emotional reaction than the more complicated, higher probability solution. This leads to the public's demands for legal interventions from the government or the seeking of clear answers for the cause. The growing threat of the white supremacist is not a mental illness problem, even though society might view this as the most reasonable, common-sense explanation that provides the false hope of an easy solution to a complex problem.

Another common mistake with a VRA is to assume that a psychological or mental health assessment is the same as a violence risk or threat assessment. A psychological or mental health assessment determines a diagnosis of a mental illness, an assessment for inpatient hospitalization, the creation of a treatment plan, recommendations for on-going therapy, and specific advice to address symptoms. A violence risk or threat assessment draws from criminology and psychology with a goal of determining the likelihood of targeted or predatory violence occurring. While a violence risk or threat assessment does not need to be performed by clinical mental health staff, there is a benefit in using professionals who have training and experience in building rapport and interviewing to aid in the violence risk or threat assessment.

The Difference Between Violence Risk and Threat Assessment

Threat and risk assessments are most often conducted by non-clinical staff and forensic professionals in law enforcement, executive protection, and human resources, or members of a BIT/CARE team. They gather information related to the events and the subject's background and interview the subject to better estimate their risk to the greater community. These assessments are not seeking to profile an individual, rather they seek to determine the risk of violence to the community by gathering information concerning risk and protective factors to determine the level of potential dangerousness. The Secret Service and FBI share:

> "The threat assessment process is based on the premise that each situation should be viewed and assessed individually and guided by the facts. Judgments about an individual's risk of violence should be based upon an analysis of his/her behaviors and the context in which they occur. Blanket characterizations, demographic profiles, or stereotypes do not provide a reliable basis for making judgments of the threat posed by a particular individual."
>
> (Drysdale et al., 2010, p. 37)

Although threat and violence risk assessments are very similar in theory, they are different in terms of application. There is general agreement that a threat assessment seeks to assess dangerousness of an individual after they issue a threat, whether the threat presents as vague, conditional, or direct, and the likelihood that threat will be carried out. A violence risk assessment (VRA) looks at general risk of violence. Meloy et al., (2011) describe the difference in this way:

> "Threat assessment and risk assessment have developed as somewhat overlapping fields. Violence risk assessment has an older provenance and is a method by which the probability of generally violent behavior is estimated for an individual based upon his membership in a particular at-risk group. Threat assessment is concerned almost wholly with the risk of targeted violence by a subject of concern and has a behavioral and observational policing focus. Risk assessment might address different domains of risk

> than threat assessment, and typically relies on more historical and dispositional (status) variables."
>
> (p. 2)

For example, if a Neo-Nazi posts on social media, "I'm going to hunt down all the Jews and create a new graveyard with my AR at sundown on this Friday," then there is a clear threat to be assessed. A VRA should be seen as a wide umbrella for an assessment when there is a concern for violence, regardless of the presence of vague, conditional, or direct threat. For our example, a VRA could have been used prior to the threat based on other posts about hatred toward specific groups, weapons and/or hostile rhetoric or memes.

The pathway to violence provides a metaphor related to understanding the progression toward violent action. O'Toole (2000) writes:

> "In general, people do not switch instantly from nonviolence to violence. Nonviolent people do not 'snap' or decide on the spur of the moment to meet a problem by using violence. Instead, the path toward violence is an evolutionary one, with signposts along the way."
>
> (p. 7)

To stop a person on this pathway, the VRA must carefully gather information and develop an intervention plan the earliest point where the potential attacker shares leakage regarding their frustration, anger, and dissatisfaction aimed at a given target.

Assessing the Pathway to Violence

Targeted violence occurs on a pathway or spectrum that is progressive. Deisinger et al. (2008) describe one approach to this progression through a four-step understanding of escalating threat moving through ideation, planning, acquisition, and implementation. Those in ***ideation*** have thoughts and ideas related to a real or perceived injustice that occurred. They experience a growing frustration and resentment, which leads to them ***planning*** how to have impact on those they blame for their underlying problems. Once they have a plan in place, they begin to obtain firearms and military supplies in the ***acquisition*** phase. This phase might also involve fantasizing about and rehearsing for carrying out the attack. At ***implementation***, they have selected the location and chosen a time to proceed. Those on this pathway offer observable clues that can be useful for law enforcement, counseling, those on a BIT/CARE team, and human resources.

For example, imagine a young man who becomes increasingly angry at low-cost labor coming into the country from Mexico. This case is demonstrated progressively in Table 12.1.

Table 12.1 Case Example of Escalating Threat

Descriptor	*Case Example*
Ideation	He begins to vent his frustrations on social media and collects grievances and injustices through stories where immigrants are taking jobs from "real Americans" or having children here to take the jobs of whites in future generations. He talks about these frustrations more and more frequently and becomes particularly enraged as more conservative politicians being to lose power due to what he perceives are illegal minority votes.
Planning	He starts to consider which people he wants to specifically harm and how to hurt as many people as possible to send a message about his agenda. He studies other attacks and thinks about the kinds of weapons, tactics, and planning he should engage in to carry out his mission.
Acquisition	He actively begins acquiring firearms and ammunition to use during the attack. He purchases these from different locations and acquires body armor, tactical gloves, kneepads, elbow pads, and harnesses.
Implementation	He chooses the time and location for the attack and takes steps to carry out final preparations, such as completing a legacy token and acquiring final weapons, ammunition, and tactical gear. He proceeds with attack.

VRAs should also follow the principle of "attending to the silence" or the times where a previously concerning individual has dropped off the proverbial radar. While we can hope they improved or found something else to draw their attention, a more realistic assessment is that they have continued to escalate and further isolate themselves. Quiet periods, or the lack of a direct threat, should not be ignored (Meloy, 2000; 2006). A lack of threat is not a reason to lower the risk as they might be quietly developing an attack plan, acquiring weapons, or conducting surveillance to learn the schedule and behaviors of their target.

Box 12.1 Attend to Quietude

The attacker at the Tuscon, AZ Safeway was quiet for close to four months between his October 4th voluntary withdrawal from Pima College and his January 8th attack (Couch, 2011). Likewise, the attacker from Virginia Tech had no reports of any concerning behaviors in the spring of 2007 prior to his April 16th assault (Virginia Tech Review Panel, 2007). This attacker obtained his weapons, rented a van, recorded a manifesto, practiced with his firearms, obtained chains and locks for doors, locked the doors with chains, and planned the other details of his deadly assault. These behaviors provided potential clues and information useful to thwarting the attack. Very few of either attackers' behaviors prior to their attacks were directly communicated threats. This serves as an important reminder to attend to ideation, planning, and acquisition phases prior to implementation. Likewise, attend to the seven approach behaviors, outlined in Table 12.6, that occur prior to a direct communicated threat.

The best hope of thwarting the plans of those on the pathway to targeted violence requires an attention to patterns and behaviors that, when viewed together as part of a larger picture, might help to illuminate the individual's path to violence. A clinician performing the assessment is in an ideal position to build trust and rapport while looking carefully for signs of escalating violence.

Violence Risk Assessment Approaches

There are numerous well-established approaches to the process of violence risk assessment. Some of these approaches outline risk factors that are important to attend to in order to accurately assess the risk of targeted violence. Others are systems of interviewing, analysis, intervention, and management of threat.

Structured Interview for Violence Risk Assessment (SIVRA-35): As part of the book *Ending Campus Violence* (Van Brunt, 2012; 2015), the SIVRA-35 expert system was created that is widely used at colleges and universities across the United States. The risk factors are summarized in Table 12.2. Of note, the first 12 items identified by the shading, are the critical items used in this measure. These carry with them an increased weight and concern in the scoring system, which assigns low, moderate, and high levels of risk. These levels of risk are then used to drive intervention plans. More information regarding the scoring and interpretation of the SIVRA-35 can be obtained by contacting www.nabita.org.

US Postal Service Threat Assessment Team Guide: In 2007 the US Postal Service developed a set of risk indicators as part of their *Threat Assessment Team Guide*. Some of these risk indicators are listed here:

- Past history of violent behaviors (e.g., physical assaults on others)
- Having a concealed weapon or flashing a weapon
- Fascination with semi-automatic or automatic weapons and their capability to cause great harm
- Odd or bizarre beliefs (magical or satanic beliefs, or sexually violent fantasies)
- Perceived loss of options
- Inspiration of fear in others (exceeding mere intimidation)
- Obsessive focus on grudge—often quick to perceive unfairness or malice in others, especially supervisor

Table 12.2 Summary of the SIVRA-35 Risk Factors

Direct communicated threat	*Acquired plans, tools and/or weapons for attack*
Violent fantasies about attack	Action plan or timeframe for the attack
Fixation and/or focus for attack	Carries deep grudges or resentments; injustices
Target described in negative written/art	Leakage about a potential attack plan
Current suicidal thoughts or plan to die	Feels persecuted or treated unjustly
Engaged in last acts; created legacy token	Hallucinations, paranoia, grandiosity
Hardened or locked point of view	Lack of options, hopelessness, or desperation
Driven to a particular action to cause harm	Recent breakup/failure of intimate relationship
Overly defensive/aggressive during VRA	Little remorse for their actions; lack of empathy
Glorification of violence	Has weapon or specialized weapons training
Externalizes blame to others for problems	Intimidates others; displays intolerance
History of impulsive, erratic, risk taking	History of conflicts with authority
Handles frustration in explosive manner	Difficulty connected with others
History of drug or substance abuse	Serious mental illness issues present
Serious mental illness *and* not in treatment	Objectification of others
Sense of entitlement; feeling owed	Oppositional thoughts and/or behaviors
Poor support and connection from others	Overwhelming stress from major life change
Drastic, unexplained behavioral change	

- Direct or veiled threats of bodily harm
- History of poor impulse control and poor interpersonal skills

(United States Postal Service, 2007, p. 39)

Risk Assessment Guideline Elements for Violence (RAGE-V): The RAGE-V was created by the Association of Threat Assessment Professionals (2006). Several risk factors are summarized here to highlight additional areas of concern.

- Beliefs, revenge, entitlement, grandiosity, need to force closure
- Drug use: methamphetamine, cocaine, alcohol, or steroids

- Head trauma
- Criminal history, including a history of violence, homicide, stalking, threats, assault, or violation of conditional release
- Prior voluntary or involuntary commitments
- Past suicide attempts, or suicide ideation, to include suicidal thoughts, statements, gestures, and attempts
- Adverse responses to authority and limit setting
- History of mental problems that compromise coping, or enhance appeal of violence, might include:

  a Depression
  b Paranoia
  c Psychopathy
  d Bipolar
  e Personality disorders (narcissistic, paranoid, borderline, antisocial)
  f Perceptions of injustice or insoluble problems.

The RAGE-V provides yet another useful list of risk factors and items to assess when conducting a threat assessment.

Threat Indicators: Turner and Gelles (2003) wrote a particularly useful and easy to understand book related to the process of violence risk and threat assessments as they are applied to human resources and workplace settings. A summary of their work, primarily drawing from pages 17–18, is provided in Table 12.3.

Table 12.3 Summary of Threat Indicators

Verbal Cues	*Bizarre Thoughts*	*Behavioral Clues*	*Obsessions*
Direct/Indirect threat	Paranoia	Physical assault	Perceived injustices
Harassing phone call	Persecutory delusions	Illegal weapon use	Grudges/ resentments
Suicide threat/ action	Self as victim	Physical intimidation	Desires certain thing
Hopelessness	General Delusions	Surveillance	Feels humiliation
Violent boasts	Command Hallucinations	Following of person	Hopelessness, trapped
Frequent profanity	Deteriorating thoughts	Short-fuse, impulsive	Weapons and killing
Belligerence	Obsessions	Destroyed property	The need for fairness
Intimidation	Substance use/ abuse	Failing self-care	Grievances and lawsuits
Challenging talk		Isolated or withdrawn	

FBI's Four-Prong Approach: In one of the first comprehensive, research-based assessments of targeted violence, the FBI (O'Toole, 2002) created a four-prong approach to threat assessment which includes 1) the personality of the student; 2) family dynamics; 3) school dynamics; and 4) social dynamics. Although this checklist was created primarily for use with K-12 schools, there are numerous overlaps with other age groups that are useful for assessing threat in the white supremacist population. The first prong in this approach is summarized in Table 12.4.

O'Toole (2000) emphasizes:

> "It should be strongly emphasized that this list is not intended as a checklist to predict future violent behavior by a student who has not acted violently or threatened violence. Rather, the list should be considered only after a student has made some type of threat and an assessment has been developed using the four-pronged model...No one or two traits or characteristics should be considered in isolation or given more weight than the others...."
>
> (p. 15)

With close to 30 personality factors that correlate with prior school shootings and a detailed account of risk factors, this provides a useful checklist to use during a VRA interview process. Caution should be taken, however, as any list brings with it the danger of false positives that can create problems differentiating true violence risk from howling and more transient threats.

The FBI further highlights three additional prongs useful in the assessment. These are outlined in Table 12.5. The prongs of family, school, and

Table 12.4 Summary of FBI Prong One: Personality Risk Factors

Leakage	*Signs of depression*	*Fascination with violence*	*Inappropriate humor*
Low Frustration tolerance	Narcissism	Exaggerated attention need	Desire to manipulate
Poor coping skills	Alienation of self	Externalization of blame	Lacking trust
Lack of resiliency	Dehumanization	Masks low self-esteem	Closed social group
Failed love relationship	Lack of empathy	Poor anger management	Change in behavior
Injustice collector	Sense of entitlement	Behavior to carry out threat	Rigid and opinionated
Intolerance	Negative role models	Unusual interest in violence	Attitude of superiority

Table 12.5 Family, School and Social Dynamics

Family	*Social*	*School*
Turbulent parent-child relationship	Student's attachment to school	Entertainment / technology
Acceptance of pathological behavior	Tolerating disrespectful behavior	Peer groups
Access to weapons	Inequitable discipline	Drugs and alcohol
Lack of intimacy	Inflexible culture	Outside interests
Student "rules the roost"	Pecking order among students	Copycat / contagion effect
No limits on TV/Internet	Code of silence	
	Unsupervised computer access	

social dynamics are useful to consider in the context of the personality risk factors. These three remaining prongs emphasize the larger context to which these risk factors should be understood.

ASIS Workplace Violence Prevention and Intervention Standards: ASIS International and the Society for Human Resource Management published *Workplace Violence Prevention and Intervention* (2011), providing standards to assist security and human resource personal to address potentially dangerous incidents. They suggest organizations would do well to be aware of the following factors:

- A history of threats or violent acts, including threats or violence occurring during employment and a criminal history suggestive of a propensity to use violence to project power and to control others, or as a response to stress or conflict
- Threats, bullying, or other threatening behavior, aggressive outbursts or comments, or excessive displays of anger
- Verbal abuse or harassment by any means or medium
- Harboring grudges, an inability to handle criticism, habitually making excuses, and blaming others
- Chronic, unsubstantiated complaints about persecution or injustice; a victim mindset
- Obsessive intrusion upon others or persistent unwanted romantic pursuit
- Erratic, impulsive, or bizarre behavior that has generated fear among co-workers
- Homicidal or suicidal thoughts or ideas
- A high degree of emotional distress
- Apparent impulsivity and/or low tolerance of frustration

- A fascination with weapons, a preoccupation with violent themes of revenge, and an unusual interest in recently publicized violent events, if communicated in a manner that creates discomfort for co-workers
- Any behavior or collection of behaviors that instill fear or generate a concern that a person might act out violently (p. 22)

Approach Warning Behaviors: Meloy et al. (2011) outline eight warning behaviors that are, "...factors which constitute change, and which are evidence of increasing or accelerating risk" (p. 5). These approach behaviors can be seen as a progressive escalation toward targeted violence. They are summarized in Table 12.6.

Structured Professional Judgement (SPJ): The SPJ process is a seven-step approach that addresses the management of threat (Hart and Logan, 2011). The process includes: 1) gathering information; 2) determining the presence of risk factors; 3) determining the relevance of risk factors; 4) developing a good formulation of violence risk; 5) developing scenarios of violence; 6) developing a case management plan based on those scenarios; and 7) developing conclusory opinions about violence risk.

Table 12.6 Summary of Approach Behaviors

Warning Behavior	*Description*
Pathway	Behaviors that are part of the research, planning, preparation, or implementation of an attack.
Fixation	Behaviors that show an increasing preoccupation, perseveration, strident opinion, negative description, impact on others, angry emotional overtone and is usually accompanied by social, academic or workplace deterioration.
Identification	Behaviors that show a "pseudo-commando" or "warrior mentality with identify with previous attackers, weapons, militaristic or law enforcement paraphernalia.
Novel Aggression	Any act of violence that occurs related to the pathway behavior for the first time with to test the subject's ability to carry out the action or measure the subject's response.
Energy Burst	Increase frequency or variety of activities related to the targeted that occur in the days or weeks prior to the attack.
Leakage	The communication to a third party of an intent to cause the target harm through an attack.
Last Resort	Behaviors with increasing desperation or distress through word or action that leaves the subject with no choice but to act.
Direct Communicated Threat	Communication of a direct threat in an oral or written manner that implicitly or explicitly conveys a desire to damage, hurt or kill a target (or individuals or things associated with the target).

1 **Gather Information:** Straightforward gathering of information is essential to the VRA process to allow for a contextual understanding of the nature of the threat. The conclusions of any VRA will be limited by the detail and breadth of information gathered regarding the subject and the nature of the risk. Interviews are one of many ways to gather contextual information during a VRA. Additional information would include past treatment, criminal records, student conduct violations, class or work attendance, social interaction, and family and peer interactions. By gathering this information, we reduce blind spots within the VRA process and can better assess the nature of the risk. **Any VRA and subsequent interventions and management will be limited if this contextual and background information is not gathered during the process.** Information should be detailed enough to provide an opportunity to better understand the nature of the threat, risk factors, and protective factors. Those conducting a VRA should make every effort to gather as much information as reasonable to provide context to the assessment.
2 **Determine the Presence of Risk Factors:** Risk factors, as discussed in Chapter 9, offer a way to conceptualize the nature of the risk. The HCR-20 version 3.0 is a VRA process that offers a useful framework to understand the historical, clinical, and current risk factors that are used in understanding potential violence (Hart and Logan, 2011; Hart et al. 2011). Several other approaches are outlined in this chapter, including the SIVRA-35 (Van Brunt, 2012; 2015), which is geared primarily toward high school and college populations.
3 **Determine the Relevance of Risk Factors:** After contextual information is gathered and risk factors are assessed, this phase weighs the risk factors for relevance to the specific case being considered. The SPJ approach balances objective data with the assessor's judgement and experience. VRAs are not just a checklist, but consider the specific, contextual environment of the threat profile.
4 **Develop a Good Formulation of Risk:** Hart and Logan (2011) encourage development of a story to better understand why this person might commit violence. Violence is goal directed, so the VRA should seek to better understand the goal and balance the various costs and benefits in the commission of violence. Does the individual desire to survive after the attack or do they plan to die in the commission of the attack? Is there anything that would deter them from their attack plan? Hart and Logan (2011) describe some concepts to consider when developing a formulation of risk. These are motivators, disinhibitors, and destabilizers. These help us better understand the 'why' behind an attacker's violent intentions.

Motivators are the ideas that push an attacker forward to their goal. Examples of these motivations for violence include a desire for status or esteem, to control or change behavior, or for justice or honor. The presence of multiple *disinhibitors* increases the risk of violence. These might include a negative self-image, unstable friends or peer groups, lack of anxiety, lack of guilt, or the encouragement of violent action by online chat groups. *Destabilizers* create imbalance in the potential attacker's life and include mental illness, disturbed perception or attention, racing thinking, and obsessive thinking.

During the VRA process, a good formulation of risk is built upon these motivators, disinhibitors, and destabilizers. This offers an insight into why a particular white supremacist might move toward violence. When building a good formulation of risk, each formulation should be individualized, testable, narrative, diachronic, ampliative, and fertile (Hart and Logan, 2011). Table 12.7 provides a summary of how each of these concepts could be applied to the case outlined in Table 12.1.

5. **Develop Scenarios for Violence:** These are imaginative stories expanding on the initial formulation of violence that outline potential ways the plan might evolve and escalate. Consider a range of options that answers questions such as: "If they planned an attack against immigrants, where might this occur?," "What local or national events might escalate this attack timeline?," "What could stop the violence from occurring?," and "What might speed up the timeline?"

Multiple scenarios are created that outline possible negative and positive outcomes. This scenario planning is often used by public safety,

Table 12.7 Case Example Describing a Formulation of Risk

Descriptor	*Case Example*
Individualized	For this person, the desire to harm others is a way to bring about national change. He sees this action as something only he is willing to do.
Testable	This can be verified and tested based on his social media posts, overheard conversations, and acquisition of weapons.
Narrative	He becomes increasingly focused his beliefs and acquires weapons and plans his attack. His life continues to deteriorate in terms of loss of friends, failing grades in classes and increased social isolation. The attack plan increasingly becomes his way of "going out in a blaze of glory."
Diachronic	Certain events, such as a pending suspension or conflict with a co-worker might escalate the plan forward more quickly. Similarly, construction at the initial attack location or increased law enforcement presence might shift the location of the attack from a Walmart with a high Mexican customer base to a local taqueria.
Ampliative	Recent news reports related to immigrant crime or a political debate occur and end up pushing forward the attack timeline.
Fertile	The time and location of attack change as he learns of a local protest concerning how immigrants are being treated at the Texas border. The presence of news and cameras give the attacker an added boost to have a national impact.

health, engineering, and the military to better prepare for potential outcomes while accounting for uncertainty. Scenario planning starts with a formulation of risk and builds to a collection of potential scenarios. These scenarios are then ordered in terms of their plausibility and likelihood.

6. **Develop a Case Management Plan Based on Scenarios:** Once the list of potential scenarios is developed, case management efforts are prioritized based on the most plausible and likely scenarios. For examples, the attacker setting off a nuclear dirty bomb at the border is possible, but unlikely. The attacker carrying out a mass shooting at a location where there are many immigrants is much more plausible.

An area of strength in the SPJ model (Hart and Logan, 2011) is the combination of assessing and managing risk. The assessment should lead to questions about what effective interventions will reduce the risk of violence. A good risk management plan considers strategies, tactics, and logistics. Strategies are the high-altitude objectives of the interventions. Tactics outline how we will accomplish the strategy. Logistics detail what we need to put the tactics into action to achieve our strategic objectives. Think about it this way, if you wanted to go a trip, the strategy is identifying the destination on a map. The tactics are whether you will walk, drive, ride a bike, or fly to the location. The logistics are the money, time, fuel, food, clothing, and suitcases needed reach your destination.

7. **Develop Conclusory Opinions about Violence Risk:** This summarizes the overall VRA and management of risk back to the referral source. Once the assessment is completed, the VRA and management suggestions are communicated by a letter, phone call, or formalized report. The conclusory phase brings together the clinical formulation for risk along with the scenarios to provide a clear intervention and management plan.

Moving Forward

This chapter provided a brief overview of the VRA process and offered a review of several examples of VRA processes. Any VRA process considers risk and protective factors to give an overall opinion on what will escalate the potential for violence and what steps could be taken to increase protective and stabilizing supports to reduce the risk of violence. The next three chapters provide the reader with three different case examples and provide both an assessment of overall risk and suggestions for interventions and management of the risk.

References

Association of Threat Assessment Professionals. (2006). *Risk Assessment Guideline for Elements for Violence (RAGE-V)*. Considerations for assessing the risk of future violent behavior. Sacramento, CA: Author.

ASIS International and Society for Human Resource Management. (2011). *Workplace Violence Prevention and Intervention: American National Standard*. Retrieved from www.asisonline.org/guidelines/published.htm.

Couch, A. (2011, January 12). Arizona shooting suspect Jared Loughner: 5 of his strange ideas. *Christian Science Monitor*.

de Becker, G. (1997). *The gift of fear and other survival signals that protect us from violence*. New York, NY: Dell.

Deisinger, G., Randazzo, M., O'Neill, D., and Savage, J. (2008). *The Handbook of Campus Threat Assessment and Management Teams*. Applied Risk Management, LLC.

Drysdale, D., Modzeleski, W. and Simons, A. (2010). *Campus attacks: Targeted violence affecting institutions of higher education*. Washington, DC: United States Secret Service, United States Department of Education and Federal Bureau of Investigation.

Hart, S. and Logan, C. (2011). Formulation of violence risk used evidence-based assessment: The structured professional judgment approach. In P. Sturmey and M. McMurran (Eds), *Forensic Case Formulation* (pp. 83–106). Chichester: Wiley-Blackwell.

Hart, S., Sturmey, P., Logan, C., and McMuran, M. (2011). Forensic Case Formulation. *International Journal of Forensic Mental Health*, 10, 118–126.

Jarvis, J. and Scherer, A. (2015) *Mass victimization: Promising avenues for prevention*. Washington, DC: Federal Bureau of Investigation.

Knoll, J.L. and Annas, G.D. (2016). Mass shootings and mental illness. In L.H. Gold and R.I. Simon (Eds), *Gun Violence and Mental Illness* (pp. 81–104). Washington, DC: American Psychiatric Association.

Meloy, J.R. (2000). *Violence risk and threat assessment: A practical guide for mental health and criminal justice professionals*. San Diego, CA: Specialized Training Services.

Meloy, J.R. (2006). The empirical basis and forensic application of affective and predatory violence. *Australian and New Zealand Journal of Psychiatry*, 40, 539–547.

Meloy, J., Hoffmann, J., Guldimann, A., and James, D. (2011). The role of warning behaviors in threat assessment: An exploration and suggested typology. *Behav Sci Law*, 30, 256–279.

National Threat Assessment Center. (2018). *Enhancing school safety using a threat assessment model: An operational guide for preventing targeted school violence*. United States Secret Service, Department of Homeland Security.

National Threat Assessment Center. (2019). *Protecting America's Schools: A United States Secret Service Analysis of Targeted School Violence*. United States Secret Service, Department of Homeland Security.

O'Toole, M.E. (2000). *The school shooter: A threat assessment perspective*. Quantico, VA: National Center for the Analysis of Violent Crime, Federal Bureau of Investigation.

O'Toole, M.E. (2002). *The School Shooter: A Threat Assessment Perspective*. Quantico, VA: Federal Bureau of Investigation.

Sunstein, C.R. (2003). *Terrorism and probability neglect. J RiskUncertainty*, 26, 121–136.

Turner, J. and Gelles, M. (2003). *Threat Assessment: A Risk Management Approach*. New York, NY: Routledge.

United States Postal Service. (2007). Threat Assessment Team Guide. Retrieved on November 30, 2019 from www.nalc.org/workplace-issues/resources/manuals/pub108.pdf.

Van Brunt, B. (2012). *Ending campus violence: New approaches to prevention*. New York, NY. Routledge.

Van Brunt, B. (2015). *Harm to others: The assessment and treatment of dangerousness*. Alexandria, VA: American Counseling Association.

Van Brunt, B. and Pescara-Kovach, L. (2019). Debunking the Myths: Mental Illness and Mass Shootings. *Journal of Gender and Violence*, 1–11.

Virginia Tech Review Panel. (2007). *Mass shootings at Virginia Tech: Report of the review panel*. Retrieved from: https://scholar.lib.vt.edu/prevail/docs/VTReviewPanelReport.pdf.

13 Overview of Treatment Approaches

Now that we have discussed the foundations of white supremacy, what contributes to vulnerability to indoctrination, the risk and protective factors, and how to assess indoctrination through the White Supremacist Indoctrination Rubric, we are shifting gears and moving into a discussion of treatment approaches to addressing those on the pathway toward violence.

Before providing direct examples for the three case studies presented in Chapter 8, this chapter will provide a review of several treatment approaches used in psychotherapy to address troubled thoughts and behaviors. These treatment approaches, along with a brief description of each, are listed in Table 13.1.

Humanistic, Person-Centered Care

On first blush, taking a person-centered approach with a white supremacist presents several challenges for the clinician. A clinician will find themselves disagreeing with and opposed to most of the viewpoints of their client in the same way a therapist would be opposed to concepts of a client advocating pedophilia. However, when considered more deeply, the core concepts found in person-centered, humanistic approach to treatment are quite well-suited to this problem.

Active listening serves as a rope of connection between the therapist and client to better understand, in a non-judgmental manner, the nature and extent of their beliefs. This does not equate to endorsing or condoning the thoughts or behaviors, but rather understanding the nature of their beliefs. Many who hold white supremacist beliefs are driven by a general fear they are worth less than everyone around them and that they do not have value. When the person-centered therapist attends to them and conveys that they are listening, it creates an environment where the client feels heard and understood. This gives an opportunity to engage with them in a non-judgmental space where they can more easily understand, explore, and change their beliefs. Learning to listen and project care to the client, while offering hope for a better tomorrow, are the most

DOI: 10.4324/9781003199656-13

Table 13.1 Summary of Treatment Approaches

Approach	*Clinician*	*Summary*
Humanistic, Person-Centered Care	Rogers (1961; 1980)	This approach is based on mutual respect and faith in the client using a stance of genuineness, unconditional positive regard, and empathetic listening.
Cognitive Behavioral Therapy (CBT)	Ellis (2007), Glasser (1975; 2001), Nay (2004)	The CBT approach to care emphasizes that we can change our behavior when we change the way we think and feel about the world around us. Two specific approaches to addressing barriers are Nay's work on addressing anger intensifiers and the Navy Seal's use of imagery and goal setting. A number of specialized CBT approaches work in relation to trauma, such as Multimodal Trauma Treatment (Amaya-Jackson et al., 2003) and Trauma Focused CBT (Cohen et al., 2006).
Rational Emotive Behavioral Therapy (REBT)	Ellis (2007)	REBT involves exploring the activating events that cause an immediate reaction, the beliefs we hold about why they occur (which might or might not be accurate), and the consequences that drive those inaccurate beliefs.
Reality Therapy	Glasser (1975; 2001)	This approach to change focuses on short-term, clearly identified, and measurable goals that are agreed upon by both the client and therapist. Deeper reasons for the behavior (or understanding the 'why') are replaced by a focus on change.
Narrative and Metaphor Therapy	White & Epston (1990), Kopp (1995)	These two approaches to change attend to the stories, metaphors, and analogies the client uses to describe their lives and worldview. By listening to and using these stories, the therapist can more easily offer alternative narratives without the defensiveness from the client.
Existential Therapy	Yalom (1980), May (1983)	This innovative and somewhat challenging approach to change requires the therapist to engage the client to face their fears of death, freedom, isolation, and meaninglessness.
Motivational Interviewing	Miller and Rollnick (1991)	This approach offers a series of concepts for the therapist to engage the client with to bring about change. These are expressing empathy, avoiding argumentation, rolling with resistance, developing discrepancy, and supporting self-efficacy.
Transtheoretical Model (TTM)	Prochaska, Norcross, and DiClemente (1994)	This approach to change outlines a series of progressive levels we each move through when attempting to change our behavior. These are pre-contemplation, contemplation, preparation, action, maintenance, and relapse.

essential concepts to bring them away from this dangerous, self-destruction indoctrination.

Carl Rogers (1961), the humanistic psychologist and father of the person-centered approach to treatment offers the following: "...when someone understands how it feels and seems to be me, without wanting to analyze me or judge me, then I can blossom and grow in that climate" (p. 62). Empathy and congruence are essential to helping the white supremacist find a new way of being. Empathy allows us to see the world from someone else's eyes, understanding from their perspective. Congruence occurs when the therapist conveys a sense of genuineness and authenticity to those they are treating; we trust those who we can understand and who seem honest and direct about their goals.

Rogers encourages us to convey a sense of understanding to our clients. Therapists should offer non-judgmental listening which leads to a fertile and supportive place for the white supremacist to share their perspective with less defensiveness and hesitation. We want to stress here, this is not an endorsement of their ideology or behavior but rather the development of a safe and nurturing space to engage in a dialogue, explore alternative thoughts, and engage in harm reduction. While there is a reasonable and visceral rejection of their thoughts, the understanding of how they came to believe what they do creates opportunities to shift these ideologies and behaviors.

Rogers offers this in his book, *A Way of Being* (1980):

> "...empathetic listening. This means the therapist senses accurately the feelings and personal meanings that the client is experiencing and communicates this understanding to the client. When functioning best, the therapist is so much inside the private world of the other that they can clarify not only the meaning of which the client is aware but even those just below the level of awareness. This kind of sensitive, active listing is exceedingly rare in our lives. We think we listen, but rarely do we listen with real understanding, true empathy. Yet listening, of this very special kind, is one of the most potent forces for change that I know."
>
> (p. 116)

As we move to explore other approaches to treatment in this chapter, consider the person-centered approach as a collaborative method with the other approaches outlined. Rogers advocates for a therapeutic stance of curiosity, non-judgement, unconditional positive regard, and exploration. It trusts in the humanistic view of our nature—our desire for connection and acceptance—and achieves change by respecting the unique personal journey that leads to our beliefs and behaviors. Through a focus on understanding and reducing the likelihood of defensiveness, the Rogerian therapist seeks to achieve their goals through the creation of a nurturing and safe place to explore their clients' thoughts, feelings, and potential behaviors. This becomes the only way people really engage in lasting change, from an internal shift in their beliefs fostered by critical self-reflection.

Cognitive Behavioral Therapy (CBT)

The CBT approach to change involves the therapist helping the client to think differently about their beliefs, negative self-concept, and actual and perceived unfair experiences with the idea that we can change our behavior when we change our thinking (Ellis, 2007; Glasser, 1975; 2001). This involves building rapport and assisting the white supremacist to learn to see things from a different point of view. This approach to care offers tools and techniques required to bring about change and assist them in shifting the way they approach their interactions. The therapist helps the client think differently about their problems and learn to behave in new ways. CBT has become a central treatment methodology in modern therapy with a high degree of empirically validated support.

Treatment starts with the identification and management of those daily challenges and frustrations the client experiences. This requires them to identify how their body is experiencing biological changes as they experience frustration and anger at those around them. These irritations and annoyances trigger biological reactions like an increased heart rate, rising blood pressure, and clenched fists. For example, if a client sees a same sex couple holding hands or kissing, a group of Black males gathered, or a Jewish man walking to a synagogue, their physiological response to their thoughts about these groups will lead to a visceral reaction. That is, they experience an increase in their heart rate and breathing, adrenaline is produced, and there is a reduced ability for creative and rational thought. Nay (2004) describes the process which starts with the stomach and GI systems emptying of blood as digestion slows or holds to free up blood for the brain and gross motor skills. This results in shallow breathing, a feeling of heaviness in the chest, and the sensation of suffocation. Senses become more reactive to stimuli, reactions become magnified, and movements might seem more threatening. Muscles tighten around the shoulders, neck, forehead, and jaw, while fine motor skills deteriorate.

Addressing the negative thought patterns will then decrease the related anger, hostility, and impulsive actions, and is likely going to be a central treatment needed for many following white supremacist ideologies. There are many activating events that occur in everyday interactions that have the potential to escalate into an explosive exchange. Nay (2004) outlines five "S" intensifiers toward anger and aggressive behavior, summarized with examples in Table 13.2. While few of these issues might be a chief complaint of the client, addressing their overall wellness, sleep, eating, stress, and substance use all have the potential to help reduce the potential for escalation.

Table 13.2 Anger Intensifiers (Nay, 2004)

Intensifier	*Description*	*Approach*
Sleep	Those who experience a lack of sleep often have difficulty focusing and experience increased frustrations. Sleep problems can come from different sources, including staying up too late, worrying about family finances, conflicts with peers, failing to get enough exercise, eating poorly and misusing substances.	Identify the cause of sleep problems through questioning and potential referral to medical services. Avoid a rush to judgement on the cause for sleep difficulties and first understand the nature of the problem.
Stress	Stress can drive us to higher production (eustress) or stop us from achieving our goals (distress). When we experience distress, it is difficult to remain focused on tasks and we become irritable, distracted, and prone to escalation.	Identify the sources of stress in the person's life and help them better understand how stress impacts academic, work, social, and emotional spheres in their lives. Help them to understand the nature of cumulative stress (e.g., stress that builds up over time) and how to reduce stress.
Substance abuse	Abuse of substances like alcohol, prescription drugs, THC, or illegal drugs such as cocaine or heroin can exacerbate our anger or reduce our impulse control in frustrating circumstances. This can also occur with other substances, such as caffeine or energy drinks.	Understand the role of substances for the client and help them better recognize how their choices to use might have a negative impact on their social, academic, work, and emotional interests. Identify times when they were angry and escalated where substances where involved.
Sustenance	Sustenance is related to how we care for our body, including the food we take in and the exercise we engage in. When our stress level rises, we might have an increasingly challenging time prioritizing diet and exercise. These remain important, however, in our ability to control our reactions and to prevent us from escalating into anger.	Identify negative patterns in their eating or exercise habits to develop a plan for improvement. This should start with small changes that are easily measured and obtainable for the person to experience growth and change.
Sickness	If we are sick, we have a harder time managing our stress and avoiding angry interactions fueled by our irritability and frustration. When we do not eat and sleep well, and choose foods and substances that are unhealthy, this also increases the risk of becoming sick.	Look for ways to engage in preventative actions to reduce the number of times the person becomes sick and thus less effective in managing their anger.

When one or more of the five are tenuous, the individual is also more vulnerable to recruitment messages. As a gardener ensures they have the right soil, sunlight, water, and nutrients for their plants, addressing anger intensifiers can be a useful backdrop to consider in our clinical work.

One approach to panning for change is outlined by the Navy SEALs, who offer some suggestions to mentally overcome the arduous physical challenges they face in their training. There are four key stress control techniques used to help the SEALs better cope with stress and stay focused on their goals (Blair, 2008). This approach is worth adapting to the extremist client.

1. **Goal Setting:** Goal setting helps the client develop a clear picture of their goals and find pathways to success. One way to accomplish this can be journaling about progress toward reaching their goals or creating a chart of times they were able to successfully navigate activating events or reduce impulsive action. The client should focus on setting immediate and measurable goals. A SEAL trainee might focus on "I need to make it to the next hill on the beach" or "I just need to stay under for another 5 seconds…I can do another 5 seconds." A client struggling with an aversion for LGBTQ+ people around them might need to focus on "I just need to avoid directly challenging them in public" or "I am going to focus on what is important to me in my relationships and stop becoming focused on what others are looking for in their relationships." Essentially, goal setting works best when it involves moving in small steps toward a larger change in thinking and behavior.

2. **Mental Rehearsal:** In the process of mental rehearsal, clients imagine themselves being successful at a particular interaction that has gone poorly in the past. If they have difficulty thinking about a problem, consider the ones related to their referral to counseling. Imagine a Navy SEAL trainee visualizing a successful mission. Sports psychologists also teach this technique for golfers when they make a swing. An example of mental rehearsal can be found in Table 13.3.

Table 13.3 Examples of Mental Rehearsal

Steps to Success	*Approach*
Identify a practical problem	Clearly visualize a conflict where you could become aggressive or continue to escalate.
Visualize a positive outcome	Imagine responding calmly and avoiding an escalation or allowing frustrations to develop. Create an image with clear details. Focus on the best possible response such as, "Well, that is certainly one way to see it. I do not see it the same way, though."
Problem Solving	Imagine obstacles to a successful interaction. Possibly imagine someone pushing or yelling back. Visualize your best possible response.
Practice	Repeat this process several times a week until you begin to see results.

3. **Self-Talk:** Positive self-talk is used to encourage clients to develop their own personal "cheerleading team" to encourage and help when they are struggling. Part of any treatment for a white supremacist includes identifying a supportive person in their life—a cheerleader—and then imagining that person mentally accompanying them during a conflict. While the conflict is escalating, the client can imagine the cheerleader saying, "You can do this. No way are they going to push your buttons. Calm and cool. The more they push; the more you relax." This positive self-talk could be used to reduce their negative reactions when they feel insulted, encounter something they feel strongly about, or other times they become triggered.
4. **Arousal Control:** This is about cycle breathing. The therapist teaches the client the importance of taking slow, deep breaths with controlled exhales. This helps them communicate to their body that this is not a panic (fight/flight/freeze) situation and allows them to maintain better control. As a point of comparison, this process is like what laboring mothers, Navy SEAL snipers, and meditating monks use to control their thoughts, feelings, and actions. This is a skill that requires practice and repetition to be successfully implemented in the long term.

Rational Emotive Behavioral Therapy (REBT)

Albert Ellis (2007) developed REBT to help clients identify irrational thoughts that occur in reaction to activating events. The REBT approach can be simplified to A-B-C: activating events, beliefs about these events, and the consequences of these beliefs. Assisting the client to challenge their perceptions regarding the connections they make from an activating event and their belief about it to their behavior in response is critical in helping them feel empowered to find alternative ways to view their world.

This process begins with the client identifying upsetting events and experiences and labeling these as activating events. These activating events can be daily hassles which they encounter in their environment (daily work stress, chronic teasing from those around them, financial worries, self-esteem), life changes (changes in status at school or work, family divorce or conflict, loss of a relationship), environmental stresses (construction noises, delays in getting something they want, chronic pain), or acculturation stress (moving from another location, living in a place where few people share their values). Few of these events can be prevented. Part of treatment involves identifying these stressful activating events and then applying techniques to improve the client's ability to cope and reduce the risk of escalation. The client is encouraged to appreciate and accept the continual presence of upsetting experiences; that they have little control over these activating events and instead must focus their energy on their reaction to them.

It is the development of alternative explanations that allows them to take better control of their reactions and choose non-violent ways to express themselves. Imagine how less likely we are to respond aggressively to the activating event of being cut off in traffic if we know the driver is rushing to the hospital to be with their dying parent. The cycle of escalation is disrupted once the aggressor can react better to the situation with empathy toward those upsetting them.

Reality Therapy

Reality therapy is a therapeutic system founded by Glasser (1975; 2001) that focuses on holding the client accountable for their behavior by creating plans with them to reach achievable goals. These are short-term plans focused on behavioral change. A plan like "David will stop being a racist Nazi in the classroom and workplace" is too broad and is not operationalized. This type of plan is difficult to put into action and monitor progress on. When the goal is subjective and broad, it is difficult to adjust or measure. The therapist would not be able to determine if David is moving forward, staying static, or moving backward. A better plan would clearly identify what behaviors contribute to David's racist and antisemitic behavior and how he could reduce these behaviors.

A good plan built upon reality therapy principles would operationalize small goals through teaching new skills and identifying obstacles that would stop the goal from being achieved. The plan would address specific behaviors such as using racial slurs or acting in a threatening or aggressive manner when they encounter people of color. The plan would identify problem areas and triggers, 'no-go' conversation topics, and help stop escalations before they reach a threatening or aggressive stage. The plan for David would encourage developing empathy and understanding why his current behaviors are off-putting and viewed as antisemitic.

Glasser (1975; 2001) provides a useful outline based on understanding of and assessing the needs of the client. This plan is abbreviated to WDEP – identifying their *wants* and needs, discussing what they are *doing* currently, *evaluating* that behavior, and *planning* and commitment to change. When reviewing plans with a client who expresses white supremacist beliefs, any treatment plans must be simple, attainable, measurable, immediate, consistent, controlled by the client, committed to by the client, and timely. Plans that are created in a hierarchical manner without being clearly outlined in measurable steps are doomed to failure.

Let's take the example of a client with several troubling misogynistic behaviors. These include street harassment or catcalling to women dressed in a perceived provocative manner and numerous complaints from females about unwanted flirtations leading to being called "sluts and whores." Addressing these behaviors from a reality therapy perspective first requires the client to catch themself in the process of getting ready to engage in a problematic behavior. Table 13.4 outlines some examples of how this approach might work.

Narrative Therapy

Everyone has a story. Narrative therapy, created by Australian family therapists Michael White and David Epston (1990), suggests that it is our client's stories about their lives that give meaning to their experiences. It is in these stories that we discover insight into the thinking, emotions, behaviors, and social and environmental experiences that shape an individual's rage and violence connected to the white supremacist movement. To shift them from these harmful beliefs, we must learn their stories. It is within these stories, formed by the individual's experience, that we become an ally to their future well-being.

Our client's stories are the manifestation of their truth. When we give value to these stories as foundational to their experience, we build a connection and open the door to change (Corey, 2001). Their stories are not static but evolving and dynamic. This provides opportunities to alter the course of the white supremacist. White and Epston (1990) write, "With every performance, persons are re-authoring their lives. The evolution of lives is akin to the process of re-authoring, the process of persons entering into stories, taking them over and making them their own" (Van Brunt, 2007, pp. 27–28; see White and Epston, 1990).

We can help our clients examine their lives within the context of the stories they tell. We can assist them in revising their stories and reconstructing

Table 13.4 A Practical Plan to Address Misogynistic Behaviors

Initial Behavior	*Negative Outcomes*	*Alternative Behavior*
Catch yourself while walking and tempted to engage in verbal callouts to a woman.	Consider the negative consequences of the behavior (e.g., dirty looks, bystander aggression, legal complication).	Consider the goal of the interaction (perhaps dating or hook up) and explore alternative, acceptable behavior to reach that goal.
Catch yourself while talking to an attractive woman in the library who tells you she would like to be left alone.	Understand that coming off as pushy or unwilling to take no for an answer will result in less interest by women in flirting or dating and can be harassing in nature.	Consider the goal of the interaction and look for settings where consensual flirtation is more appropriate (parties, bars, concerts).
Catch yourself when tempted to use negative language to describe women when rejected or frustrated.	Consider the negative consequences, including conduct actions or legal problem and negative reputation with others.	Given the anger is present, look at walking away or using a practiced, less negative script, "Ok, I understand."

narratives better adapted to their well-being. We can assist them to separate from negative, damaging stories and instead take ownership over them that leads to a more healthy and productive future. White and Epston (1990) describe these new, hopeful stories being shared between therapist and client. They provide numerous examples and techniques for building these new stories supporting the client's overall health in their book, *Narrative Means to Therapeutic Ends*.

The externalization of the story from the client becomes a first step in the narrative therapeutic approach. White (1988, 1989) writes, "Externalizing is an approach to therapy that encourages persons to objectify, and at times, to personify, the problems that they experience as oppressive" (p. 5). White and Epston (1990) posit that behavior, fears, and worries must be separated from the client prior to any attempt to reconstruct them. It would be reasonable for the indoctrinated white supremacist to clench their stories tightly out of fear they would lose the fabric of their life's meaning, purpose, and direction. "As persons become separated from their stories, they are able to experience a sense of personal agency; as they break from their performance of their stories, they experience a capacity to intervene in their own lives and relationships" (1990, p.16). When we externalize the story, it becomes like taking the carburetor out of the engine to repair it. By taking this action, we create the freedom to examine the nature of the problem, allowing new and unique outcomes to their stories. By adding detail, sensation, and emotion to their narratives, this process of "storying" offers insight into how the client creates meaning in their life.

Kopp (1995) offered a similar approach to narrative therapy. He suggests the therapist focus on the language, examples, metaphors, and analogies the client uses in descriptions of their life. It is in these narratives where we gain critical insight into how the white supremacist has come to believe what they do. Dr. Corsini describes it this way in the forward of Kopp's (1995) text:

> "the client and therapist, acting like detectives, look for clues to understanding the essence of the mystery by exploring and transforming the client's metaphoric language, hoping to find something that has little significance either to the client or to anyone who does not know the secret of the metaphor, but which, when the secret is revealed, becomes the key that opens the lock of the door that has stood between the person and freedom."
>
> (pp. ix–x)

As they follow these breadcrumbs of metaphor and language, the therapist gains the ability to help craft more optimistic and constructive outcomes.

Kopp (1995) gives the example of a patient who describes her husband's poor behavior. She talks of his poor attention, disrespectful communication concerning his coming and goings, and his laziness about looking for work. She shares, "he barges into the house like a locomotive" (p. xiv). Kopp used this description to gain insight into the client's dissatisfaction with the marriage and feelings of disempowerment. He asks her, "If he is a locomotive, what are you?" She clarifies what was being asked and replies with, "a tunnel" (p. xiv). Kopp asks, "What if you could change the image so that it would be better for you, how would you change it?" She thinks a moment and then suddenly exclaims, "I'd be the derailer!" (p. xv). This "self-as-derailer" metaphor becomes a shared construct between the therapist and patient. It provides scaffolding to support the client moving from a passive model (the tunnel) to an active model (the derailer). This gives them a way out; an opportunity to see their problems with new, unique, and optimistic outcomes.

For the white supremacist, the stories they tell themselves about being superior to other people, or powerless and enslaved to the Jews who control the banks, are essentially repeated messages that reinforce their existing stories from earlier in their life. By understanding and engaging in their story, the therapist creates opportunities to enter into a more powerful dialogue about the validity of these stories without having them tied directly to the client's self-worth and ego.

Existential Therapy

In a novel approach to engaging clients, Irvin Yalom (1980) outlines an approach to change in his book *Existential Psychotherapy* where behavior is seen as related to four ultimate concerns in life, dealing with the vastness of the freedom of our choices, the anxiety that exists when contemplating death, wrestling with what it means to relate to others yet being ultimately alone, and coming to terms with an ultimate meaning in our existence. Yalom offers these a broad landscape with an awareness that there is some overlap among the four domains.

These four challenges correspond well with the struggles faced by the white supremacist. While a more advanced therapeutic concept, we believe it will be helpful to see how some of these struggles directly relate to the struggles they face in leaving this ideology. The approach provides some keen understanding into the core factors that underpin the white supremacist's sadness and rage.

1 **Freedom:** While freedom might seem to be a positive concept, Yalom encourages us to look at the other side of freedom: How do we approach freedoms we have? What do we see when we stare into the abyss of limitless choices? Everywhere you look, you are faced with more options. How can someone investigate the infinite options for life and choose a path that they can feel confident about? Yalom (1980) writes: "'Freedom' in this sense, has a terrifying implication: it

means that beneath us there is no ground— nothing, a void, an abyss. A key existential dynamic, then, is the clash between' our confrontation with groundlessness and our wish for ground and structure." (p. 9). The white supremacist self-labeling as the superior race offers a comfort against the fear of freedom; it provides them with the highest amount of power and control when they see themselves as the best of all humanity.

2 **Death:** Even though we exist now, there will be a day we will cease to exist. Death waits us all and we are powerless to escape it. The famous Dutch philosopher, Benedict de Spinoza suggests, "Everything endeavors to persist in its own being." With this idea in mind, it becomes important for the therapist to help the client resolve "the awareness of the inevitability of death and the wish to continue to be" (1980, p. 8). Again here, the superiority of their existence as a member of the dominant race provides a comfort against the ultimate death that awaits us all. The stoic philosopher Lucretius offers a calming statement: "Where I am, death is not; where death is, I am not. Therefore death is nothing to me" (1980, p. 45). This might require the client to face some difficult realities about their own mortality. We can look for ways to help our clients explore their own mortality and find a larger sense of direction and meaning.

3 **Isolation:** While many of us have close connections with others, there is always a distance. For some that distance is a constant state. We are individuals in community. As humans, we seek human connection; it's part of our existence. Those who subscribe to the white supremacist ideology attempt to justify isolation by claiming domination over others. Yalom offers the following, "I believe that if we are able to acknowledge our isolated situations in existence and to confront them with resoluteness, we will be able to turn lovingly to others. If, on the other hand, we are overcome with dread before the abyss of loneliness, we will not reach toward others but instead will flail at them in order not to drown in the sea of existence" (1980, p. 363).

4 **Meaninglessness:** If we all must die, and if we are also ultimately alone in a universe of infinite choice; what meaning do our lives really have? The white supremacist is looking for meaning in a universe with no meaning. This existential dread drives their fantasies of being part of a something larger, more powerful, and dominant. This position provides a temporary respite against the meaninglessness of their existence. By offering an alternative way to conceptualize this dilemma, the therapist helps the client finds alternative ways to process their lack of meaning in life and helps them find healthy connections during their time on earth.

Box 13.1 Learning to Swim

Imagine you have an intense fear of the water. When learning to swim, this fear must be put aside. Facing this fear allows a swimmer to hold their breath and submerge. We cannot learn to swim until we wrestle and overcome our fear of the water, our fear of drowning. As we release our fear, we obtain mastery over the water; it has lost its ability to evoke fear. It is only through releasing our fears we can truly enjoy life. Yalom quotes Tolstoy early in the book saying, "he is dying badly because he has lived badly" (p. 33). The white supremacist might benefit from this approach to treatment in the same way. It is reasonable to understand their connection to the movement as part of a fear response. If minorities gain power, does that not them take away their power? As a therapist helps them address these fears, they work to become less threatened by concepts such as critical race theory, equity, the strength in the diversity of culture. We would suggest this is critical in the treatment approach to addressing white supremacist indoctrination.

Related to Yalom's work, Rollo May's (1983) book *The Discovery of Being* approaches change through a similar existential lens. May's work encourages emphasis on the immediacy of the moment and the corresponding power that lives in our freedom of choice. Individuals are not cast onto some deterministic path by their experience, and therapists should encourage their clients to take responsibility for their thoughts and actions. The client's task becomes finding meaning rather than feeding their obsession with superiority.

May introduces the term *dasein*, a German word meaning "being there," and how this can be used to develop a real encounter between client and therapist. This work should seem family to Rogers' concepts of genuineness and congruence in the therapeutic contact. May sees the client in terms of *potenia*, or "being" as a source of potentiality. He writes: "'being' is the potentiality by which the acorn becomes the oak or each of us becomes what he truly is" (1983, p. 97). May would encourage the therapist to ask the client who subscribes to white supremacist beliefs, "Where are you?" as opposed to "How are you?" This focus on where the client is now and where they are headed encourages focus on their potential rather than on their behaviors. It is here that the pain of exploration and introspection becomes a path to healing. To be successful in this approach, we see the moon, not the finger pointing to the moon. The therapist sees what the client can become, not their current state.

It is through our focus on direction, or "becoming," that takes us beyond the symptom reduction of CBT techniques and calls attention to the nature of the human connection present in client/therapist interaction. Given that we are each human entities, true *dasein*, we must be willing to experience each other's humanness first, rather than becoming solution focused. May (1983) says it this way:

> "Knowing another human being, like loving him, involves a kind of union, a dialectical participation with the other. This Binswanger calls the 'dual mode.' One must have at least a readiness to love the other person, broadly speaking, if one is to be able to understand him."
>
> (p. 93)

Here, it is the relationship that is healing, as Rogers writes (1961, 1980), rather than any advice or solutions. May (1983) quotes Fredia Fromm-Reichmann "The patient needs an experience, not an explanation."

The anxiety experienced by the white supremacist, and make no mistake they experience an intense amount of anxiety, is "the loss in the range of possibility" (May, 1983, p. 45). We are on our way to deprogramming someone from a white supremacist ideology when "the patient [can] focus on some point in the future when he will be outside his anxiety or depression" (1983, p. 135). It is this anxiety that can be seen as a manifestation of fear of non-being. As a result, treatment focus should move away from mere symptom relief to helping the white supremacist face their fear and place it in the appropriate context. We cannot explain away pathological anxiety by argument, mesmerism, or medication. To do this work successfully from an existential approach, we must nod across from the client and say, "You are correct. Death is terrifying. There are too many choices. We are out of control." Change comes from acknowledging the pain as they gain power and comfort over their life choices and find solace in the revelation we are in this together, that we are the same, whether a Jew, person of color, gay or lesbian, Muslim or female.

We acknowledge that this might be a controversial shift for many readers, particularly given the prevalence of the CBT treatment approach. However, our work cannot merely be symptom relief, whether it is the redirection of needs or supplanting of desires. We must examine the true underpinnings or the purpose behind the symptoms. May (1983) offers this example to encourage us to focus on our client's potential, writing that you are "teaching a farmer irrigation while damming up his streams of water" (p. 164). This kind of direct connection is overly simplistic. We can teach white supremacists to keep their intense beliefs to themselves if they wish to stay enrolled in school or employed in the workplace, but if we silence them, this provides no real solution.

Motivational Interviewing

Motivational interviewing, or motivational enhancement therapy (MET), was developed by Miller and Rollnick (1991) as treatment for defensive clients with alcohol dependency and/or abuse. The approach has been used to work with other clients who are resistant to treatment or behavioral change, which makes it a proactive approach to working with white supremacist clients who are often unwilling to shift their core beliefs or are unsure how to untangle themselves from their past connections related to this ideology. Miller and Rollnick's approach outlines five, non-progressive, non-hierarchical concepts that can be applied well to working with clients who are mandated to treatment. An application of this approach with a white supremacist client who aligns with the Ku Klux Klan (KKK) is included in Table 13.5.

• **Express Empathy:** The expression of empathy requires not only the experience of empathy with a client, but also conveying to the client that you are seeing their perspective. This expression of empathy respects the client's point of view, freedom of choice and ability to determine their

Table 13.5 Addressing KKK Indoctrination through Motivational Interviewing

Stage	*Therapist Task*
Express Empathy	Explore where these beliefs originated for the client. Use open ended questions to gain perspective. How have they been treated by others for holding these beliefs? What is it like for them to feel that way?
Avoid Argumentation	Avoid direct arguments about their thoughts, but instead focus on understanding and clarifying their position and how they support their ideas. Explore exceptions to the rule (e.g., "Have there been times where you met a Black person who surprised you by the way they were?")
Roll with Resistance	When they push back on change or concepts, consider alternative ways to engage them in conversations. If they are locked strongly in an opinion, explore times where they saw these ideas differently. Consider exploring times they use terms like "all," "everyone," and "always." Attend to the push/pull nature of their having to constantly defend their point of view preventing them from considering alternative points of view.
Develop Discrepancy	Explore, through curious, open-ended questions, how these beliefs have helped or hurt their experiences in school, work, and relationships. Help them see ways their beliefs might be limiting their choices and options.
Support Self-efficacy	Find times where you have points of agreement and praise them when they exhibit qualities you have been encouraging such as critical thinking and finding exceptions to the rule, or when they show vulnerability and/or a willingness to consider alternative perspectives.

own self-direction. Suggestions from the therapist for change are subtle and the responsibility for change lies with the client.

Box 13.2 Empathize with the KKK?

There are significant challenges to working with the white supremacist. There are reasonable parallels to the challenges working with someone who engages in domestic violence, drunken driving, or child abuse. There is no sympathy for those who express hatred, seek to marginalize, silence, of commit violence against others. There can be no quarter given to justify or redirect blame for these individuals' actions. People have choice in these matters, regardless of their trauma experience, upbringing, or difficulties in life. When using treatment approaches that advocate understanding the client's perspective, the therapist must share this understanding without endorsing the ideology that advocates hate and violence toward others. We struggle in our writing to convey the importance of understanding with the purpose of bringing about change, which can seem like a less than vigorous condemnation of their ideology. However, if we do not create an environment that fosters change, we are essentially risking the lives of those very people we are working hard to protect.

- **Avoid Argumentation:** When you argue with your client, neither of you are listening to the other and any change remains elusive. The client is considering counter arguments to your points as you consider how to react to their arguments. There is a power in taking a break if you find yourself arguing with the client. Take some time to explore more deeply what they are saying. Open ended, exploratory questions often reduce the client's defensiveness and provide an opportunity to shift and clarify beliefs without first having to overcome that defensiveness.
- **Roll with Resistance:** As with the cautions expressed with avoiding argumentation, rolling with resistance encourages the therapist to avoid direct confrontation, but instead stay focused on goals and outcomes. The therapist should look for ways to address a client's resistance to change by engaging them in new and innovative ways of thinking. When clients present with a lack of motivation or an unwillingness to embrace change, this should be seen as part of a normal developmental responses. Our interventions should not be mired down in the client's unwillingness to change, but rather focus on supporting their developmental growth and personal responsibility to change.
- **Develop Discrepancy:** Developing discrepancy encourages the therapist to engage the client in a debate when the client presents with ideas that do not logically lead them to a desired outcome. By

exploring the consequences of the client's behavior in a neutral manner, avoiding sarcasm or a condescending tone, the therapist helps clients understand that the current behavior will not help them achieve the desired goal. The goal is increased awareness from the client as they increase their ability to take ownership in their choices and begin to explore the advantages to choosing a different way to behave.

- **Support Self-efficacy:** Supporting self-efficacy has the therapist praise the client when they take actions in a positive direction. There is an acknowledgement that change can occur and a more positive future is possible. The therapist finds occasions and opportunities to "catch them doing well," praising this behavior to shape future positive behavior.

Transtheoretical Change Theory

Transtheoretical change theory was created by Prochaska, Norcross, and DiClemente (1994). In their book, *Changing for Good*, they offer an excellent overview of this process we all experience when try to make changes in our lives. This theory is helpful when wrestling with the question "Why is it so hard for the white supremacist to see the harm they are causing and just learn to appreciate individual differences?"

Change theory can help the client gain a sense of perspective and understanding about why they repeat difficult or frustrating behaviors. Consider a behavior you have tried to change in your life to think about while reading. This could be a current struggle or something you have tried to change in the past, perhaps smoking, watching too much TV, or not getting enough exercise. As you read this section, keep your example in mind to better understand this process.

1 Pre-contemplation: At this stage, the client is unaware they have a problem and has not considered change. Our goal is to increase awareness about the need for change. The therapist adopts a non-judgmental, non-directive open discussion aimed at helping the client see how their behaviors might be impacting their life and those around them. There is no sharing advice at this stage since they do not believe they have a problem and have no desire to change. Until the client wants to change their behavior, the therapist's advice or positive suggestions will be ignored.
2 Contemplation: We find ourselves in this stage most often. Here, your client might have thought about change and might be considering doing something different soon. They have started to understand that their current behavior is not in their best interest. However, while they are not happy with their current situation and wish things could be different, they are not ready to actually

implement changes at this stage. The therapist's goal here is to encourage and motivate their client to consider how their behavior is affecting themselves and those around them. The client should explore ways they might begin to plan to make change and assess what resources they might need to make that change happen. The therapist should not focus on the specifics of *how* the plan would be implemented, but rather explore *why* they might want to behave differently.

3 Preparation for Action: Here, the client knows they have a problem and is ready to develop a plan to bring about change. Plans and goals will work best when they are short-term, focused, and able to be adapted to ensure their success. Goals should be measurable and easy to monitor in terms of their progress. The therapist is most useful at this stage assisting the client brainstorm and update their plans to improve their success once the action phase begins.

4 Action: This stage involves the client putting their plans into action. They will attempt to alter their negative behaviors and develop new positive behaviors to replace them. The therapist can support the client by helping them implement action steps and encouraging them to remain resilient in their efforts, particularly when things might not progress as easily as the client might like.

5 Maintenance and Relapse Prevention: The main tasks here are to continue successful plans and repeat those action steps that are working while adjusting the parts of the plan that are not working. Change has occurred and the client has had some success achieving their goals. They need to maintain their progress and seek to mitigate the risk of returning to negative behaviors. The therapist helps support their success by identifying and encouraging an awareness of potential obstacles that could lead to relapse.

Moving Forward

This chapter provided an overview of the treatment approaches that might be used to help when working with those who are at-risk of or already enmeshed in white supremacy indoctrination. The next three chapters will review the case studies from Chapter 8, completing a violence risk assessment for each and offering treatment recommendations using the approaches outlined here.

Discussion Questions

- After reviewing the various treatment ideas suggested in this chapter, which ones resonate the most with you in terms of offering help and bringing about change?

- Give an example of how you might apply one of these techniques to a case discussed so far in the book.
- Is there a treatment method you have used that was not mentioned that you believe would work with this population?
- Using the change theory model discussed in this chapter, pick a behavior in your life that you have either successfully changed or have struggled with changing. Map out this behavior using the five levels of: pre-contemplation, contemplation, preparation, action, relapse/maintenance.

References

Amaya-Jackson, L., Reynolds, V., Murray, M.C., McCarthy, G., Nelson, A., Cherney, M.S., and March, J.S. (2003). Cognitive behavioral treatment for pediatric posttraumatic stress disorder: Protocol and application in school and community settings. *Cognitive and Behavioral Practice*, 10, 204–213. doi:10.1016/S1077-7229(03)80032-9.

Blair, C. (2008). Better test performance the Navy SEALs way. Retrieved from http://studyprof.com/blog/2008/11/25/better-test-performance-the-navy-seals-way.

Cohen, J.A., Mannarino, A.P., Murray, L.K., and Igelman, R. (2006). Psychosocial interventions for maltreated and violence-exposed children. *Journal of Social Issues*, 62, 737–766.

Corey, G. (2001). *Theory and practice of counseling and psychotherapy*. Belmont, CA: Brooks/Cole Thompson Learning.

Ellis, A. (2007). *The Practice of rational emotive behavior therapy*. New York, NY: W.W. Norton & Company.

Glasser, A. (1975). *Choice Theory: A New Psychology of Personal Freedom*. New York, NY: Colophon Books.

Glasser, A. (2001). *Counseling with choice theory: The new reality therapy*. New York, NY: Colophon Books.

Kopp, R.R. (1995). *Metaphor Therapy*. New York, NY: Brunner/Mazel, Inc.

May, R. (1983). *The Discovery of Being*. New York, NY: W.W. Norton & Company.

Miller, W.R. and Rollnick, S. (1991). *Motivational Interviewing: Preparing People to Change Addictive Behavior*. New York, NY: Guilford Publications.

Nay, R. (2004). *Taking Charge of Anger*. Guilford Press.

Prochaska, J., Norcross, J., and DiClemente, C. (1994). *Changing for Good*. Harper Collins.

Rogers, C. (1961). *On Becoming a Person*. New York, NY: Houghton Mifflin.

Rogers, C. (1980). *A Way of Being*. New York, NY: Houghton Mifflin.

Van Brunt, B. (2007). *The Thematic Apperception Test (TAT): Administration and interpretation*. Prescott, AZ. Borrego Publishing.

White, M. (1988–1989). The externalizing of the problem and the reauthoring of lives and relationships. *Dulwich Centre Newsletter*, pp. 5–28.

White, M. and Epston, D. (1990). *Narrative Means to Therapeutic Ends*. New York, NY: W.W. Norton & Company.

Yalom, I. (1980). *Existential Psychotherapy*. Basicbooks.

14 Treatment Approaches for Hank

These next three chapters were written as if the case detail presented in Chapter 8 was an actual case referred for assessment and treatment. This approach will provide the reader with a look at how a therapist, psychologist or other practitioner can blend the risk and protective factors in each scenario with the White Supremacist Indoctrination Rubric (WSIR) to form a violence risk assessment (VRA). The approach outlined is one of many ways to organize the case data and is presented as an example useful for those new to the VRA process to better understand the flow throughout the VRA and treatment recommendation.

For those looking to improve their interviewing skills needed to conduct a VRA in person, we would recommend reading *Harm to Others: The Assessment and Treatment of Dangerousness* (Van Brunt, 2015). The book was written primarily for therapists, clinicians, social workers, and psychologists who are increasingly being asked to conduct VRAs as part of their practice. While a clinical license is not required to conduct a VRA, these should always be conducted by those with 1) an in-depth knowledge of threat assessment principles; 2) the proper training on assessment, rapport building, deception detection, and interviewing skills; and 3) adequate supervision and focus on quality improvement and scholarship in the ever-evolving field of threat assessment.

The VRA is made up of six steps:

1 **Gather thematic case data.** When conducting a VRA, the first step is to review the case details in a written format. This helps the assessor gather the relevant case details to categorize them for later analysis. Imagine a blank piece of paper or an empty Microsoft Word document. This is our opportunity to outline pertinent case details prior to moving forward in the analysis. This organization of the fact pattern from the case often takes the longest and is what the other sections directly reference. For the purpose in this chapter, the thematic case data pulls together the facts of the case into a more accessible format.

DOI: 10.4324/9781003199656-14

2 **Identify risk factors.** Based on the thematic analysis (or interview) of the case details, the next step is reviewing the presence of risk factors outlined in Chapter 9. For clarity, these are separated into three categories: 1) present; 2) in need of further exploration; and 3) not present. These risk factors should be seen as one side of the preverbal teeter/totter and will be balanced with the corresponding protective factors outlined in Chapter 10. As mentioned in Chapter 12, a good VRA considers both risk and protective factors when assessing the nature of risk. The risk factors provided should also be seen as a floor, rather than a ceiling of factors. Quality VRA work requires continual review of threats and attacks and should be continually evolving.

3 **Identify protective factors.** Once the risk factors are identified, then next step is identifying the protective factors that serve to scaffold or offset the potential risk of an attack. As Dr. Murphy outlines in Chapter 10, these protective and stabilizing factors serve to mitigate the impact of stressful life events and reduce the overall risk of an escalation on the pathway to violence. Later in the VRA process, the goal becomes to address the escalation caused by the risk factors and increase the number and nature of the protective factors to further reduce the risk of violence.

4 **Apply the White Supremacist Indoctrination Rubric (WSIR).** When assessing the risk of a particular population such as incels, terrorists or sexual offenders, it is useful to gauge the specific nature of those risks related to the unique views of these attackers. It is critical to understand the WSIR is a small part of the overall VRA when assessing a white supremacist for an escalation in violence. The WSIR provides insight related to level of indoctrination in the ideology based on past attacks. This is useful both in contextualizing the nature of the risk factors as well as tailoring treatment and intervention techniques.

5 **Create risk narrative.** This step involves taking the above data and telling a story of the potential violence in natural and accessible language. This does not mean simplistic, but rather crafting the story of potential violence in a way that is useful, likely, and supported by the risk and protective factors as well as the WSIR.

6 **Develop and implement interventions.** The intervention step outlines a go-forward strategy for the referral source. These interventions are varied and should address specific risk factors that should be reduced along with protective and stabilizing factors to be increased. These interventions should include therapeutic treatment, address social and peer influences, conduct and law enforcement involvement, family, and community support. Interventions should be holistic in nature and address all the areas that impact the individual.

In the remainder of this chapter, we will review the case of Hank using this six-step model and then offer some additional therapeutic treatment recommendations based on Chapter 13. The cases of Jessie and Dawson will be discussed in subsequent chapters using the same model.

The Case of Hank

1 Thematic Case Analysis of Hank

Location and People

- High school student at a small (200 students) school; rural, conservative community with high gun ownership rates and hunting is common
- Hank is identified at risk
- Father is manager of factory in town

  a Gets angry at David teasing Hank, throws a dinner roll and says, "I'm not gonna tolerate that kind of language at my dinner table. Particularly when you can't even get a full-time job, Mr. Football."

- Mother works as administrator at church
- Two younger sisters, not much known about them
- David is brother:

  a Athletic, numerous friends, dating cheerleaders
  b Graduated and works part time at hardware store in town
  c Teasing Hank about being gay, about how Hank cannot find a girlfriend
  d Argues with Hank and uses incel language "Ha, I never had any problem with the girls—maybe it's because you are a beta-cuck, little fag-bitch. Probably need to stop sucking meat with your two wanking Nazi friends."

- Chris is only mentioned as a friend of David and Austin
- Austin

  a Childhood friend of Hank and Chris
  b His father is involved in Proud Boys movement and has become more active when a Chinese-based factory moved to town.
  c o Austin shares father's frustration with the factory, complains about immigrants taking hard-working Americans' jobs.
  d He disparages the Black Lives Matter movement by claiming it was funded by Jewish interests to destabilize the country.
  e o Austin says, "All the immigrants and blacks think about is how bad it is for them and how everything is about slavery. It's

the same with the Jews...freaking Anudda Shoah and everything is about the holocaust. Like we don't have it hard."

f Pressures Chris and Hank to "man up" and do something about the overtaking of our country.

g o Talks at school with Chris and Hank about how girls are attracted to "money, like the Jews, or the athletic, dumb blacks".

- Hank

a o Talking with Chris and Austin, Hank says, "They keep dating these freaking Chads who treat them like shit. I swear, these bitches get what they deserve. Nice guys always finish last."

b o Socially isolated, not athletic, has not dated much

c o Junior in high school

d o Recently joined online chat rooms to learn more about white supremacy

e o Posts on Twitter a quote from the Charleston Shooters manifesto ""I see all this stuff going on, and I don't see anyone doing anything about it." (Chapter 7: case 54)

f o Hank says to Chris and David, "I can see how all this works. Everything is set up against us. Something needs to change. They're taking over."

g o Hank argues with his brother David when teased about fake media and how girls at the high school chase the wrong guys

h o After an argument at the dinner table, retreats in tears after father throws a roll at his brother's head

i o Begins to isolate self, misses school, perhaps depressed

j o Learn he has been wearing cap with 88 on it and a shirt with RAHOWA

k o He is being bullied by other students

l o Calls another student a Jewish slur in the cafeteria

Of Note

- Austin (one of Hanks friends) use the term "Anudda Shoah", which is a white supremacist phrase used to mock Jews by implying that anytime something goes wrong they bring up the holocaust. This is both a highly insulting phrase and also demonstrates a high degree of insider knowledge of white supremacist doctrines to use such an insult so casually.
- There is frequent incel language referenced demonstrating that Hank has a good knowledge of this and might be researching this on the internet to find support for his lack of success at dating.

a Chad is defined as genetically superior male who is desirable to Stacie.

  b Stacie is the ideal, genetically superior white female that is taken by Chad.

- David, Hank's brother, also uses this incel and homophobic language

  a Beta-cuck defines males who are taken advantage of by women and are less than the genetically superior Chad.

- Mentions of Hank wearing a cap with 88 on it. This references the eighth letter of the alphabet (H) and refers to Heil Hitler, a symbol of the white supremacist movement.
- Mentions of Hank wearing a shirt with RAHOWA which is another symbol of the white supremacist movement and means RA=Racial, HO=Holy, WA=War.

2 Identify Risk Factors for Hank

Present Factors

- **Hardened point of view.** Hank has certainly begun to develop a hardened point of view concerning immigrants, fake media, why he is unsuccessful dating and his affiliation with a past attacker in Charleston.
- **Drivenness and a justification for violent action.** While there is not a specific fixation or focus to an attack plan or violent action, the recent isolation, teasing, and escalating behaviors should be seen as cause for concern.
- **Grievance or dangerous injustice collection.** It would be reasonable to see Hank's frustration at women to be an injustice that he perceives as something he must unfairly endure.
- **Feelings of isolation and hopelessness.** There is current evidence of increased isolation and sadness, without direct mention of suicidal thoughts. The recent tearful retreat from the dining room table and the missing of school leads to a reasonable assumption that this area is increasing.
- **Marginalization.** The bullying and teasing Hank is experiencing from his brother and at school give evidence to this area increasing. Hank likely feels different from others and particularly marginalized when it comes to his perceived rejection from women.
- **Objectification and depersonalization.** These are central to Hank's feelings as he interacts with others. More and more, there is evidence he sees other students who are black, Jewish, or female as undeserving of agency or personhood.
- **Catalyst events.** The increase in teasing from his brother and continued frustration with successfully dating likely are driving an

escalation in his behavior. There are likely pending conduct actions for his cafeteria slur to the girl that could result in suspension.

- **Experience of teasing and bullying.** The school officials share Hank is experiencing more bullying from other classmates. This also happens at the hands of his brother.
- **Free fall.** There does seem to be a movement in Hank's experience to a general worsening of his life in several different areas (school, home life, dating, academics).
- **Decrease in academic or work progress.** There is a lack of interest and assumed corresponding drop in grades related to Hank's school. The potential school discipline actions are also pending and create a potential for further academic problems.
- **Social isolation.** While Hank does have connections with Chris and Austin, these connections are potentially complicated as they escalate his behavior. Hank's experience with rejection by the girls at the school further leads to his isolation, loneliness, and potential hopelessness.
- **Lack of empathy and remorse for actions.** Hank seems to lack an awareness of how his behaviors impacts others. Examples of this are his broad, angry statements to friends and escalations using the Jewish slur in the school cafeteria.

In Need of Further Exploration

- **Actionability.** There is not a clear mention of Hank specifically having his own firearm, but as Hank's father and brother are frequent hunters, there are guns in the house. Hank has gone hunting with his dad, but it is unclear if he observed or hunted using a firearm.
- **Suicidal.** There is growing evidence of Hank's anger, frustration, sadness, and impulsivity that should lead to a deeper exploration of suicidal thoughts and ideas.
- **Desire for fame.** Thought there does not seem to be desire for fame or glory, this might be present in his internet usage and should be explored.
- **Fantasy rehearsals.** There is no direct evidence that Hank is escalating in any type of attack plan. It would be worthwhile to explore his internet chat room discussions to determine if there is more here that is unknown school officials.

Not Present

- **Threats.** There do not appear to be any direct or indirect threats of violence presented in this case.
- **Use of substance.** There is no current evidence of substance use or abuse. Given Hank is a high school junior, it would be worth

exploring his potential use with his friends Chris and Austin, and their desire to keep that hidden to not get into trouble with school officials, police, or family.

- **Mental illness.** There is no current evidence of mental illness beyond Hank's need for a deeper suicide assessment and recent increase in isolation and sadness.
- **Fascination with violence.** There is no evidence in this case that Hank is showing a focus on violence or a fantasy rehearsal related to violent themes. More details could be obtained from his internet usage.

3 Identify Protective Factors for Hank

- **Environmental and emotional stability.** Hank is part of a large family (one of four children) with a mother and father who are both employed with all basic needs being met. There is some friction between Hank and his brother, which will need to be further explored to determine if this is a historical issue with them or if this has worsened with David's graduation and lack of moving out of the house. Hank does not appear to be working and lacks engagement with school in terms of a career and his current academic progress. There is little stability in his emotions and change seems to further escalate Hank toward frustration. Overall, this factor seems somewhat present for Hank, but it could be strengthened in terms of employment and/or future career aspirations (particularly with David having challenges moving on from the house). There seem to be opportunities for improvement, particularly with the school noticing the escalation in the behavior and making a request for therapeutic intervention.
- **Social health and connection.** This is a central struggle for Hank, particularly around his difficulty dating and the teasing about him being gay. The incel exploration in the online space will increase challenges with social health and connection to others. Hank seems to have little social connection with others beyond Chris and Austin and lacks a healthy view of masculinity. Social relationships at the school remain strained and difficult. He also lacks any club, organization, or sports connection with others.
- **Access and satisfaction with non-violent outlets.** Hank lacks these connections and appears to be receiving most of his socialization from outlets that increase his risk of escalation toward violence (internet chat rooms, Chris, and Austin). There is little going on in his life that is stimulating, rewarding, engaging or fun.
- **Empathy.** Hank lacks empathy toward others and has recently been escalating in behaviors that are likely to increasingly raise this risk moving forward. It is likely he would have the ability to consider the perspective of others, but has few opportunities at home, with friends and at school to be encouraged to do this.

- **Cognitive clarity and pluralistic awareness.** This area should be seen in context of a young man's developmental process as a sixteen-year-old. It is likely Hank would be open to these ideas and this protective factor would be useful for him to engage in perspective taking and potentially caring for others. At this time, this is a protective factor that is not present, yet might be a potential area of future growth.

4 Apply the White Supremacist Indoctrination Rubric for Hank

Overall, Hank scores in the 2–3 range on all five of the WSIR scales. This should be seen as someone who has a casual but growing interest in the white supremacist movement.

Hank is confronted by the school for wearing an 88 cap and a shirt with "RAHOWA" on it, both concerning white supremacist symbols representing *Casual Collection* (3) on **Appearance**. He does not appear to be overly connected with any group beyond a *Passing Interest* (2) on **Affiliation**. Hank looks online for materials and would likely be at the *Casual Exploration* phase (3) on **Absorption**. Hank's father takes him hunting, so this would lead to *Casual Exploration* (3) on **Acquisition**. Hank seems to have a *Passing Interest* (2) in terms of **Appointment** to a mission.

5 Create Risk Narrative for Hank

Hank has been identified as someone early on the pathway to violence. While he lacks a current attack plan with any fixation or focus on a target, his behavior is concerning and getting worse. Without intervention, it is likely that Hank will escalate to committing increasingly violent actions towards women, Jews, Blacks, or immigrants. Based on the lack of focus and narrowing to a specific group, it would be more likely to see an escalation with incidents of aggression and threats like we saw in the cafeteria with the Jewish slur.

Hank retreats into his online group support through his online conversations and usernames. This might serve as a fantasy rehearsal where he sees himself as someone with a sense of purpose, authority, and dominance; all attractive qualities for someone teased, isolated, and rejected. There are also indications that this online connection might relate to incel ideology, which is likely to increase Hank's anger at the

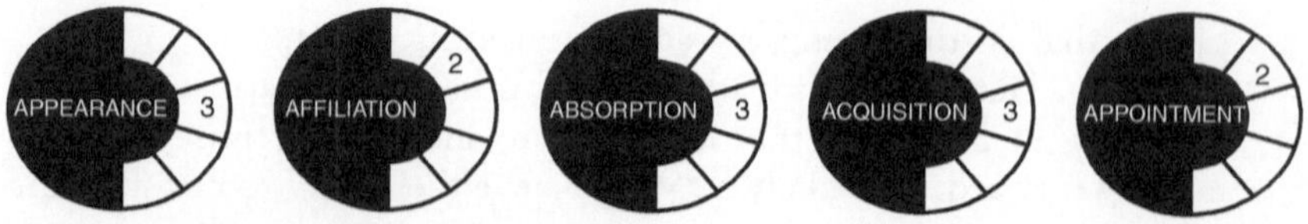

Figure 14.1 WSIR: Hank

rejection he experiences from women. This, in turn, exacerbates feelings of hopelessness, worthlessness, and potential suicidality, a particular concern in a home where there is easy access to firearms.

Hank's clothing indicates support of white supremacist ideas. It would be advisable to further explore where these items (hat with 88 and RAHOWA shirt) came from to see if there are larger connections to the white supremacist movement related to these purchases. There should be a further assessment of his knowledge and access to firearms. Likewise, given Hank's close connection to Chris and Austin, any exploration around weapons access should involve all three boys.

Hank might be motivated to escalate his violence by his frustration at being over-looked by his female classmates. Future violence might be motivated by an upsetting event which arouses and upsets him, triggering an impulsive reaction. Likewise, he might feel motivated to act violently to save face and convince Chris, Austin, or those in the online conversations that he is committed to the ideology. His violence could be an attempt to control or change his circumstances or to gain a sense of honor, justice, and self-esteem, as he often feels bullied, teased, and marginalized.

There are several disinhibitors for this violence including a negative self-concept, lack of integration socially with others, and increasing negative attitudes about the future. Two disinhibitors for violence of particular concern are a lack of anxiety and lack of guilt related to the incident in the cafeteria. Hank does not to appear to have any pressing destabilizers such as obsessive thoughts, inability to reason, impaired memory, or disturbed perception.

Overall, Hank's current risk for violence would be estimated as low, with a strong concern that without intervention this would increase to moderate soon. Hank's incident in the cafeteria should be used as leverage to connect him to counseling to address the growing concerns of his academic progress, along with the potential approach behaviors for violence. These escalating approach behaviors would include his use of the slur directly to a female student and his increased absorption of white supremacist ideology manifested by his acquisition and display of imagery on his clothes. Hank would strongly benefit from encouragement to connect with different social groups, clubs, organizations, or athletic teams. He should look to develop increased interpersonal skills related to dating as well as identify academic and future goals. To put it simply, he is a lost boy who has been found by a dangerous group. Interventions should focus on both separating him from this group, finding new ways he can connect, and identifying pathways to a better future.

6 *Interventions for Hank*

Clear limits set by the school around any future behavior. While a zero-tolerance policy[1] would not be supported by literature or best practice, clear and consistent disciplinary action attuned to the behavior is warranted. There is an excellent opportunity to leverage counseling with his ability to stay engaged in school. Obtaining parental buy-in for this process is critical.

There should be efforts to address the risk of Chris, Austin, and Hank encouraging and supporting each other in more extreme interactions.

Austin presents another risk of escalation, and a separate assessment of this risk would be recommended based on his interactions with Hank. There is little information shared about the third friend, Chris, but exploring his involvement and ideology would be recommended as well.

The school should review and monitor these events through its campus Behavioral Intervention Team (BIT) or CARE team to ensure timely and proper follow-up. This might include obtaining release of information forms from Hank's therapist to ensure progress and compliance with expectations.

An intervention goal is to identify and connect Hank to alternative social outlets where he feels connection and support from his peers.

There should be an exploration of a restorative justice student conduct process to address Hank's cafeteria incident, provided the other student and her parents are amenable to this as an option and that it does not cause further harm.

Guns should be removed from the home if the parents are willing. If removal is not an option at this time, ensure his parents have guns locked and safe. If there is an existing safe or locks, encourage them to change the combination or location of the keys. Chris and Austin's access to firearms should also be assessed.

The school should develop or use its existing process related to bullying and teasing reduction. The bullying and teasing that Hank, Austin, and Chris might experience could contribute to an environment of further marginalization, isolation, and frustration.

Areas of Further Exploration

- Further explore the online conversations and usernames, including social media posts. Are there multiple usernames? Does he serve in an administrator or moderator capacity? Have these connections resulted in any in-person meet ups, conventions, or social engagements? This could be accomplished through coordination with law enforcement or third-party security groups to conduct an open-source intelligence process to assess his social media and online activities.
- Given his absorption of white supremacist ideology online, there should be efforts to further identify key elements that motivate his focus. For example, is he driven by thoughts of Black men taking the women he should rightfully have or Jews taking opportunities from him for a better future?

- There should be further exploration of where Hank obtained his clothing and hat with white supremacist logos and markings. There might be additional connections through these purchases, perhaps over the internet, dark web or in person. Determine if the parents knew about this and if the items delivered to the house.
- Disinhibitors related to a potential lack of guilt, anxiety, or remorse about the racial slur in the cafeteria should be explored. Consideration should be given to determine if this was an assignment from an online or in-person group to test Hank's commitment to the cause. Further, was this an unprovoked comment or a response to teasing? How did he feel after the incident? Was there a sense of empowerment?
- While Hank's father throwing a dinner roll at David does not necessarily lead to an assumption of violence in the home, it is worth future exploration. Similarly, little is said about Hank's sisters. Their relationship to Hank is an important area of exploration.

Counseling and Therapeutic Interventions

A referral to therapy should address some of these general concepts:

- Discussing impulse control and frustration tolerance
- Identifying triggers for his anger and developing alternative ways he could behave when upset or frustrated
- Identifying and encouraging academic or career interests as a source of positive connection
- Exploring online connections to determine the extent of indoctrination and the motivations of the behavior (e.g., does it provide social support Hank is lacking?)
- Discussing family life, including developing coping and response skills to David's teasing in the home
- Social skills training related to dating along with an identification of irrational beliefs and expectations
- Exploring his absorption of white supremacist ideology
- Developing additional resiliency skills to address bullying and teasing from others at school
- Assessing potential suicidal thoughts or behaviors
- Developing empathy skills and encouragement to better understand the experience of others
- Developing critical thinking skills that allow for multiple perspectives, alternative beliefs, and a reduction in Hank's hardened perspective

Treatment Notes for Hank

Therapeutic suggestions for treatment are typically not included in these types of VRA assessments beyond suggestions for the type and frequency of therapeutic treatment. These recommendations are included above. For the purpose of this book, the authors provide some suggestions based on the therapeutic approaches outlined in Chapter 13. These are organized based on the counseling and therapeutic interventions provided in the VRA above. As mentioned previously, it will be uncommon to receive this level of therapeutic direction in most VRAs, typically the comments are "outpatient therapy recommended." If there is lack of direction from the VRA, the clinician will first begin with drafting these treatment recommendations based on their review of the VRA.

- **Impulse control and frustration tolerance.** Much of our reactions to the events around us can be seen through the lens of REBT's A-B-Cs (Ellis, 2007). The therapist would first assist Hank in seeing the activating events that trigger him. Next, they would explore the beliefs he has about these occurring around him. For example, seeing a Black male talking to a white girl as directly reducing his chances at dating. Next, the therapist would encourage Hank to share his current behaviors in terms of the consequences of his beliefs. Finally, they would begin to explore alternative beliefs that lead to alternative consequences.
- **Identify anger triggers.** Leaning into the Rogerian (1961,1980) counseling approach, this goal could be accomplished by open-ended questioning about the nature of the things that make Hank upset around him. By using open-ended questions and engaging in active listening, the therapist would be able to explore the triggers that get Hank upset and begin a discussion of alternative ways of seeing these triggers. Helping Hank understand the role of anger intensifiers (Nay, 2004) in his life would be another way to help decrease the chance of a negative reaction by improving his frustration tolerance and impulse control.
- **Identify academic/career interests.** Too often in this type of therapy the focus becomes on the reduction of triggering events. While these are important first steps, additional exploration of future goals and identifying ways for Hank to connect to his schoolwork and potential college or first job would help provide a sense of hope and accomplishment. Here the therapist could draw on reality therapy planning skills (Glasser, 1975; 2001) and explore the existential dilemma of too much freedom of choice (May, 1983; Yalom, 1980) when considering future career options. To aid this process, a direct referral to career counselors and the use of computer software designed to identify potential careers that Hank would enjoy and find fulfilling would be helpful.
- **Explore online activity.** This should be approached by looking at a cost/benefit analysis of the positive and negative consequences of his online use. What is a common experience for him online? What

friends has he made? What are the things he finds positive about these chat groups? What things has he seen that made him feel uncomfortable that he would disagree with? Explore his online connections to determine the extent of indoctrination and the motivations of the behavior (e.g., does it provide social connections or a feeling of larger group affiliation). Once these are identified, exploring alternatives for connection such as in-person clubs, organization, or sports is key, perhaps even looking for online gaming communities or discussion groups related to his career goals.

- **Family assessment.** This would involve a more explorative set of questions to better understand Hank's family experiences. There is little mention of his younger sisters and clear mentions of bullying from an older brother who remains in the house after graduation. Both parents work and there is mention of the mother working for a church that the family might attend. Examples of exploratory questions could include: Have you thought about your sisters following in your footsteps related to white supremacy? Your brother is critical of you and remains living at home after high school graduation. Does it make sense that you would take his criticism and advice, given he remains out of school and working part time? What was your experience growing up with your mother and father in terms of discipline and limit setting?
- **Dating skills.** The REBT method (Ellis, 2007) of care could be helpful to aid Hank in understanding the beliefs he attaches to his dating goals. The term catastrophize refers to taking an unfortunate event and reacting to it in a way that gives it a large amount of space and power in your life. It is likely Hank has viewed small setbacks when talking to women with a belief that leads to negative consequence such as feeling he is unworthy, unattractive, or unable to ever date women. He might have experienced an unfortunate rejection or two and believes that since he was unsuccessful with those attempts, he has nothing to offer and will always be unsuccessful. Aside from the practical skill development, there also could be an application of existential therapy (May, 1983; Yalom, 1980) to help Hank explore why dating is important to him related to his self-worth and larger sense of meaning in life.
- **Absorption of white supremacist ideology.** This will be an assessment of what Hank has been exposed to so far and how deeply he is invested in these concepts. A central hypothesis in the VRA is that the movement provides him a larger group connection and affiliation to offset his lack of meaning, success in dating, social integration, and career goals. It would be possible he resonates with these ideologies for other reasons and a careful exploration of his reading, interactions, and understanding would be helpful. Given this has been a source of teasing and bullying at school, this exploration by the

therapist should be approached after a rapport is established and with awareness this is likely a topic he will be defensive and guarded about. The therapist should employ skills related to motivational interviewing (Miller and Rollnick, 1991) to avoid argumentation and roll with any resistance that might be expressed.

- **Resiliency skills.** These skills will help Hank have additional options when he experiences teasing or bullying by other students for his beliefs or lack of dating experience. This process should include an exploration of alternative reactions when confronted, learning to shift his beliefs when experiencing an active event to lead to better consequences, and to be aware of anger triggers.
- **Suicide assessment.** A suicide assessment is warranted with Hank given his recent isolation, lack of academic progress, and the pending student discipline actions. Access to firearms in the home is another heightened risk factor for suicide. The clinician should apply an idea to action approach to assessment and consider Hank might be hesitant and/or defensive when replying to questions that would make him seem weak or in need of help.
- **Empathy development.** Perspective taking and increasing empathy skills are critical areas of treatment that will help Hank better understand the groups that the white supremacists express such hatred toward. For the Rogerian therapist, there is often a parallel process that occurs in treatment where Hank can experience someone listening to him in an active manner, providing an authentic and genuine presence and treating him with unconditional positive regard (Rogers, 1961; 1980). The central tenet of humanism is having faith in Hank's ability to behave well when free of obstacles and negative experiences in his own life. Essentially, the goal is the therapist teaching Hank how it feels to be heard and understood with the hope this is something Hank can practice with others.
- **Critical thinking skills.** The development of critical think skills is central to the cognitive behavioral approach. The therapist helps Hank understand the choices that are in front of him and how his emotions are related to his feelings, thoughts, and actions. This also provides an opportunity to introduce the process of change as it occurs over precontemplation, contemplation, preparation, action, maintenance and/or relapse (Prochaska et al., 1994). By understanding this progression of change, Hank can work on his behavior and see the results that help reduce difficulties he might be experiencing. Another key component of this approach would be the development of discrepancy found in the motivational interviewing approach to change (Miller and Rollnick, 1991). The question for Hank becomes, is what you are currently doing getting you closer or further from your goals? Further, Hank would be tasked with considering alternative thoughts and behaviors rather than those not beneficial to him.

Moving forward

In the next chapter, we will explore the case of Jesse and follow a similar process as we did in this chapter. This will provide you an additional set of examples related to the application of the WSIR, the assessment of risk and protective factors, the formulation of a risk narrative, and interventions.

Note

1 Zero-tolerance policies refer to a separation from school based on a single incident of violence, weapon possession, or threat. Separating a student from school under a zero-tolerance policy poses a risk of escalating an upset, frustrated student and may serve as a catalyst event driving an isolated, rage-filled, vengeful attacker. Assessment, intervention, and monitoring are more effective in mitigating threats of violence in the community (Van Brunt, 2012). While separating a student from school may give an illusion of safety, there are numerous examples where angry, disgruntled, and disempowered individuals came back to campus or the workplace to seek their revenge (O'Toole, 2000; Scalora et al., 2010).

References

Ellis, A. (2007). *The Practice of rational emotive behavior therapy*. New York, NY: W.W. Norton & Company.

Glasser, A. (1975). *Choice Theory: A New Psychology of Personal Freedom*. New York, NY: Colophon Books.

Glasser, A. (2001). *Counseling with choice theory: The new reality therapy*. New York, NY: Colophon Books.

May, R. (1983). *The Discovery of Being*. New York, NY: W.W. Norton & Company.

Miller, W.R. and Rollnick, S. (1991). *Motivational Interviewing: Preparing People to Change Addictive Behavior*. New York, NY: Guilford Publications.

Nay, R. (2004). *Taking Charge of Anger*. Guilford Press.

O'Toole, M.E. (2000). *The School Shooter: A Threat Assessment Perspective*. Quantico, VA: National Center for the Analysis of Violent Crime, Federal Bureau of Investigation.

Prochaska, J., Norcross, J., and DiClemente, C. (1994). *Changing for Good*. Harper Collins.

Rogers, C. (1961). *On Becoming a Person*. New York, NY: Houghton Mifflin.

Rogers, C. (1980). *A Way of Being*. New York, NY: Houghton Mifflin.

Scalora, M., Simons, A., and Vansly, S. (2010, February). *Campus Safety: Assessing and managing threats (FBI Law Enforcement Bulletin)*. Washington, DC: Federal Bureau of Investigation.

Van Brunt, B. (2012). *Ending Campus Violence: New Approaches to Prevention*. New York, NY: Routledge.

Van Brunt, B. (2015). *Harm to Others: The Assessment and Treatment of Dangerousness*. Alexandria, VA: American Counseling Association.

Yalom, I. (1980). *Existential Psychotherapy*. Basic Books.

15 Treatment Approaches for Jesse

This chapter outlines the violence risk assessment (VRA) and treatment recommendations for Jesse. Table 15.1 serves as a reminder of the steps used to conduct the VRA and outline treatment recommendations. For more detail about each of these stages, please refer to the beginning of Chapter 14. The chapter concludes with treatment notes for Jesse to provide the reader with some practical examples of how a therapist, psychologist, social worker, or clinician could address the treatment interventions outlined in the last step.

The Case of Jesse

1 Thematic Case Analysis of Jesse

Location and People

- Small liberal arts college
- Jesse is identified risk

Table 15.1 Steps in a VRA and Treatment Process

	Step	*Summary*
1	Gather Thematic Case Data	Gather a summary of key facts in the case that provides an easily organized set of details to support the subsequent steps.
2	Identify Risk Factors	Risk factors related to the case are listed and described here.
3	Identify Protective Factors	Protective factors related to the case are listed and described here.
4	Apply the WSIR	The White Supremacist Indoctrination Rubric (WSIR) is applied to the case.
5	Create Risk Narrative	A story about the nature of the overall risk of the case is included in this step.
6	Develop and Implement Interventions	Specific interventions relevant to the case are included in this step.

DOI: 10.4324/9781003199656-15

- Classmates in his Introduction to Political Thought class
    - a Argue with Jesse
    - b Call him a neo-Nazi, racist, and ignorant
- Jesse challenges a social justice group
- No mention of friends, family, or other supportive people in his life
- A student at the free speech rally punches him

Jesse

- First semester freshman
- Openly expresses nationalistic politics, advocates for
    - a Stronger immigration policies
    - b States' rights, including segregated schools
    - c Strong voter ID laws
- Uses slurs and enflaming language like "those people," "illegals," and "aliens"
- Says in class "I argue for individuals to take pride in their own heritage and cultural experiences. Whites should not be made to feel guilty for things their ancestors did, nor be ashamed or taught critical race theory, which lacks scientific rigor."
- Confronts Black Lives Matter with "all lives matter"
- Argues against critical race theory to a classmate and says to his therapist, "I came to this school because it claimed to be a place to engage in critical thinking and explore ideas. What I get instead is violence and hatred. I really don't understand this at all."
- Supports Kyle Rittenhouse
- Posits the antisemitic idea that Jews own most of the wealth in the US and are not a marginalized group
- Wears a swastika to a free speech event and when confronted argues, "It's actually a Hindu symbol of peace that was co-opted by the German Nazi Party."
- Wears an empty holster to the same event
- After being punched by a fellow student, goes to the counseling center

Of Note

- While many of his actions come across as trolling (he likely knows how the swastika will be interpreted), when talking to the therapist, he seems puzzled by the reaction. This disconnect should be explored.

- There is not mention of any support systems or other protective factors. These need to be explored.
- There is also no mention of weapons access or any affiliation with white supremacist groups. Most of what he says is in line with mainstream right-wing Republican thought (aside, perhaps, from his thoughts on segregation). It would be worth exploring his sources of information and if he spends time on overt white supremacist sites.

2 Identify Risk Factors for Jesse

Present Factors

- **Hardened point of view.** Jesse expresses a consistent viewpoint that is strongly held on several topics. These include taking stances against immigrants, critical race theory, and white supremacist theory. To some extent, however, it would be useful to explore these ideas to an end. Is the true desire here to offend and upset others or are these truly his beliefs?
- **Marginalization.** There is outright anger and frustration at Jesse's perspectives and speech. He certainly feels different from many students on campus and particularly marginalized when it comes to his perceived rejection at being allowed to have his own beliefs.
- **Catalyst events.** Being hit by another student might be a catalyst event for Jesse to begin considering how he might defend himself during future arguments. It could also lead to further feelings of isolation, sadness, and potentially hopelessness.
- **Experience of teasing and bullying.** Jesse is taunted, teased, bullied, threatened, and physically assaulted by others for expressing his beliefs. There is, of course, the larger question of how much he brings these reactions on himself by continually confronting the core values of other groups, but there is no doubt he is experiencing teasing and bullying from others.
- **Social isolation.** There are few friends or other supports of connections mentioned by Jesse in this scenario. He is experiencing social isolation from others.
- **Lack of empathy and remorse for actions.** Jesse is surprised by the reaction to his behaviors, speech, and challenging of others' core values. There is a lack of empathy, insight, or awareness for why others would be upset about his behavior.

In Need of Further Exploration

- **Grievance or dangerous injustice collection.** Jesse expresses frustration to his therapist about having his beliefs challenges by other people and being upset about being made to feel guilty for being white. This seems to be a recurrent surprise and/or area of conversation and question for Jesse, rather than something that he is expressing an intense anger about.

- **Feelings of isolation and hopelessness.** Jesse feels increasingly surprised and frustrated by others due to his beliefs. His thoughts and ideas are generally in the minority, and this results in him having fewer connections with people. While isolation is clearly present, more questions would need to be asked to develop a better understanding of how deep these feelings go, particularly after the violence of being physically assaulted.
- **Free fall.** Jesse does seem to be experiencing increased isolation and challenges in his social connections with peers. His academics are not directly mentioned and should be an area of further exploration.
- **Decrease in academic or work progress.** This is not mentioned directly in the scenario and should be explored moving forward.
- **Mental illness.** There is no current evidence of mental illness beyond Jesse's need for challenging other's core beliefs and, potentially, not being aware that the questions he asks, symbols he wears, or statements he makes carry consequences. Exploration of an underlying developmental disorder such as autism spectrum disorder or a personality disorder should be considered.
- **Use of substance.** There is no current evidence of substance use or abuse, but this might be worth exploring.

Box 15.1 "They are on the spectrum"

Because the diagnosis of autism spectrum disorder (ASD) or Asperger's is occurring more commonly and being talked about increasingly in social media, there is a heightened opportunity for misunderstanding and misattribution of behavior. This has occurred the recent past in the context of the Sandy Hook school shooting with Adam Lanza. Following this attack, many in the Autism community found themselves talked about as potentially dangerous or capable to similar violence. The comment around a potential ASD diagnosis for Jesse is made as a potential explanation for his difficulty and surprised responses to why others would react aggressively or violently to his statements. A lack of awareness of 'normal' social reactions to these statements could be related to a processing or developmental disorder. This is not to imply those with ASD or Asperger's more commonly buy into white supremacist beliefs or violence in general.

Not Present

- **Fantasy rehearsals.** There is no evidence that Jesse is escalating in any type of attack plan. His expression of beliefs seems more driven to debate and argument on intellectual levels.
- **Objectification and depersonalization.** While there appears to be a lack of empathy and awareness as to why his speech and perspectives are upsetting to others, it does not appear that Jesse returns the name calling and negative descriptions other hurl at him, but rather he responds in a calculated, calm manner.
- **Threats.** There do not appear to be any direct or indirect threats of violence presented in this case.
- **Actionability.** There is not a clear mention of Jesse having access to a firearm. This would be an area useful for further exploration if there were any threats of violence or he expressed a need to defend himself from future attacks.
- **Drivenness and a justification for violent action.** While there is a drivenness for conflict and trolling others with his beliefs, this lacks any escalation toward violent action and is limited to debate.
- **Desire for fame.** There does not seem to be desire for fame or glory. There is a desire for debate and potentially trolling others that seem to be a driver for Jesse's behavior. There is an unspoken desire for attention, albeit as a firebrand.
- **Suicidal.** There is no direct mention of this. If there is more hopelessness and frustration expressed, then it would be useful to follow up with a suicide risk assessment.
- **Fascination with violence.** There is no evidence that Jesse displays a fascination with any kind of violence. In fact, it seems more likely he is focused on principled debate and dialogue.

3 *Identify Protective Factors for Jesse*

- **Environmental and emotional stability.** Jesse is experiencing a large amount of friction between himself and almost all other students on campus. There is not much information shared about his academic major, current academic progress, relationship goals, hobbies, social clubs, organization, or athletics. While he seems calm and reasonable in his desire to express and share his beliefs with others, there lacks an insight and awareness to how these controversial beliefs and behaviors will be received. While Jesse might initially describe himself as stable and that he is doing well at college and in his interactions with others, most of us would not see this as the case.
- **Social health and connection.** There is little connection with others and Jesse's social health and positive peer interactions are non-existent.

- **Access and satisfaction with non-violent outlets.** There are no places mentioned where Jesse feels free to express his ideas without immediate judgement and negative interactions. Therapy could be one place where this can occur for him and will be a critical aspect to his interventions.
- **Empathy.** Jesse lacks empathy and understanding as to why others would be upset about his statements and ideology. He also has a history of challenging others on their core beliefs and then is seemingly unaware why they might be upset by this.
- **Cognitive Clarity and Pluralistic Awareness.** While Jesse can express his viewpoints in a clear manner, there is a total lack of awareness of any perceptive beyond his own. The wearing of a Swastika, despite the appropriation of the symbol from the Hindus, demonstrates a critical lack of awareness and insight.

4 Apply the White Supremacist Indoctrination Rubric for Jesse

Jesse has a deep absorption of the facts and details related to the white supremacist movement but is driven to debate and potentially troll others with these ideas, rather than to advocate violence.

Jesse has worn a swastika on his clothes representing *Passing Interest* (2) on **Appearance**. He is knowledgeable about many different groups but does not appear be overly connected with any group beyond a *Passing Interest* (2) on **Affiliation.** Jesse has detailed and cataloged knowledge of white supremacist thought and would likely be at the *Historian/Marketer* phase (5) on **Absorption**. Jesse does not appear from the case study to have any knowledge or experience with weapons so this would lead to *None* (1) on **Acquisition**. Jesse seems to have an *Active Directive* (3) in terms of **Appointment** to a mission.

5 Create Risk Narrative for Jesse

Two central aspects of this case are 1) Jesse has a deep knowledge white supremacist ideology, and 2) Jesse frequently engages others in debate, challenging their core beliefs, and receives insults, threats, teasing, bullying and physical violence in return. Given his higher cognitive ability and the ease at which most people would predict this type of reaction when

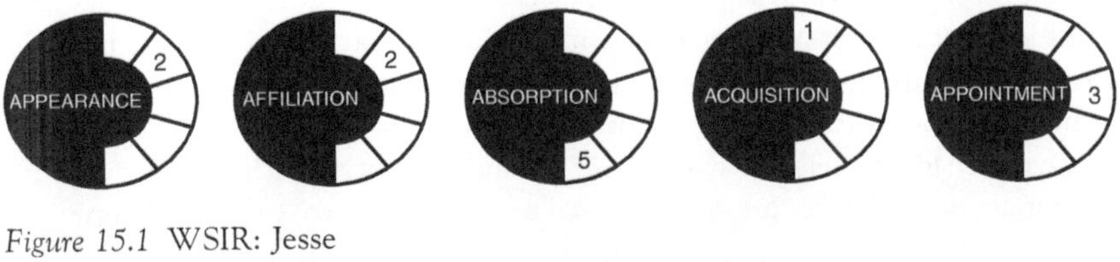

Figure 15.1 WSIR: Jesse

publicly challenging others core beliefs, it seems incongruous that Jesse is surprised at these reactions, so it will be critical in this VRA to better understand if Jesse does this intentionally to 'troll' others or if he is truly surprised by their reactions.

Since Jesse lacks any current attack plan with fixation or focus on a target, the central concern is an 'in-kind' relative response as he continues to experience teasing, bullying, threats and physical violence in response to his challenging and upsetting others. There are few unexplored aspects of the scenario, namely what he is studying and how he is progressing in his course, which are important to explore.

Jesse experiences social isolation and marginalization. While it would be reasonable to assume this could have a negative impact on his mental health, it is not clear if this will lead to retaliation, a re-doubling of his efforts to challenge and debate others, or acquiring a gun or weapon to defend himself from future attack. Does Jesse experience increased sadness, hopelessness, or suicide thoughts because of his conflicts and increased social isolation? While there have been no threats made by Jesse, it would be equally useful to assess his access to firearms.

Some motivators for Jesse to escalate his violence include his expression of frustration at being insulted threatened and physically assaulted. Future violence might be motivated by an upsetting event which arouses and upsets him, triggering an impulsive reaction. He could begin to see violence as a more viable option to control or change his circumstances as he often feels bullied, teased, and marginalized.

There are several disinhibitors for this violence including a lack of integration socially with others and a lack of anxiety about his actions. Jesse does have several pressing destabilizers, such as a disturbed perception of those around him including a disturbed perception of how his actions are viewed by others, and difficulty remaining rational and reasonable in his interactions. There seems to be few motivators for violence, yet it is useful to consider his aggressive actions towards others through a lens of potential escalation. In this case, he might increase his aggressiveness out of a desire to right past wrongs out of a sense of justice or honor protecting his right to expression. This might also contribute to a sense of status or esteem as an outspoken firebrand such as a Howard Stern, Joe Rogan, or Rush Limbaugh. There is evidence he is excited or aroused by others expressing a viewpoint he disagrees with and the aggressiveness in that sense might be related to the proximity or a release of expression. While it is unlikely Jesse would see his arguments and conflicts with others as leading to a change in hearts and minds, but this assertive arguing and trolling might be related to a desire to change others' opinions (or at least confront them).

Overall, Jesse's risk for violence would be estimated at low with no evidence of a desire on his part to act violently to others. There is a concern the increased marginalization, conflict, and recent physical violence he experienced might lead to a potential in-kind response. It is worth mentioning that there is a highly unlikely potential that he is radicalized towards violence by the groups he is associating himself with and exploring online. In a thorough evaluation and treatment plan, it would be recommended to talk more with him about is affiliation with those who see violence as a path forward for their agenda and how his thoughts and ideas align or depart from this ideology.

Jesse would strongly benefit from encouragement to examine his behavior related to his desired outcomes. For example, if he wishes to engage in debate, is there an appropriate time or place to do that? If he wishes to change the minds of others through education or persuasive argument, is there a more effective way to reach this goal? It would be advised to explore his ability to understand his behavior as other's experience it as well as the disconnect between his actions and the surprise at how others perceive him. To put it simply, it is more likely Jesse will be harmed by others who find his behavior insulting than to have him physically hurt someone else. Interventions should focus on helping him find new ways to define and meet his goals through his behaviors.

6 *Intervention for Jesse*

Reassurance to Jesse that the physical violence he experienced, unrelated to the reason, is not ok and will not be tolerated by the school. He should be made aware of the process in place to address physical assaults and be involved, as appropriate, in the process moving forward.

There should be a discussion related to time, place, and manner as it applies to free speech. While Jesse should be encouraged to express his ideas, free speech is not always free of consequences. This should be approached carefully, as the physical violence that occurred should not be condoned or expected in the future.

Jesse should be reminded of the conduct code as it applies to his behavior related to potentially harassing and unwanted conversations with other students on campus. While he has free speech rights, others have the right to exist without intimidation or threats, direct or otherwise, related to their safety.

There should be a review of the college conduct policy as it relates to hate speech and symbols on campus. What is consider free speech and expression and what is considered hate speech and threatening symbols? This would be a good policy to review apart from Jesse. For example, how will the college respond the an art project involving a noose in a tree, an image of a burning cross, or a swastika symbol?

Jesse appears to be surprisingly unaware and taken aback when people react poorly to his conversation and displays of images that most would consider offensive. Exploring the reasoning for this and determining if he

is truly unaware or engaging in intentional trolling with his behaviors would help better determine a course of action.
The school should review and monitor these events through its campus Behavioral Intervention Team (BIT) or CARE team to ensure timely and proper follow-up. This might include obtaining release of information forms from Jesse's therapist to ensure progress and compliance with expectations.
An intervention goal is to identify and connect Jesse to additional outlets for his thoughts that are more appropriate in time, place, and manner.
There should be an exploration of a restorative justice student conduct process to address the physical assault that occurred.

Areas of Further Exploration

- A discussion is warranted to determine if there are deeper connections to white supremacist ideology and actions. Many of these groups advocate violence to further their causes and it would be helpful to better understand how Jesse connects to these concepts. In other words, his absorption rating of a 5 on the WSIR indicates an almost encyclopedic knowledge of these concepts. What is the rationale for his time spend on this topic? When did he begin to explore these ideas?
- There is also evidence of a rather wide expression of ideas related to white supremacist ideology. It would be helpful to ask Jesse more directly about which ideas he personally holds and what his thoughts are on the group's encouragement of violence to further their agenda.
- There should be a exploration of disinhibitors related to a potential lack of guilt, anxiety, or remorse about the advancement of ideas that many find threatening and offensive.

Counseling and Therapeutic Interventions

A referral to therapy should address some of these general concepts:

- A conversation about the physical assault and his well-being following this kind of violence, including a contextual exploration of whether this had happened before (being punched) and how he handled it then
- Exploring the nature of his ideology, where this developed and developing a better understanding of what core ideas and actions he is currently committed to
- Identifying and encouraging academic or career interests as a source of positive connection, including future political study, forensic debate, or communications
- Discussing family, friends, and his social life to determine if they are supportive

- Social skills training related to dating along with an identification of irrational beliefs and expectations
- Developing additional resiliency skills to address the growing disconnection between Jesse and others at school
- Assessing potential suicidal thoughts or behaviors that might develop because of his marginalization and likely teasing and threats of violence that might be occurring
- Developing empathy skills and encouragement to better understand the experience of others and why his behaviors are seen with such disdain
- Developing critical thinking skills that allow for multiple perspectives, alternative beliefs, and a reduction in Jesse's hardened perspective

Treatment Notes for Jesse

Therapeutic suggestions for treatment are typically not included in these types of VRA assessments beyond suggestions for the type and frequency of therapeutic treatment. These recommendations are included above. For the purpose of this book, the authors provide some suggestions based on the therapeutic approaches outlined in Chapter 13. These are organized based on the counseling and therapeutic interventions provided in the VRA above. As mentioned previously, it will be uncommon to receive this level of therapeutic direction in most VRAs, typically the comments are "outpatient therapy recommended." If there is lack of direction from the VRA, the clinician will first begin with drafting these treatment recommendations based on their review of the VRA.

- **Support post-assault.** While a potentially challenging area to start with given Jesse's troubling beliefs, there should be direct and immediate conversations around his reaction to the assault. This should include providing support and empathy related to his experience of physical violence. This kind of genuineness and concern for others is central to Rogers' (1961, 1980) work in person-centered therapy. Any potential comment related to the idea of "well, this was to be expected given what you said and have been doing" should be avoided. There might be a useful parallel process that could develop over therapy where the support and empathy Jesse receives from his therapist could be a springboard to him understanding this empathy is something he should be demonstrating; however, it would be recommended to address this later in treatment.
- **Assessment and developing supports.** It is unclear from the narrative what social and family supports might be available to Jesse. Does he have many friends? Has he made friends before? What is his family background? Are they supportive? How have those close to Jesse handled his thoughts and ideas? This can be seen as building up

potential resiliency skills and addressing the conflict growing between Jesse and many of the students on campus.

- **Discussion of offensive behaviors.** A core question related to Jesse's motivation is the disconnection between his words and actions and his surprise at how offended others are. This should initially be an exploratory, non-judgmental discussion of what Jesse's expectation are when he says something offensive to them. He should be asked where these expectations came from and if they are still serving him well. The reality therapy approach to treatment (Glasser, 1975; 2001) offers some insight on how to intervene and better understand these cognitive distortions and lack of insight regard the response of others. Additionally, a focus on the development of discrepancy, outlined in motivational interviewing (Miller and Rollnick, 1991), would be important to challenge Jesse on his current behavior and how it is out of step with his goals.
- **Identify academic/career interests.** Exploration of future goals and identifying ways for Jesse to explore academic and career interests would be useful to encourage his progress towards his stated goals. This might involve the study of communications, forensic debate, public policy, or politics. Each of these fields stresses the importance of purposeful communication related to the outlined goals. Here the therapist could draw on reality therapy planning skills (Glasser, 1975; 2001) to help Jesse identify next steps such as making an appointment, anticipating obstacles, and establishing small achievable goals. To aid this process, a direct referral to career counselors and the use of computer software designed to identify potential careers that Jesse would enjoy and find fulfilling would be helpful.
- **Absorption of white supremacist ideology.** Given the high level of knowledge Jesse has demonstrated in this area, the next area of exploration would be understanding how much of this ideology Jesse subscribes to and to what degree he resonates with the call to violence present in much of the writing. It would be possible he resonates with these ideologies as they create an opportunity for him to be unique and receive negative attention from others. Given all human behavior is purposeful, exploring the underlying goal of his mastery of white supremacist ideology would be useful to better explore alternative goals or paths to existing goals.
- **Suicide assessment.** While no direct suicide statements were made, an assessment would be helpful given the increase in marginalization and physical assault. The clinician should apply an idea to action approach to assessment and consider that Jesse might be hesitant and/or defensive when replying to questions that would make him seem weak or in need of help.
- **Empathy development.** Perspective taking and increasing empathy skills are critical areas of treatment that will help Jesse understand

why his statements are so offensive to those he talks with on campus. Using the Rogerian approach, Jesse might learn from the way the therapist responds to him in an active manner, providing an authentic and genuine presence and treating him with unconditional positive regard (Rogers, 1961; 1980). The central tenet of humanism is having faith in Jesse's ability to behave well when free of obstacles and negative experiences in his own life. Essentially, the goal is for the therapist to teach Jesse how it feels to be heard and understood with the hope this is something he can practice with others.

- **Critical thinking skills.** The development of critical think skills is central to the cognitive behavioral approach. The therapist helps Jesse how his current behavior is out of step with his current goals. The motivational interviewing approach to change (Miller and Rollnick, 1991) would help Jesse explore what he is currently doing and if it is getting him closer or further from his goals. Further, Jesse could consider alternative thoughts and behaviors rather than those not beneficial to him. This provides an opportunity to introduce the process of change as it occurs over precontemplation, contemplation, preparation, action, maintenance and/or relapse (Prochaska et al., 1994). By understanding this progression of change, Jesse can work on his behavior and see the results that help reduce difficulties he might be experiencing.

Moving Forward

In the next chapter, we will explore the case of Dawson and follow a similar process as we did in this chapter. This will provide you an additional set of examples related to the application of the WSIR, the assessment of risk and protective factors, the formulation of a risk narrative and interventions.

References

Ellis, A. (2007). *The Practice of rational emotive behavior therapy.* New York, NY: W.W. Norton & Company.

Glasser, A. (1975). *Choice Theory: A New Psychology of Personal Freedom.* New York, NY: Colophon Books.

Glasser, A. (2001). *Counseling with choice theory: The new reality therapy.* New York, NY: Colophon Books.

May, R. (1983). *The discovery of being.* New York, NY: W.W. Norton & Company.

Miller, W.R. and Rollnick, S. (1991). *Motivational Interviewing: Preparing People to Change Addictive Behavior.* New York, NY: Guilford Publications.

Nay, R. (2004). *Taking Charge of Anger.* Guilford Press.

O'Toole, M.E. (2000). *The school shooter: A threat assessment perspective.* Quantico, VA: National Center for the Analysis of Violent Crime, Federal Bureau of Investigation.

Prochaska, J., Norcross, J., and DiClemente, C. (1994). *Changing for Good*. Harper Collins.

Rogers, C. (1961). *On becoming a person*. New York, NY: Houghton Mifflin.

Rogers, C. (1980). *A way of being*. New York, NY: Houghton Mifflin.

Scalora, M., Simons, A., and Vansly, S. (2010, February). *Campus s: Assessing and managing threats (FBI Law Enforcement Bulletin)*. Washington, DC: Federal Bureau of Investigation.

Van Brunt, B. (2012). *Ending campus violence: New approaches to prevention*. New York, NY: Routledge.

Yalom, I. (1980). *Existential Psychotherapy*. Basic Books.

16 Treatment Approaches for Dawson

This chapter outlines the violence risk assessment (VRA) and treatment recommendations for Dawson. Table 16.1 serves as a reminder of the steps used to conduct the VRA and outline treatment recommendations. For more detail about each of these stages, please refer to the beginning of Chapter 14. The chapter concludes with treatment notes for Jesse to provide the reader with some practical examples of how a therapist, psychologist, social worker, or clinician could address the treatment interventions outlined in the sixth step.

The Case of Dawson

1 Thematic Case Analysis of Dawson

Location and People

- Community college automotive welding program
- Dawson is identified risk

Table 16.1 Steps in a VRA and Treatment Process

	Step	*Summary*
1	Gather Thematic Case Data	Gather a summary of key facts in the case that provide an easily organized set of details to support the subsequent steps.
2	Identify Risk Factors	Risk factors related to the case are listed and described here.
3	Identify Protective Factors	Protective factors related to the case are listed and described here.
4	Apply the WSIR	The White Supremacist Indoctrination Rubric (WSIR) is applied to the case.
5	Create Risk Narrative	A story about the nature of the overall risk of the case is included in this step.
6	Develop and Implement Interventions	Specific interventions relevant to the case are included in this step.

DOI: 10.4324/9781003199656-16

- Has "few friends" at school
- Works at a local bar, though no friendships here are mentioned
- In an on again, off again relationship

    a The two argue often, with yelling and threats
    b History of domestic violence where Dawson choked her to teach her "her place"

- Classmates

    a Tells one about his weapons collection
    b Initially laugh him off, but are growing more concerned

- Instructor is asked to intervene, asks Dawson to stop talking about his beliefs

    a Reports Dawson to campus BIT

Dawson

- Studying automotive welding and crash repair at community college
- Works in a local bar, position unnamed
- Clothing marked with white supremacist symbols (88, pit bull, radiation warning [Atomwaffen], "I have nothing to say," "RAHOWA")
- Shaved head and tattoos of white supremacist symbols (88, pit bull)
- Owns several weapons, including shotguns and AR-15, and stocks ammunition
- Member of several unnamed white supremacist groups
- Has attended rallies and protests
- Refers to white supremacist concepts: three-percenters, racial holy war and day of the rope
- Refers to previous attacks on James Byrd and Matthew Shepard
- Quotes well-known white supremacist [Richard] Spencer
- Has a history of domestic violence, having once choked his girlfriend
- Makes a vague conditional threat at a progressive rally ("I swear if anyone pushes me on this today, we are gonna have a day of the rope f-*king tomorrow. I'll pull some James Byrd and Matthew Shepard shit.")
- Makes a vague threat toward Jews (says his ammunition store could "give those ovens in WWII a run for their money")
- According to other students, threatens to "start hanging" Black and Jewish people

Of Note

- It is interesting that Dawson is initially ignored or at least tolerated by other students, despite his comments and the outward symbols he displays. This implies an escalation in his rhetoric which should be explored.

- His weapons access and knowledge should be more deeply examined. Have his weapons been purchased legally? Does he have interest in or has he acquired other weapons, like bomb making materials? What kind of training does he have?
- The case study mentions a volatile relationship that should be explored, both to determine the extent of the violence present and whether his partner is a source of support or exacerbates his issues. There might also be Title IX implications, especially if she is a fellow student.
- While it is mentioned that Dawson has a few friends, not much is known about protective and anchoring factors in his life. Does he have support systems outside the white supremacist groups he belongs to?

2 Identify Risk Factors for Dawson

Present Factors

- **Hardened point of view.** Dawson has clearly defined belief set supporting white supremacy that he expresses to others around him and in the clothing and symbols he wears.
- **Drivenness and a justification for violent action.** Dawson's mannerisms, speech, clothing, and affiliations point toward an internal rage and justification for violent action. He also makes several threats as people or groups annoy or frustrate him.
- **Threats.** Dawson makes multiple threats in public such as, "his ammunition store could give those ovens in WWII a run for their money," and ""'I swear if anyone pushes me on this today, we are gonna have a day of the rope f-*king tomorrow. I'll pull some James Byrd and Matthew Shepard shit." He does not mention a specific place of attack or individual he or his groups are directly planning to attack. He has made specific threats toward and physically assaulted his girlfriend for speaking out of turn.
- **Grievance or dangerous injustice collection.** Dawson frequently expresses his frustration and anger and makes comments and white supremacist rants about keeping the nation pure.
- **Objectification and depersonalization.** Dawson mentions his dislike of certain groups and how they dilute white purity. He talks about the need for a racial holy war. He also stated that women need to know their place in the world and has choked his girlfriend for her actions.
- **Desire for fame.** The symbols Dawson wears representing his white supremacist beliefs and his threatening and aggressive behavior to others is indication of a desire for attention and to provoke others'

reactions to him. It would be worth exploring further the nature of his connection within his white supremacist groups and how these issues of hierarchy are handled.

- **Social isolation.** Dawson does seem to be experiencing a fall from his initial connections with those around him, but the case does not discuss this directly as a problem in his mind.
- **Lack of empathy and remorse for actions.** Dawson does not care how his actions are seen by others and appears to enjoy sharing how he feels regardless of how people around him react. He seems to lack an awareness of how his behaviors impact others. Examples of this are his threats, attitudes toward women, and comments on racial purity.
- **Fascination with violence.** Given the number of weapons and the symbols he wears, there is evidence Dawson shares a fascination with violence and thinks often about racial holy wars and changing/purifying our nation.

In Need of Further Exploration

- **Free fall.** There is not much said about Dawson's life outside of school. This would be an area of further exploration, particularly how he feels about his relationship with his girlfriend.
- **Decrease in academic or work progress.** There is no evidence of Dawson struggling in his classwork, but this would be an area worthy of future exploration. He works in a bar, but no details are provided, so this would be another area of exploration.
- **Actionability.** Dawson talks openly about his many weapons and makes a direct reference his stockpile of ammunition being allocated for killing Jews. Dawson's anger at a recent rally is also cause for concern. Additionally, automotive welding is a career that has the potential to involve skills and abilities that could be used in preparation of para-military equipment and materials. While there is no evidence of this, this should be an area of exploration.
- **Fantasy rehearsals.** Dawson wears the symbols of the white supremacist movement and talks frequently about desires for racial purity, for women to know their place, and about starting a racial holy war.

Not Present

- **Suicidal.** There is no current evidence of Dawson feeling suicidal.
- **Feelings of isolation and hopelessness.** There is no current evidence of isolation or feelings of hopelessness from Dawson.
- **Catalyst events.** There do not appear to be clear catalyst events in this case that are escalating Dawson's behavior moving forward.
- **Experience of teasing and bullying.** There is no evidence of teasing or bullying.

- **Marginalization.** There is little evidence of Dawson being marginalized by others. In fact, he seemed to get along well with many in his class until his comments, clothing, and threats increased. He has some social skills and ability to form relationships (such as with his girlfriend).
- **Use of substance.** There is no current evidence of substance use or abuse.
- **Mental illness.** There is no current evidence of mental illness.

3 Identify Protective Factors for Dawson

- **Environmental and emotional stability.** Little is known about Dawson's background in this area beyond some comments he has few friends and an abusive relationship with his girlfriend.
- **Social health and connection.** Little is known is this area as well. While Dawson seems to have some ability to form friendships and has a charismatic side, the offensive nature of his beliefs and expression of white supremacist ideas sour people to him quickly.
- **Access and satisfaction with non-violent outlets.** As Dawson is attending college, there is likely some interest and future goals related to a career. It is unclear how invested he is in automotive welding.
- **Empathy.** There is a clear lack of empathy and understanding given his clothing, speech, and threats that are made. It is unclear in the scenario if he has the ability to talk with others and understand their perspective and chooses not to do this, or if he is unable to do this. In either case, his behavior shows a lack of empathy and understanding for how his clothing, speech and threats are harmful to others.
- **Cognitive clarity and pluralistic awareness.** Again, it is not overly clear for the case study if Dawson is aware of his actions and how they impact others, yet chooses not to care, or if he is unaware of these perceptions. He shows little regard for others around him to the extent he argues for a structure that limits diversity and actively harms those different from himself.

4 Apply the White Supremacist Indoctrination Rubric (WSIR) for Dawson

Overall, Dawson scores in the 4–5 range on all five of the WSIR scales. This should be seen as high level of concern and indoctrination into the white supremacist ideology.

Dawson wears multiple symbols of concern including the pit bull, 88, RAHOWA, and the Atomwaffen symbol. He also has several visible racist tattoos. This represents a *Consistent Style* (5) on **Appearance**. He is knowledgeable about many different groups and claims membership in several of them indicating *Active Membership* (4) on **Affiliation**. Dawson

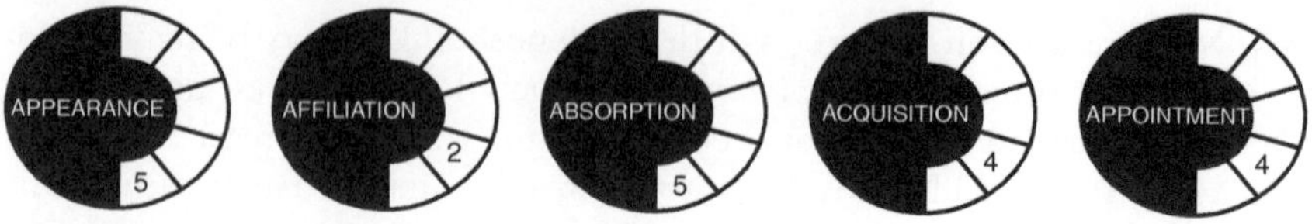

Figure 16.1 WSIR: Dawson

has detailed and cataloged knowledge in white supremacist thought and casually references previous attacks as justification for his anger. This would likely be at the *Historian/Marketer* phase (5) on **Absorption**. Dawson mentions owning multiple firearms and gives the impression he is preparing for violence, indicating a *Soldier* phase (4) on **Acquisition**. Dawson seems to have an *Active Directive* (4) in terms of **Appointment** to a mission.

5 Create Risk Narrative for Dawson

Dawson presents a significant risk for violence. He shows little empathy for those around him and engages others on topics of ideology without thought for how this might make others feel uncomfortable or threatened. He has a history of physical violence toward a girlfriend and clear attitudes of antisemitism and misogynistic thought, ideas and action. Dawson has access to weapons and brags about them to others.

While there seems to be a lack of fixation and focus on a particular target, Dawson seems open to the possibility of causing problems with multiple targets with a possible fixation on Jews and women. He has the desire to challenge and/or convert others to his thinking and engages in these activities often. The consistency of his style and presence of white supremacist clothing, tattoos, and markings demonstrates his commitment to these beliefs. His threats, while vague, bring with them an added concern, as he had shown the ability to act in a lethal manner to others. Given his impulsive control difficulties, it is likely Dawson will act violently again based on his history of violence toward his girlfriend, the substantive nature of his threats against Jews, referencing his stockpile of ammunition and his calls for a racial holy war.

The lack of a clear social support network leaves Dawson particularly vulnerable to recruitment into extremist groups as they offer him connection to others who hear his point of view. He wears the clothes and symbols of his tribe (the pit bull, 88, RAHOWA, and Atomwaffen) along with several racist tattoos.

There are several disinhibitors for this violence including a negative attitude, lack of anxiety, and a lack of guilt related to his speech and threats shared with others. He does not seem to appreciate or care about how his thoughts and worldview are seen by others. Likewise, a sense of disturbed perception and inability to reason are affecting the way he interacts the world, creating destabilizing influences. Dawson is obsessed with his beliefs, frequently challenges those around him, and has acted violently based on and in support of these beliefs.

The main causes for concern, however, are the numerous motivators for violence. Dawson is motivated by a sense of justice and honor to elevate the white race into its rightful place of power. This provides a direct profit gain for Dawson, along with an elevation in his esteem. There is the potential for him to be motivated toward violence due to his proximal affiliation with several white supremacist groups, and his rhetoric and threats offer a clear release and expression of his internal grievances. As a man on a mission, Dawson engages in actions designed to intimidate and control those around him to bring about a change he wants to see in the world. Finally, Dawson is motivated toward violence in defense of his people, purpose, and goals. He views the world as changing and negatively effecting the rightful place of white people. Violence becomes justified in his mind in reaction to this perceived marginalization.

These motivators, the depth of his indoctrination into the white supremacist ideology, his previous violent behavior, and his access to numerous weapons all make him a high risk for future violence. While Dawson lacks a clear mission and/or fixation or focus on a particular target with an intent to kill, he has numerous groups he has objectified and feels justified hurting. Combined with his lack of anxiety or guilt in relation to his escalating behaviors, violence is a likely outcome.

It will be difficult to engage Dawson, though one path could be through the creation of a hostile academic environment that could be used to raise the issue of mandated assessment and treatment to shift his behavior. Interventions should focus on understanding why this path seems so appealing to Dawson and how alternative futures, such as completing his degree, could provide a more positive outcome. Alternatively, the school or therapist could focus on the reduction of negative outcomes such as his behavior leading to an expulsion, criminal charges, and further closed doors, all of which limit his options. In either case, clear boundaries and expectations should be placed on his behavior in the classroom as it relates to the creation of a hostile environment and violates most student behavioral codes of conduct.

6 *Interventions for Dawson*

Steps should be taking to ensure the safety of the girlfriend who was physically assaulted. The school will have a different responsibility depending on how it came into this knowledge and where the assault occurred. While much of Dawson's behavior is concerning related to his white supremacist beliefs, the physical assault should be a focus of the interventions.

The campus should hold Dawson accountable for any behavior that violates the student code of conduct. Specifically, this will pertain to threats made against other individuals or groups, physical violence, or any actions that creates a hostile academic environment. While a zero-tolerance policy[1] would not be supported by literature or best practice, clear and consistent disciplinary action attuned to the behavior is warranted. There is some opportunity to leverage counseling with his ability to stay engaged in school, though more should be explored as to what his career goals are.

The school should review and monitor these events through its campus Behavioral Intervention Team (BIT) or CARE team to ensure timely and proper follow-up, which might include obtaining release of information forms from Dawson's therapist to ensure progress and compliance with expectations.

A background check determining the nature of Dawson's previous criminal behavior should be explored. This should include past student conduct actions as well as Title IX allegations or processes. Efforts should be made to determine how he acquired his weapons and if they are owned legally (which often changes state-to-state).

Given the nature of the threats made to others, it would be advised for campus law enforcement to discuss Dawson with local police, the FBI, Homeland Security, and the Fusion Center. Connecting with the Secure Community Jewish Security Operations Command Center would be another opportunity to determine if he has previously engaged in these activities. Given the nature of the threats and the violence risk, these communications would likely be allowed under FERPA's[2] emergency exemptions policy.

Areas of Further Exploration

- The assault on his girlfriend might require further follow up under campus Title IX policy. In any case, given the nature of the "women should know their place" comment, efforts should be made to monitor Dawson's behavior around women to quickly address inappropriate comments and/or threats. This assault might also provide an opportunity to set limits on Dawson's behavior and/or as a leverage into counseling assessment or treatment (specifically around anger management and impulse control).
- Little was shared regarding Dawson's social media profile, which might provide better context to his white supremacist activities. There should be an exploration of his online conversations and usernames, including social media posts. Are there multiple usernames? Does he serve in an administrator or moderator capacity?

Have these connections resulted in any in-person meet ups, conventions, or social engagements? This could be accomplished through coordination with law enforcement or third-party security groups to conduct an open-source intelligence process to assess his social media and online activities.

- Given his absorption of white supremacist ideology online, there should be efforts to further identify key elements that motivate his focus. For example, is he driven by thoughts of Blacks taking the women he should rightfully have or the Jews taking opportunities from him for a better future?
- There should be an exploration of those disinhibitors related to a potential lack of guilt, anxiety, or remorse about his open conversations and rather controversial concepts and threats made to marginalized groups. Dawson has a host of motivators that provide reasons for him to escalate to violence. Given the large number of these potential triggers, more intentional and proactive efforts should be taken in this case.
- The automotive welding degree is one that has the potential to be weaponized. Some examination of this potential should be considered.
- Many colleges and universities have explored the limits of what they allow on their campuses in terms of speech or symbols associated with hate. These expectations are typically outlined in the student code of conduct or under the Office of Equity and Inclusion. These range from state to state and among different private and public campuses. Determining if any of Dawson's language in class or symbols and phrases on his clothing violates these community standards would be useful in setting limits and perhaps encouraging counseling.
- Given Dawson's seeming willingness to engage in unfiltered conversation with other students, it would be a good investment to follow up with some students in his class to gather information about his potential threats and hate speech.

Counseling and Therapeutic Interventions

A referral to therapy should address some of these general concepts:

- Exploration of his lack of anxiety and guilt over racist and bigoted comments in class.
- Development of alternative strategies he could use when he encounters a person who he sees as a challenge.
- Identifying and encouraging academic or career interests as a source of positive connection.
- Discussing his job and what drew him to that kind of work. It is implied in the scenario that Dawson has an affable and charismatic

side. Identifying ways to strengthen those stabilizing factors in his life would be helpful to further off-ramp him from the pathway toward violence.

- Discussing his negative attitudes toward women and the escalation that involved assaulting his girlfriend. This should include impulse control and anger management.
- Exploration of online connections to determine the extent of indoctrination and the motivations of the behavior.
- Discussion of relationships and his past forming of intimate connections.
- Explorations around his absorption of white supremacist ideology and if this is escalating to violent action.
- Development of empathy skills and encouragement to better understand the experience of others, even those he disagrees with.
- Putting into practice harm reduction skills that will help Dawson avoid a disruption to his school progress, student conduct violations, Title IX reports, and/or criminal proceedings.

Treatment Notes for Dawson

Therapeutic suggestions for treatment are typically not included in these types of VRA assessments beyond suggestions for the type and frequency of therapeutic treatment. These recommendations are included in the intervention section of the VRA. For this book, the authors provide some suggestions based on the therapeutic approaches outlined in Chapter 13. These are organized based on the counseling and therapeutic interventions provided in the VRA above. If there is lack of direction from the VRA, the clinician will first begin with drafting these treatment recommendations based on their review of the VRA.

- **Impulse control and anger management.** Despite the numerous areas of concern in this case, the one clear instance of physical violence that occurred was focused on his girlfriend. It was shared they have trouble communicating and often escalate into threats. As Ellis (2007) describes, the frustrating behaviors that occur around us should be seen as activating events that lead to our beliefs that, in turn, fuel our consequences. The therapist should encourage Dawson to first list the things his partner or past partners have done to frustrate him and to eventually help him feel more empowered to choose his belief about these events and better control the outcome and consequences.
- **Intimate relationship dynamics.** Asking Dawson some explorative questions about his past and current relationships might be useful in understanding how better to augment his social supports and

protective factors. Helping Dawson explore the larger existential questions of what his goals are in life, what makes him happy, and what he is looking for in a relationship will help him gain better control of his current behaviors and feel more in control of his future.

- **Anger triggers.** Many things frustrate Dawson. One way to address these is to create a list ranging from 1–100 of the things that upset him in the world, a classic cognitive behavior therapy (CBT) technique (Glasser, 1975; 2001; Ellis, 2007). Using this list in a more thematic analysis will likely provide a better understanding of which motivators for violence are triggered for him in different scenarios. Another approach borrows from Rogers (1961; 1980), where the therapist would use a more non-linear, explorative technique relying on open-ended questions. By using this technique, the therapist could build out a similar list of upsetting scenarios and look for alternative ways of seeing these triggers.
- **Academic/career interests:** Little is known about Dawson's larger career goals and what he is setting out to accomplish by working in automotive welding. This focus would help strengthen the protective and supportive factors missing from Dawson's life. While finding a job is a good starting place, an exploration of future goals and identifying ways for Dawson to reach them might help him more easily to identify alternative actions moving forward. A warm hand-off referral to career counseling might be useful. More likely, someone like Dawson would respond better to someone older in the field of his desired study to give him advice and guidance.
- **White supremacist group connections.** It would be useful to better understand what drew Dawson to the groups he belongs to and to assess the current utility of such groups in his life. In other words, are these group connections bringing him closer to his overall goals or drawing him further away from them? This should be approached by looking at a cost/benefit analysis of the consequences of his affiliations. What is a common experience for him at group meetings? What friends has he made? What are the things he finds positive about these encounters? Have there been any situations that have made him feel uncomfortable or that he disagrees with during the meetings? The therapist could then employ a development of discrepancy (Miller and Rollnick, 1991) to further help Dawson understand the harm of these groups. As he feels more comfortable with the idea of change, the therapist can help him through the stages of change (Prochaska et al., 1994). Developing an awareness that change might be a one step forward and one step backward process will help build a better sense of resiliency and grit.
- **Family assessment.** While the details of Dawson's school and family history are not mentioned, these would be important to explore.

Human behavior is purposeful and developing a better understanding of what early influences impacted Dawson's development might provide insight into what he is looking for. Chapter 6, *Lost and Looking*, defines these cognitive openings that are exploited by hate groups. Has Dawson come from an isolated childhood, lacking connection or opportunities for growth and positive relationships? The therapist might be able to identify the void that created a cognitive opening for those extremists offering friendship, support, and shared experiences.

- **Empathy development.** A potential dissonance in Dawson's life exists between his job, along with the inference that he was a "good guy" before he started talking about all the white supremacist stuff, and how his later threatening and racist behavior is so at odds with these earlier impressions. The hypothesis here is Dawson is capable of empathy and caring when it is in his interest but comes off poorly when he is ranting or leaning into his white supremacist ideas and threats. Helping Dawson connect these two parts of himself is a critical area of treatment that will assist him to better understand the groups white supremacists hate. This is an example of a parallel process that can be exploited in treatment, modeling for Dawson someone listening in an active manner, providing an authentic and genuine presence and treating him with unconditional positive regard (Rogers, 1961; 1980). While likely difficult for most therapists given Dawson's violent actions and hate speech, the humanistic approach to treatment requires a dedication to the idea Dawson can behave well when free of obstacles and negative experiences in his own life. Our therapeutic goals become helping Dawson see how it feels to be heard and understood with the anticipation he would further develop these skills as he interacts with others on campus.
- **Critical thinking skills.** The development of critical think skills is central to the cognitive behavioral approach. Dawson has adopted a philosophy of hate that stands against a pluralistic and diverse society. Even as there might be room for difference in reasonable debate, Dawson has chosen extremist viewpoints that reject compromise, demand separation and violence. These underlying beliefs drive his choices and his emotions, thoughts, and actions. One approach is to help Dawson better explain his life philosophy and further test this ideology in the world based on his current experiences. The Gestalt approach to therapy (Perls, 1969), living in the existential area of clinical practice, might be helpful in challenging Dawson's assumptions that some people have more worth than others, that violence will provide a path to change, and that this ideology and approach to living is the one that will help him best meet his overall goals.
- **Process of change.** Assuming the above techniques are successful, and Dawson is ready to engage in the process of change, helping him

understand change comes slowly and with obstacles will allow him to remain realistic in his objectives. While change theory outlines a process of precontemplation, contemplation, preparation, action, maintenance and/or relapse (Prochaska et al., 1994), the simple commitment that occurs at preparation and action need to be understood realistically. Plainly stated, if Dawson has found solace in these white supremacist groups that offers him support, acceptance, and meaning, then abandoning these groups will be difficult. The process is like the one employed in Alcoholics Anonymous. The commitment to discontinuing drinking is bound with a replacement of the social group and support that is lost when the social benefits of drinking and spending time in a bar are stopped. This should not be presented as an impossible challenge or burden for Dawson, but rather helping him to understand the twists and turns in the path ahead.

Notes

1 Zero-tolerance policies refer to a separation from school based on a single incident of violence, weapon possession or threat. Separating a student from school under a zero-tolerance policy possess a higher risk of escalating an upset, frustrated student and might serve as a catalyst event driving an isolated, rage-filled, vengeful attacker. Assessment, intervention, and monitoring are more effective in mitigating threats of violence in the community (Van Brunt, 2012). While separating a student from school could give an illusion of safety, there are numerous examples where angry, disgruntled, and disempowered individuals came back to campus or the workplace to seek their revenge (O'Toole, 2000; Scalora et al., 2010).

2 Family Educational Rights and Privacy ACT www2.ed.gov/policy/gen/guid/fpco/ferpa/index.html

References

Ellis, A. (2007). *The Practice of rational emotive behavior therapy*. New York, NY: W.W. Norton & Company.

Glasser, A. (1975). *Choice Theory: A New Psychology of Personal Freedom*. New York, NY: Colophon Books.

Glasser, A. (2001). *Counseling with choice theory: The new reality therapy*. New York, NY: Colophon Books.

May, R. (1983). *The discovery of being*. New York, NY: W.W. Norton & Company.

Miller, W.R. and Rollnick, S. (1991). *Motivational Interviewing: Preparing People to Change Addictive Behavior*. New York, NY: Guilford Publications.

Nay, R. (2004). *Taking Charge of Anger*. Guilford Press.

O'Toole, M.E. (2000). *The school shooter: A threat assessment perspective*. Quantico, VA: National Center for the Analysis of Violent Crime, Federal Bureau of Investigation.

Perls, F. (1969). *Gestalt theory verbatim*. Lafayette, CA: Real People Press.

Prochaska, J., Norcross, J., and DiClemente, C. (1994). *Changing for Good*. Harper Collins.

Rogers, C. (1961). *On becoming a person*. New York, NY: Houghton Mifflin.

Rogers, C. (1980). *A way of being*. New York, NY: Houghton Mifflin.

Scalora, M., Simons, A., and Vansly, S. (2010, February). *Campus s: Assessing and managing threats (FBI Law Enforcement Bulletin)*. Washington, DC: Federal Bureau of Investigation.

Van Brunt, B. (2012). *Ending campus violence: New approaches to prevention*. New York, NY: Routledge.

Yalom, I. (1980). *Existential Psychotherapy*. Basic Books.

17 Prevention and Educational Programming

Educators are in the position to offer prevention and intervention programs at the earliest stages of white supremacist thought and guide a nascent white supremacist on another path. They can also build a foundation of empathy, equality, and morality that can prevent later indoctrination. This chapter will begin with a review of prevention and developmental models, followed by specific programming advice for educators and others.

Theoretical Frameworks for Prevention and Intervention

Gordon's Operational Classification

Gordon's operational classification system (Gordon, 1963) is used by both the National Institute on Drug Abuse and the United States Institute of Medicine and is particularly helpful in providing a common language and framework to prevention efforts.

The system defines three parts to the continuum of care, prevention, treatment, and maintenance, with a focus on prevention programs, initiatives, and messaging. There are three populations addressed by this programming. *Universal* programming looks at the entire population at the highest level appropriate. *Selective* programming focuses on those portions of the population at greatest risk. *Indicated* programming targets individuals showing signs or symptoms of being affected. There are three levels of prevention. *Primary* prevention attempts to avoid the problem occurring at all. *Secondary* prevention occurs after the problem arises in order to reduce the prevalence and stop growth. Finally, *tertiary* prevention is focused on slowing the spread and growth (Gordon, 1963).

The Public Health Model

The primary goal of the public health model is to benefit the most people possible in the population. The multidisciplinary approach, drawing from education, psychology, sociology, medicine, epidemiology, criminology,

DOI: 10.4324/9781003199656-17

and economics (Dahlberg and Krug, 2002), focuses "on the safety and well-being of entire populations" (Centers for Disease Control and Prevention, 2016a, p. 1).

The public health model can be applied using the following four steps:

1 **Define and monitor the problem.** Here, we must understand the issue, including who or what is impacted, the timeline of the event(s), any underlining causes, and if there are specific locations affected.
2 **Identify risk and protective factors.** While the presence of risk factors does not cause health conditions, it is important to look at these factors when determining where to focus prevention efforts. These efforts can then involve strengthening protective factors and mitigating risk.
3 **Develop prevention strategies.** Using knowledge of risk and protective factors, as well as community surveys, focus groups, needs assessments, and stakeholder interviews, develop and test prevention programs that are evidence-based and can be evaluated for effectiveness.
4 **Disseminate and evaluate these strategies.** The final step is to assure widespread adoption of the prevention strategies, which involves training, technical assistance, and networking. Procedures should be regularly evaluated for effectiveness and adjusted as needed.

Bronfenbrenner's Ecological Systems Theory

Bronfenbrenner's ecological systems theory (1979) was created to explain the complex interplay between personal and contextual factors, and how those factors impact the individual. By extension, the theory describes the interrelation between the individual and their surroundings. Given that we do not develop in a bubble, it makes sense that the outside world in all its complexities has an impact on the individual.

Picture concentric circles with the individual in the middle. The influences closest to the individual making a direct impact comprise the **microsystem.** This includes siblings, parents, peers, friends, teachers, grandparents, and all immediate influences surrounding the person. Their direct conversations, interactions, and relationships to these individuals are factors creating an immediate impact on the individual.

The next level of influence, the **mesosystem**, comprises members of the microsystem that interact with one another. For example, if an individual's parents are fighting with one another, even if the individual is not involved in the conversation, that conflict will impact their child. With friendships, this influence can occur as someone gets caught in the middle of friends who have conflict with one another that began independent of their relationship to the individual.

The **exosystem** is outside of the mesosystem. Think of the world swirling around us. The political climate, institutional/school rules, and anything going on in the world that someone does not participate in, but nonetheless has an impact on that person, is within the exosystem.

But that is not all. External influences like one's culture, socioeconomic status, race, religion, and various ideologies create the **macrosystem**. To use race as an example, the experiences of minoritized groups are likely quite different than the majority. Our cultural background, socioeconomic status, and the aforementioned defining features exert an influence on who we become.

The outermost circle of influence is the **chronosystem,** which refers to the influence of timing and time on the individual. Timing refers to the impact an event has on a person depending upon at what point it happens in their lifetime. Someone who loses a loving parent at the age of 16 would be impacted differently than someone who loses a loving parent at the age of 60. Losing a parent at 16 is a non-normative life event, an event we do not expect to endure when we're young. Losing a parent at 60 is a normative event, as we know within our mid- to late-adulthood that we will lose a parent. While both grieve, the young person will be hit harder with the realization their parent will not see them graduate, will not meet their partner, and will be missing from other big events. Another aspect in the chronosystem is the time period in which one grows. Think of toddlers in the pandemic. They are likely unaffected by wearing masks, as they do not know life without them. Now think of the angry reactions of some adults when faced with the mask requirement. This is new to them and they know what it feels like to go without. Timing and time are impactful though in different ways, yet both are part of the chronosystem.

Social-Ecological Model

The social-ecological model works in conjunction with Gordon's system to describe environmental approaches and the interactions between individual, relationship, community, and societal factors (Centers for Disease Control and Prevention, 2016b). Each of these is targeted with strategic prevention efforts specific to its needs.

1. **Individual.** Here, we look at such factors as age, education, socioeconomic status, health, and living conditions to educate and train individuals and encourage healthy attitudes, beliefs, and behaviors.
2. **Relationships.** Mentoring and peer programs address unhealthy relationships with peers, partners, and family members and promote healthy relationships that can positively influence thoughts and behaviors.
3. **Community.** This level looks to the community, including schools, workplaces, and neighborhoods, and how the community can affect

the individual. Prevention efforts at this level look to address climate and policies that negatively affect individual health and wellness.

4 **Society.** Finally, we broaden the exploration to look at the society as a whole and its climate and norms, looking for ways to prevent social and economic inequalities.

Educational and Developmental Models

Chickering's Theory of Identity Development

Perhaps the most well-known, widely used, and comprehensive model of psychosocial development, Chickering's theory is made up of seven vectors of identity development. These are not linear or progressive, but instead movement occurs along each at different rates and in conjunction with others (Chickering and Reisser, 1993).

The seven vectors are (Robinson, 2013)

1 **Developing competence.** The individual develops intellectual (reasoning and critical thinking), physical (wellness, artistic, and athletic), and interpersonal (working with others and communication) skills.
2 **Managing emotions.** The individual is able to recognize and manage their emotions and reactions to events.
3 **Moving through autonomy toward interdependence.** The individual develops an independent outlook but recognizes the importance of interdependence in successful relationships.
4 **Developing mature interpersonal relationships.** The individual develops the acceptance of others, respect for differences, and tolerance for those around them.
5 **Establishing identity.** The individual develops a healthy self-concept.
6 **Developing purpose.** The individual has a sense of fulfillment or movement toward fulfillment in work, interests, and relationships.
7 **Developing integrity.** The individual develops personal values and can apply them to their behavior.

The student's environment affects these vectors in a variety of ways including through institutional objectives, institutional size, student-faculty relationships, curriculum, teaching, friendship and student communities, and student development programs and services (Robinson, 2013).

Educators should be actively aware of differences and create environments where students can learn from one another. Students should have the opportunity to stretch their thinking and learn to understand themselves and others.

Bloom's Taxonomy of Critical Thinking

Bloom's taxonomy of critical thinking (1956) classifies the learning objectives that educators set for students into three areas, cognitive (knowledge), affective (emotions), and psychomotor (skills). Within each area, there is progressive learning and skill building (Orlich et al., 2004) with the goal of holistic education.

Within the *cognitive* domain, which involves the intellectual skills for understanding and retaining knowledge, there are six levels of cognition that are generally progressive in nature, with each level mastered before moving to the next. These levels are knowledge, comprehension, application, analysis, synthesis, and evaluation. The *affective* domain looks at emotional growth and the ability to understand the emotions and attitude of oneself and those of others, moving through the five stages of receiving, responding, valuing, organizing, and characterizing. Lastly, the *psychomotor* domain focuses on building physical skills (Bloom did not create subcategories for this domain) (Bloom, 1956).

While traditional education is often focused on the cognitive and psychomotor domains, developing the affective domain, especially empathy, is an important part of preventing and changing white supremacist thought and should be part of any curriculum.

Sanford's Challenge and Support Theory

Sanford's theory is based on balancing challenges and support (Sanford, 1966). Environments that offer suitable challenges with adequate support offer the best opportunity for growth and development. Too much support without challenges can seem comfortable but lead to boredom and does not provide engagement. Conversely, overly challenging environments without enough support can be toxic and promote anxiety.

Kohlberg's Theory of Moral Development

Kohlberg's theory defines six stages of moral development and posits that morality is primarily focused on seeking and maintaining justice (Kohlberg, 1973).

- **Level 1: Preconventional morality.** This early stage is centered around the expectations of authority figures and the consequences of breaking rules.
    a **Stage 1: Obedience and punishment.** Rules are obeyed to avoid punishment. This stage is most common in children, but adults sometimes also use this reasoning.

b **Stage 2: Individualism and exchange.** Rules are obeyed for personal gain. Actions are judged by how they serve individual needs.

- **Level 2: Conventional morality.** In this next level, the moral standards of role models and society are internalized.

  a **Stage 3: Developing good interpersonal relationships.** Conformity is emphasized and the focus is living up to social expectations and roles.
  b **Stage 4: Maintaining social order.** Society as a whole is considered, and the focus is maintaining law and order and respecting authority.

- **Level 3: Postconventional morality.** At this level, abstract ideas of morality come into play.

  a **Stage 5: Social contract and individual rights.** Individuals recognize the differing values, opinions, and beliefs of others. While laws are important in a society, they should be agreed upon by all the members of the society.
  b **Stage 6: Universal principles.** In the final stage of moral reasoning, individuals are guided by universal ethical principles even if they conflict with laws and rules.

According to this theory, these stages cannot be taught directly and are not the product of socialization (Crain, 1985). The stages emerge from individual thinking about moral dilemmas. However, social connections can stimulate these mental processes as we discuss and debate issues with others. When we are questioned or challenged, we develop new and more comprehensive positions.

Putting Theory Into Practice

Programming Basics

When planning intervention programming, it is important to:

- **Assess needs.** Use climate surveys, focus groups, anecdotal information, and program assessments to find gaps in current prevention strategies.
- **Connect to institutional mission and goals.** Ensure the program aligns with other institutional goals and efforts. Work with the diversity, equity, inclusion office and within the diversity and safety goals in the strategic plan.
- **Consider the relationship to compliance.** There could be compliance requirements related to Title IX, VAWA, student conduct code or criminal codes.

- **Identify stakeholders and partners.** Think about the individuals, departments, and programs that are stakeholders in the program. Make sure your programming supplements but does not duplicate work already being done. Find on- and off-campus partners for involvement.
- **Determine a budget and source of funding.** Consider local grants and program stakeholders for funding and think about financial timelines.
- **Determine your target audience.** Think about Gordon's classifications above—is your audience universal, selective, or indicated? Identify the characteristics of your audience.
- **Decide on related models and theories.** Using this chapter as a guide, consider the models discussed and which would apply to your program.
- **Develop program goals, objectives, and learning outcomes.** The program goal is a broad statement about the desired results of the program. Program objectives should be SMART (specific, measurable, achievable, relevant, and time bound) (Doran, 1981). Learning outcomes identify the skills or knowledge participants will gain from the program.
- **Coordinate with third-party vendors.** Review any third-party content or presenters you plan to use for customization and institutional fit. Research their references and feedback. Be sure to follow your institution's contracting and procurement guidelines.
- **Select and train presenters and facilitators.** If possible, include practice opportunities and role-plays.
- **Confirm logistics.** This includes locations for the program, technology support, food and beverage, parking, signage, etc.
- **Create and implement a marketing plan.** Use diverse marketing and promotional strategies, including print, social media, and special promotions and incentives.
- **Present the program.** Be prepared for issues that might arise and leave time to deal with last-minute needs.
- **Assess the program.** Design assessment and feedback opportunities based on the learning outcomes. Analyze the data and share it with your program partners.

Engage Students in Prevention

For prevention programming to be effective, there must be buy-in, support, and involvement from students during the planning and implementation. Students are invaluable resources on how to use marketing and promotions to engage other students, what language is appropriate, and the timing and locations that will reach the widest audience. Assisting in the planning will be a beneficial learning opportunity for students outside the classroom.

Peer educators are valuable in disseminating prevention concepts and need to be trained on the risk and protective factors discussed in Chapters 9 and 10, as well as the WSIR outlined in Chapter 11. As part of their training, peer educators should be given a chance to discuss their own experiences and perceptions, as they might be unaware of their own biases.

There are student groups on most campuses that are involved in activism on issues of social justice, racial equality, gender equity, and other related issues. Engage with these groups and understand their goals and priorities. While administrators can easily misstep with these groups by taking an adversarial stance or out of concerns about neutrality, it is possible and valuable to work with these students on prevention.

Address Microaggressions

Sue (2010) defines microaggressions as "brief, everyday exchanges that send denigrating messages to certain individuals because of their group membership" (p. xvi). The slights are often unintended but have a strong and repeated impact on those of a different country, ethnicity, culture, sexual identity, disability, or mental illness (Van Brunt et al., 2015). Microaggressions can be difficult to address because the people making the comments might not understand why they are offensive and might be defensive when confronted.

It can be helpful to explain the cumulative impact of microaggressions. Sue (2010) uses thumbtacks and raindrops to illustrate that the volume of these experiences can overwhelm a person. When addressing a particular microaggression, it is important to remind the person responsible that it is not just this one comment that matters, but all the comments and experiences affected the person each day.

Educational programming should address the unintentional impact of racially insensitive jokes, stereotypes, and slurs, separate from the intent. Even if no harm was meant, it can be a result of these microaggressions. When possible, educators should make these learning opportunities without shaming or punishing.

Bystander Intervention Efforts

Bystander intervention strategies should be specifically tailored to each audience and the obstacles to intervention that they face. Students must be trained in an awareness of and the ability to identify problematic behavior and understand the harm that will result.

The Southern Poverty Law Center (2017b) offers four key steps that should be part of any bystander intervention training.

1. **Know what public harassment looks like.** Harassment takes many forms, from microaggressions to hurtful comments to violence. It can stem from many types of bigotry, including racism, sexism, xenophobia, homophobia, or religious discrimination.
2. **Be aware of your identity before acting.** As discussed in Chapter 3, we all define ourselves in different ways and often in the intersectionality of more than one. Intervening could escalate the situation if the harasser targets you as well. If you share the same identity as the harasser, are in authority, or are part of the dominant culture, you might be in a better position to de-escalate the situation.
3. **Recognize your blocks, or reasons why you may not intervene.** There are many reasons you might be hesitant to intervene. You might be scared or might feel like you cannott make a difference. Being aware of your blocks will help you tailor your intervention and choose one of the methods described in step 4.
4. **When an incident occurs, choose one of the five Ds of bystander intervention.** Each of these offers a path of action.

    a. **Direct.** Directly address the incident. Before you respond directly, be sure that it is safe for you to do so. Ask yourself the following: Are you safe from harm? Is the person being harassed safe? Is it unlikely the situation will escalate? Does the person being harassed want someone to speak up? If the answers are "yes," you might choose a direct response. Keep it succinct and do no argue or debate the harasser, as that can escalate the situation.
    b. **Distract.** Use distraction to stop the incident. This is more subtle and involves interrupting the incident. Do not address the harassment directly, but instead talk about something unrelated, like asking for the time or directions.
    c. **Delegate.** Ask for help from a third party. Here, you find someone with authority to intervene.
    d. **Delay.** Take action after the fact. If you are unable to intervene during the incident, you can check in afterward with the people who were targeted, offering assistance or resources.
    e. **Document.** Record the incident. Start with the other Ds to give aid to the person being harassed. However, if someone else is already helping, or if you are unable to intervene otherwise, recording the incident as it happens can be valuable. After the incident, ask the person harassed what they would like to do with the recording and do not use it without their consent.

Teaching Empathy

As we have discussed, white supremacists generally lack empathy and depersonalize those outside of their ideals. Teaching empathy must be an element to any prevention programming. Empathy skills are key to a student's willingness to engage in prevention efforts, recognize micro-aggressions, and step up as a bystander. A lack of empathy impacts their perspective of problematic behavior and the harm caused by it.

Students must not only learn empathy but be willing to act on it. Many times, we might care about a person or a situation, but not do anything to help. This is related to the bystander interventions we discussed above. Educators can model and encourage this empathetic action.

The Making Caring Common Project (Jones et al., 2018) suggests five steps educators can take to build empathy in their students.

1. **Model empathy.** When frustrated by a student, look at the situation from their perspective before responding. When a student is upset, reflect back their feelings. Follow up on non-verbal cues and address them rather than moving first to reprimands. When appropriate, ask students for their input and really listen. If you can, incorporate their feedback into your classroom or curriculum.
2. **Teach what empathy is and why it matters.** Give students a clear understanding of what empathy is and how it improves their environment and relationships. Talk about having empathy not only for people they care about or who are like them. Give examples of how to act on empathy.
3. **Practice.** Take to time to practice empathy using role playing and "what would you do" case studies. Use social and emotional learning (SEL) programs and teach calming routines and dispute resolution skills.
4. **Set clear ethical expectations.** Be clear in your expectations about how students should treat one another. Establish clear guidelines for unacceptable language and behavior. Teach students to hold each other accountable and use restorative justice and peer mediation to resolve conflicts.
5. **Make school culture and climate a priority.** Take a climate survey annually to see if students and staff feel safe and respected and implement changes as needed.

A Systems Approach to Prevention

If you're a practitioner, educator, or working in a related field, you know the importance of a theoretical framework that drives our approach to counseling or teaching. For this reason, we are providing an intervention based on Bronfenbrenner's theory. With this approach, we cannot ignore any of the systems impacting the individual.

Let's think hypothetically. You are a school counselor tasked with creating a prevention program geared toward preventing recruitment and protecting targeted students. What would Bronfenbrenner advise you to do? The suggestions below are not a fully comprehensive program, but they are suggestions easily put into practice.

Microsystem Level

1 Prior to the beginning of the academic year, provide parents/caregivers with a newsletter that shares the school's goal of addressing white supremacy.

 (A) Describe the efforts being made to safeguard students and protect them from recruitment.
 (B) Share information from Chapter 4. Be sure parents/caregivers can readily identify phrases, concepts, and symbols of white supremacy and are willing to have a conversation with their kids about white supremacy.
 (C) Share information on the dangers of unsupervised social media use and the sites that are havens for white supremacists (see Chapter 5). Educate parents/caregivers on the use of social media if they are unfamiliar.

2 Schedule several assemblies for the academic year to discuss interpersonal relationships and the importance of reporting concerns.
3 Work with at-risk students. If an outside agency is needed, do not shy away from seeking help. As stated by Divecha and Brackett (2019), "at the micro-level, we need to address children's individual needs, including those who engage in bullying behavior, as well as the targets of, and witnesses to bullying" (p. 2). Social isolation and alienation can play a role in susceptibility to recruitment. Students need to feel accepted and welcome, so it is important to have these conversations.
4 Utilize teacher in-service at least twice per year to bring in an expert who can provide training on identifying risk and protective factors as well as other information from within this text.

Mesosystem Level

Bronfenbrenner spoke of the dangers of the breakdown of the mesosystem, which can lead to devastating circumstances. If the microsystems that work together to create a particular aspect of the mesosystem break down, it can lead to "a breeding ground of alienation" (Bronfenbrenner, 1979, p. 231).

As stated by Divecha and Brackett (2019), "Developmentally supportive mesosystems have common goals, positive orientations, emotional and trusting relationships, bidirectional communication, and an evolving balance of power in favor of the child" (p. 9).

1 Partnerships are key. Parents should communicate with schools and vice versa. When the relationships among those in a student's life are good, the likelihood of starting on the pathway to violence lessens.
2 If you're working as an educator, administrator, or mental health professional within a school, have an open door policy, even if you limit the office hours to a particular day and timeframe.
3 Encourage parents to share any emergency concerns by calling a monitored emergency phone line, whether it is 9–1-1 or a district-wide phone number. It is important that certain behaviors of concern can be addressed immediately.
4 Ideally, the school should have community policing in addition to a school resource officer (SRO) or campus safety department who provides a friendly face within a school. Officers should refrain from getting involved with disciplinary decisions unless the potential for a health and safety emergency is heightened. We want students to trust the SRO/campus safety to the extent they will report concerns about classmates.
5 Communication among systems is of great importance. If the school works in silos, the silos and walls need to come down to ensure partnerships in maintaining a peaceful school climate. If there is not a CARE or threat team, we encourage you to get training through one of the key resources mentioned in the next chapter (e.g., InterACTT or a similar agency). A single individual or two should not be assessing a student's likelihood to be recruited or to harm themselves. There have been instances in which disciplinary decisions have been made by a single administrator or mental health professional that went awry and resulted in tragedy.

Exosystem Level

Laws, policies, and procedures are part of the exosystem, as is the internet. These are outside forces that the student does not interact with, but impact the student nonetheless. Work on developing policies toward improving the social climate within the school.

Re-think those policies and procedures that have a negative impact on those students already facing life struggles. Many school policies were developed long before we realized the importance of threat assessment, reporting concerns, and preventing bullying and related alienation. For example, consider how the absence policy impacts those students who do not have a ride to or from school. Consider the bullying, harassment, and intimidation policy is drafted. Look for state mandates and create policy and procedures that align with your state. If there is not a policy, be sure to create one that allows anonymous reporting, restorative justice practices, and getting help for the targets and perpetrators of bullying behaviors. Ensure the policy does not benefit only those students who have little, if any, risk factors. ALL students deserve to feel safe and protected while in school. When they do, they are less likely to seek out the camaraderie of extremists and the "protection" they offer.

Macrosystem Level

As mentioned in our summary of Bronfenbrenner's theory, we are impacted by what defines us. We learn the values of the groups to which we belong, but as humans, it is not enough. Minoritized groups need to be understood, advocated for, and protected from harm. The following suggestions are not geared toward those students vulnerable to being recruited; instead they are protecting those who are targeted most often. We need to ensure everyone feels valued and are learning in the least restrictive environment, a place where they feel accepted and without fear.

1 Create a Gay-Straight Alliance (GSA). This will encourage students to interact with one another and show solidarity among students.
2 Adhere to GLSEN'S Policy Recommendations on Gender Nonbinary Students. Visit www.glsen.org/activity/model-local-education-agency-policy-on-transgender-nonbinary-students for more information.
3 Do more for Black students. Specifically, work Black history into the curriculum as often as you can. Black History Month diminishes the great contributions of Black Americans throughout our history. It should not be a month. The entire year should allow students to see themselves in the good parts of our history.
4 Dispel myths associated with minoritized groups. These conversations might not be happening at home despite your best efforts. Myths and ignorance lead to stereotypes and prejudice. Increasing awareness and education is key.

Chronosystem Level

Timing and time are perhaps the most challenging systems, as there are life events that happen outside of our control. We cannot ensure parents live well into late life or stop pandemics from happening. What we can do is ensure we are supportive. Whether it be familiarizing yourself with local grief counselors or diminishing false information surrounding COVID-19, we can and should be there as a stable base and connection for students.

How to Fight Hate

Should you be in a role in which formal education and counseling are not within your job expectations, there remain ways you too can work toward preventing hateful rhetoric, crimes, and recruitment. The

Southern Poverty Law Center (2017b) provides suggestions for anyone within a community in an information brief titled, "Ten Ways to Fight Hate." The ten principles are summarized below along with suggestions on how to put them into practice:

1 **Become active in the fight against hate.** That is, we are stronger as a united front with a common goal. Talk to friends and family about the issue, as many might be unaware of the severity.
2 **Join to arrange information sessions and engage in activities such as painting over neo-Nazi or other hate-related graffiti in your community.** All too often community agencies work in silos. Preventing and addressing hate requires the silos to come down to allow a synergy among local schools, campuses, law enforcement, and other stakeholders as they provide the education and take action.
3 **Reach out to minoritized groups that might be impacted by hate and hate crimes.** If you are being targeted by an individual or hate group, we encourage you to seek help. As suggested by the Southern Poverty Law Center, report every incident. If you are hesitant to do so alone, seek someone safe to join you. Related to this, community members must recognize the most vulnerable groups. Be there for them as an advocate and an ally. Keep hate symbols fresh in your mind so you can recognize if hate is present within your community. This is true whether you are a target or advocate. The SPLC recommends that all victims report each incident, speak to the media, and know their rights. Without reporting, law enforcement will not know to be extra vigilant in relation to hate groups and protecting those targeted. Going to the media is a way to spread the word and raise awareness by doing so, and it is key to remember there are hate laws that can be applied should the act be a crime.
4 **Use your voice.** Though this is important, it is key that the conversation remain calm. There is a way to denounce hate while simultaneously enlightening and empowering others. Regardless of how we feel about media at times, they are a way into the homes of others who might not realize the threat of white supremacy. If you have a cohesive community group fighting hate, seek information on the impact of hate within your community. The Southern Poverty Law Center stresses the importance of humanizing those impacted by a hate mindset. The more we raise awareness, the greater the likelihood knowledge will be shared, and hate will not be tolerated. The media also needs to realize the impact of naming perpetrators of violence and giving attention to the groups. Talk to reporters about the value of sharing how to fight hate rather than how to perpetrate it.
5 **Increase your knowledge of facts.** In addition to readily identified hate groups such as the Proud Boys and Atomwaffen Division,

recognize there are individuals who act alone on hate philosophies, especially as they move up the pathway to recruitment and violence. In reading the previous chapters, you are on your way to recognizing not only the hate mindset (e.g., "The Great Replacement), but also the symbols, gestures, and terms that might be on the clothing or in the speech or writing of a particular community member. The earlier we recognize the outward manifestation of hate, the better equipped we are at thwarting any potential violence.

6 **Face hatred in the interest of helping rather than hurting** It is likely, if you are reading this book, that you are working toward fighting hate and might feel anger and resentment toward those individuals believing in the hateful rhetoric. Violence is not the solution. Even if a hate group plans a rally in your community, stay away from the event. Things can escalate quickly, and you have to stay safe and healthy if you are to take action the right way. As suggested by the SPLC, what you can do it organize a peaceful event simultaneous to the hate rally, one that sends the message that hate will not be tolerated.

7 **Work with local government officials and enlighten them as to the state of hate in our nation.** Some will vehemently oppose your ideals and that is to be expected. However, it will serve as a reminder to elect those who oppose intolerance. Forming a connection and shared dedication to keeping hate out of your community will result in a higher likelihood of leaders taking a strong stance against hate groups. Having a conversation about hate crimes and the need to take them seriously will result in protecting targets from crimes that might otherwise be deemed random.

8 **Maintain a united front.** Communities that share a common goal and interest in peace have a greater likelihood of dissuading those with a propensity for violence. Give at-risk individuals the opportunity to feel a connection to others within the community to prevent their need to band with hate groups. Interfaith groups and celebrations are a good way to connect those of different cultures, races, and religions and convey a message of strength and unity.

9 **Foster a climate of acceptance.** The Southern Poverty Law Center offers many that can be shared at schools, on campuses and with parents. Check into the course content offered within the school to be sure it provides accurate information and contributions made from diverse groups. Parents and teachers can also investigate the type of organizations that can be forged at school related to advocacy for the rights of others.

10 **Engage in introspection.** Innate biases must be addressed within us to ensure our hearts and minds are dedicated to doing what is right. Introspection is key to ensuring our own intentions are good and that we are advocates for the right reasons. In addition to working on

ourselves, we should be aware of those in our lives who influence us. There's an old Italian proverb, "Tell me who you are with and I will tell you who you are," which summarizes why we have to choose our friends and allies wisely.

Moving Forward

Prevention and education efforts related to white supremacy can and should start young and center on a climate of caring and empathy toward all people. Educators are able to model and teach these concepts and involve students in programming, peer accountability, and bystander intervention. Students who learn to address microaggressions, bystander intervention strategies, and empathy toward others have a foundation to help guard them against white supremacist indoctrination throughout their lives.

References

Bloom, B.S., ed. (1956). *Taxonomy of educational objectives. The classification of educational goals. Handbook I: Cognitive domain*. New York, NY: David McKay.

Bronfenbrenner, U. (1979). *The sociology of human development: Experiments by nature and design*. Cambridge, MA: Harvard University Press.

Centers for Disease Control and Prevention. (2016a). The public health approach to violence prevention. Retrieved on February 22, 2016, from www.cdc.gov/ViolencePrevention/overview/publichealthapproach.html.

Centers for Disease Control and Prevention. (2016b). *The social-ecological model: A framework for prevention*. Retrieved on February 22, 2016, from www.cdc.gov/ViolencePrevention/overview/social-ecologicalmodel.html.

Chickering, A.W. and Reisser, L. (1993). *Education and identity* (2nd ed.). San Francisco, CA: Jossey-Bass.

Crain, W. (1985). *Theories of Development*. New York, NY: Prentice-Hall.

Dahlberg, L. and Krug, E. (2002). Violence—a global public health problem. In *World report on violence and health*. E. Krug, L. Dahlberg, J. Mercy, A. Zwi, and R. Lozano, eds. Geneva: World Health Organization, pp. 1–56.

Divecha, D. and Brackett, M. (2019). Rethinking school-based bullying prevention through the lens of social and emotional learning: A bioecological perspective. *International Journal of Bullying Prevention*. https://pureedgeinc.org/wp-content/uploads/2020/06/Divecha-Brackett2019_Article_RethinkingSchool-BasedBullying.pdf.

Doran, G.T. (1981). There's a S.M.A.R.T. way to write management's goals and objectives. *Management Review*, 70(11): 35–36.

Gordon, R. (1963). An operational classification of disease prevention. *Public Health Reports*. 96(2), 107–109.

Jones, S., Weissbourd, R., Bouffard, S., Kahn, J., and Ross, T. (2018). How to Build Empathy and Strengthen Your School Community. https://mcc.gse.harvard.edu/resources-for-educators/how-build-empathy-strengthen-school-community.

Kohlberg, L. (1973). The claim to moral adequacy of a highest stage of moral judgment. *Journal of Philosophy*. 70(18), 630–646.

Orlich, D., Harder, R., Callahan, R., Trevisan, M., and Brown, A. (2004). *Teaching strategies: A guide to effective instruction* (7th ed.). Boston,MA: Houghton Mifflin.

Robinson, M. (2013). Chickering's seven vectors of identity development. Retrieved on February 22, 2016, from https://studentdevelopmenttheory.wordpress.com/chickerings-seven-vectors.

Sanford, N. (1966). *Self and Society*. New York, NY: Atherton Press.

Southern Poverty Law Center. (2017a). Ten Ways to Fight Hate: A Community Response Guide. Retrieved on February 21, 2022, from www.splcenter.org/20170814/ten-ways-fight-hate-community-response-guide.

Southern Poverty Law Center. (2017b). SPLC on Campus: A guide to bystander intervention. Retrieved on January 31, 2022, from www.splcenter.org/20171005/splc-campus-guide-bystander-intervention.

Sue, D. (2010). *Microaggressions in everyday life: Race, gender, and sexual orientation.* Hoboken, NJ: John Wiley & Sons.

Van Brunt, B., Murphy, A., and O'Toole, M. (2015). The dirty dozen: Twelve risk factors for sexual violence on college campuses (DD-12). *The Journal of Violence and Gender*. 2(3), 1–16.

18 It Takes a Village

A Review of Organizations and Resources to Help

This chapter will provide a summary of some of the major organizations and resources that will aid the reader in developing their abilities to assess, intervene and manage the risk associated with extremist violence. This will be similar to an annotated bibliography in both offering a summary as well as information regarding how to contact the group.

Anti-Defamation League (ADL)

www.adl.org

The ADL works to eliminate prejudice and hate via multiple resources. The group puts policy into practice, as their reports and resources provide enlightening data that highlights current issues including extremism. Their website also features helpful tools for parents and educators via www.adl.org/education-and-resources/resources-for-educators-parents-families.

The PROTECT Plan is the ADL's most comprehensive approach to battling white supremacy to date. Released shortly after the January 6th attack on the Capitol, this initiative addresses white supremacy from a variety of angles. PROTECT is an acronym for *Prioritize* preventing and countering domestic terrorism; *Resource* according to the threat; *Oppose* extremists in government service; *Take* domestic terrorism prevention measures; *End* the complicity of social media in facilitating extremism; *Create* an independent clearinghouse for online extremist content; and *Target* foreign white supremacist terrorist groups (ADL PROTECT Plan to Fight Domestic Terrorism). PROTECT adopts a "whole of government" and "whole of society" plan of attack that involves state and national levels of government including, but not limited to, the Office of the President, the National Security Council, and the Federal Bureau of Investigation. For detailed information on PROTECT, visit www.adl.org/protectplan.

The ADL also introduced the REPAIR plan. Like PROTECT, it is geared toward addressing the issue of white supremacy through policy. In Chapter 5, we addressed the failures of the majority of mainstream social media channels related to providing an open platform for white supremacy groups. REPAIR is ADL's attempt at encouraging policy among mainstream sites with the ultimate goal of pushing hate groups toward non-mainstream platforms (ADL Repairing Our Internet Ecosystem to

DOI: 10.4324/9781003199656-18

Push Hate and Extremism Back to the Fringes of the Digital World). Specifically, REPAIR is an acronym for *Regulation* and reform; *Enforcement* at scale; *People* over profit; *Access* to justice; *Interrupting* disinformation; and *Research* and innovation. For more information on REPAIR, visit www.adl.org/media/16037/download.

Center for American Progress (CAP)

www.americanprogress.org/

CAP focuses on improving the human condition. Their goals include rescuing the planet from further harm as well as promoting peace worldwide. CAP prides itself on changing policy and encouraging debate on key issues such as extremism, LGBT rights, and climate change. The organization often seeks signature support from like-minded individuals to encourage policy change.

Educate Against Hate

https://educateagainsthate.com

Educate Against Hate takes a holistic approach to providing resources and guidance to various groups. Specifically, Educate Against Hate's primary goal is to protect youth from being radicalized by terrorist organizations and other hate groups. Their strategy is to encourage resilience in order to prevent susceptibility to radicalization. Resources are available to parents, teachers, and school administrators.

Higher Education Case Management Association (HECMA)

www.hecma.org

HECMA is an excellent resource for those in need of case management guidance. Case management is especially important when an individual is at risk of being recruited by an extremist group. HECMA offers document resources, training, and consulting.

Human Rights Campaign (HRC)

www.hrc.org

HRC focuses on fighting for equality for the LGBTQ+ community advocacy and legislative action. They provide myriad resources to parents, educators, law-makers, employers, and others through their website and at www.thehrcfoundation.org/professional-resources?_ga=2.12304372.1591952181.1644013799-2077682420.1644013799.

Indivisible

https://indivisible.org/resource/standing-indivisible-against-white-supremacy

Made up of thousands of local groups, Indivisible fights to resist right-wing policies and agendas. Indivisible recognizes that our democracy favors the white and wealthy and fights to build a fair and equitable system through grassroots action.

Institute for Strategic Dialogue (ISD)

www.isdglobal.org

ISD strives to reverse negative events transpiring around the world. Their key goals are to eradicate polarization, disinformation, and extremism. ISD has forged strong partnerships with local and federal agencies and communities. In addition, a great deal of research is conducted to educate practitioners and the public. ISD also provides related trainings via their Strong Cities Network. They have created data-based intervention models geared toward protecting the globe from issues involving social media, gaming, and other forms of technology.

International Alliance for Care and Threat Teams (InterACTT)

www.interactt.org/

InterACTT is an alliance of mental health professionals, professors, researchers, law enforcement, threat assessors, case managers, and other like-minded individuals. The overarching goal of InterACTT is to provide threat assessment and other tools focused on providing intervention guidance. InterACTT is the first group of its kind to offer an online threat assessment that provides the user with an algorithm-based case management plan via the Navigator. Threat assessment tools are readily available, but the unique and innovative Navigator is groundbreaking. InterACTT also hosts two peer-reviewed journals, blogs, and other media geared toward addressing extremism and other difficult issues.

The Jewish Federation of North America (JFNA)

www.jewishfederations.org

The mission of the JFNA is to safeguard Jews across the globe. The organization has operations in North America with branches that extend far beyond. The Jewish Federations provide trainings and lifesaving information to various agencies toward saving lives. The agency informs policy and provides guidance via newsletters and ongoing extremism data updates via their website.

The Leadership Conference on Civil and Human Rights

https://civilrights.org/heres-10-things-you-can-do-to-stop-white-supremacy

This agency brings attention to white nationalist groups in effort to shed light on the extent of the problem. On their website, they provide ways anyone can help fight against such issues as extremism, justice reform, and immigration. The Leadership Conference on Civil and Human Rights is one of many organizations putting pressure on the US government to create stricter laws against nationalist crimes.

Life After Hate

www.lifeafterhate.org

Life After Hate is unlike most of these organizations in that it was founded by former extremists. That alone lends credence to the fact that the pathway to recruitment and related violence can be addressed and mitigated. In their own words, the founders of Life After Hate state "We were founded by former violent far-right extremists who were once committed to the idea that violence is the best way to make lasting change. Today we believe that this way of life is counterproductive, exhausting, and dangerous." Life After Hate members work to free individuals from the clutches of hate groups, giving them a new view of culture and the world. The agency conducts research related to extremism and also provides training, outreach and intervention.

Moonshot

https://moonshotteam.com

Moonshot prides itself on taking an ethical approach to policy making. In addition, their work centers on providing educational resources addressing such issues as the incel movement and domestic terrorism. Moonshot is dedicated to finding those engaging in harmful online behaviors, work to understand the driving forces of the individuals, and develop content geared toward helping those involved with harmful internet activity. Moonshot does so by providing safety resources, mental health counselors, and those resources necessary to keep them away from the harm of unsafe online content.

Muslim Advocates

https://muslimadvocates.org

Founded after the passage of the Patriot Act, Muslim Advocates fights against bigotry and discrimination. They chiefly provide legal council both in court and in the policy making process. They also track incidents of discrimination and provide resources on issues affecting the Muslim American community.

National Association for Behavioral Intervention and Threat Assessment (NABITA)

www.nabita.org

NABITA provides resources and trainings to BIT/CARE teams as they work to prevent violence on campuses and workplaces. NABITA provides training in BIT operations, violence risk assessment, case management, and disruptive and dangerous behavior.

Not in Our Town (NIOT)

www.niot.org

NIOT addresses various forms of violence such as bullying, racism and hate. One of the greatest resources on the site is a live map that continuously updates efforts used to fight hate. The site provides links to schools, campuses, and other agencies and institutions that have used their approach. This provides the opportunity to look at how similar agencies are fighting hate, so others can get information on how to work with NIOT.

Secure Community Network

www.securecommunitynetwork.org

SCN is the official safety and security organization of the Jewish community in North America. They have built a team of security directors throughout North America to offer critical infrastructure assessments, active shooter and safety trainings and emergency preparedness coordination. They operate a 24/7, 365 days-a-year Jewish Security Operations Command Center that takes the full spectrum of reports from anti-semitic voicemail messages to targeted attack response to events such as the Tree of Life shooting in Pittsburg and the Colleyville Hostage standoff in Texas. They can be contacted at 844-SCN-DESK and dutydesk@securecommunitynetwork.org

Southern Poverty Law Center (SPLC)

www.splcenter.org

SPLC provides research and data on topics impacting marginalized groups. SPLC digs deep into the various hate groups and their actions to allow SPLC to inform the public, educate media sources, and those responsible for protecting the safety of our nation (i.e. law enforcement). SPLC is an excellent resource for informative publications on current issues including, but not limited to, domestic terrorism. The agency is skilled at information sharing and training.

Stop AAPI Hate

https://stopaapihate.org

The COVID-19 pandemic brought with it a sharp rise in hate and violence against Asian American and Pacific Islander communities. The Stop AAPI Hate coalition was formed on March 19th, 2020, to combat this growing problem. The coalition tracks incidents AAPI discrimination and violence and recognizes that to affectively fight AAPI discrimination, we must work to end all forms of structural racism. The site allows users to report incidents, provides ways to get involved, and includes resources and educational materials.

Tanenbaum

https://tanenbaum.org/about-us/combating-extremism

Tanenbaum fights hate in many forms with a special focus on extremism, bullying, and marginalization. Specifically, the organization utilizes a public educational approach to sharing knowledge and resources. The information they provide is free and geared toward assisting educators, parents, school personnel, churches, and those who benefit from the knowledge. This is done through their *Combating Extremism* initiative.

The Violence Project

www.theviolenceproject.org

The Violence Project is dedicated to lowering the rates of many forms of violence. The organization is funded via the National Institute of Justice. Extremism, school/youth violence, and gun violence are issues targeted by the Violence Project. The approach used by The Violence Project is somewhat different than traditional threat assessment, as they look at various levels of contributing factors: the individual, institutional, and societal. Resources related to this approach are available on their site.

White Nonsense Roundup (WNR)

https://whitenonsenseroundup.com/

As Dr. Fitch said in Chapter 3, "White people, come get your people." WNR is a site created by white people, for white people to address racism in society. WNR roundup recognizes that people of color should not have to educate white people on issues of racism and privilege, so WNR provides resources to help white people confront racism on social media, at work, at school, among friends and family, and wherever they see white nonsense.

Appendix: The White Supremacist Indoctrination Rubric

The White Supremacist Indoctrination Rubric (WSIR) was developed by Drs. Brian Van Brunt and Lisa Pescara-Kovach as a research-based, reliable, and easy-to-use approach to assessing the subject's level of white supremacist indoctrination. This is useful in violence risk assessment and developing treatments and interventions.

The WSIR rates five areas of indoctrination on a scale of 1 to 5: appearance, affiliation, absorption of knowledge, acquisition of weapons, and appointment to mission.

Table 1 Appearance

Level	*Label*	*Description*
1	None	Here there are no indications of tattoos, clothing, hair styles or symbolism related to the white supremacist movement.
2	Passing Interest	They show interest in tattoos, symbols, clothing or imagery associated with the movement. They may reference or wear tentatively some small affectation.
3	Casual Collection	They have some items of clothes that include symbols from the white supremacist movement. They wear these occasionally. They may have tattoos related to the movement, but they are small and in easily concealable locations.
4	Conscious Display	They have many items of clothing with white supremacist symbols, logos, or phrases. They may also have multiple tattoos that are visible and difficult to conceal. They may shift clothing or conceal tattoos to fit into a work setting or social setting, but often they can be found communicating a clear message through their clothes (e.g., Identity Evropa triangle, blood drop cross symbol).
5	Consistent Style	They are regularly found in clothing with white supremacist logos, phrasing or images and/or have visible tattoos, often on the neck or forearm, that are not easily concealed and convey their connection to the movement. They have adopted a hair style and other mannerisms connected to the white supremacist movement. They encourage others to wear and display white supremacist symbols.

Table 2 Affiliation

Level	*Label*	*Description*
1	None	They have no affiliation (online or in -person) with any group that expresses extremist, white supremacist, or hate-based ideologies.
2	Passing Interest	They have looked at some groups online but have not requested more information or joined any newsletter or membership. Their online exploration exists on mainstream sites. They maybe have considered attending a local meeting, protest, or convention, but have not done so in person.
3	Casual Exploration	They have downloaded some online materials and are actively learning about the movement. They may have a local connection, group, or organization they have begun talking to and have attended a meeting, protest, or convention to learn more about the movement.
4	Active Membership	They have connections to several online resources with white supremacist content, many on "dark web" sites and forums, and have attended meetings, protests, or other group activities. They may have multiple accounts to hide their identity and follow those who hold white supremacist beliefs and/or active hate content directed to targeted groups (e.g., Blacks, Jews, LGBTQI+).
5	Leadership/ Recruitment	They maintain active membership to groups both online, especially on "dark web" sites and forums, and in-person where they have administrator, moderator, or other leadership status. They have acquired written materials, pamphlets or flyers and share these with others. They have an active social media presence that expresses white supremacist beliefs and/or active hate content to targeted groups (e.g., blacks, Jews, LGBTQI+). Their profile photo is a hate symbol or personal photo with their hate group.

Table 3 Absorption of Knowledge

Level	*Label*	*Description*
1	None	They know very little about the white supremacist movement and may suggest that it was over with the German Nazi Party.
2	Passing Interest	They have reviewed some material, perhaps read a book or manifesto, related to the movement. This is done more out of passive curiosity rather than direct pursuit.
3	Casual Exploration	They have acquired some knowledge about the movement and are looking to learn more. This may be through conversations with members in-person or through online chat groups or membership websites. They may have some materials, images or documents saved, but these are limited to just a handful.

Level	Label	Description
4	Focused Learning	They have a good amount of knowledge about the movement and have read several key texts. They have saved images, documents, and manifestos regarding white supremacy and hate to better defend their points. They share and talk with others about their study.
5	Historian/ Marketer	Their knowledge of the movement, ideologies and beliefs is detailed and well-researched. They make use of a catalog or classification system to store information and are always looking to acquire more. They have sophisticated counterarguments to those they debate and adopt a creative and manipulative use of social media. They publish and/or sell materials, logos, patches, stickers, and insignias to others.

Table 4 Acquisition of Weapons

Level	Label	Description
1	None	They have no interest and little knowledge related to weapons or dangerous materials. They have not previously fired a gun.
2	Passing Interest	They own no they weapons but have used a firearm on occasion at a range or while hunting. They have a basic knowledge of weapons.
3	Casual Exploration	They own or have easy access to firearms. They have the firearm for personal protection or hunting. They have taken basic firearm safety courses or have the equivalent knowledge. They show interest in other dangerous materials. They may have begun to acquire a few secondary items such tactical gear.
4	Soldier	They own multiple firearms or other weapons and have acquired them out of concern to use the weapons to be prepared for the coming conflicts. They have studied tactics and have taken combat firearm courses. They have multiple weapon systems. They practice with others and stockpile ammunition and/or do their own re-loading. They belong with a group or militia to support their training and work as a collective.
5	Specialist/ Officer	They have acquired deep knowledge of firearms and have stockpiled dozens of weapons. They may have a narrow area of expertise. They teach/support others in their acquisition of weapons skills. They train frequently and have specific plans detailing how weapons and gear will be used against specific groups. They study previous attacks to learn how to be more effective in their killing.

Table 5 Appointment to Mission

Level	*Label*	*Description*
1	None	There is no mission considered and no commitment to any type of action against any group.
2	Passing Interest	They have a partial understanding and perhaps even agree with some of the white supremacist group's ideology, but have not joined a group, attended a protest or are considering action.
3	Casual Exploration	They have researched various groups, protests, and rallies and have expressed interest in attending. They either have attended event(s) or have plans to attend one soon. They feel aligned with the group's goals and mission yet are hesitant to become fully immersed or committed to action.
4	Active Directive	They are connected to a group and looking for ways to assist the group's mission forward. They align with the group's ideology, and they may have engaged in protests, rallies, harassing behavior or pseudo-militaristic tactics and training. They target other groups or protests to counter their messaging and look for ways to harm and disenfranchise those who they stand against.
5	Pathway to Violence	They are connected to a group or sub-group committed to violent action against those they hate. They have acquired weapons and engage in training and tactics to carry out a mission. The time, location and date may not be chosen yet, but they are certain it will occur and may be actively involved in recruiting and/or training of others to engage in violence to bring their vision of how the world should be to fruition.

Index

Note: Locators in *italic* and **bold** refer to figures and tables, respectively; Locators followed by "n" indicate endnotes.